NEVER BEEN RICH

The major published works of Harry Harrison Kroll

Mountainy Singer (William Morrow & Co., 1928)
The Cabin in the Cotton (Long & Smith, 1931)
Three Brothers and Seven Daddies (Long & Smith, 1932)
Return Not Again, with Annette Heard (Bobbs-Merrill, 1936)
The Ghosts of Slave-Driver's Bend (Bobbs-Merrill, 1937)
I Was a Share-Cropper (Bobbs-Merrill, 1937)
Keepers of the House (Bobbs-Merrill, 1939)
The Usurper (Bobbs-Merrill, 1942)
The Rider on the Bronze Horse (Bobbs-Merrill, 1943)
Perilous Journey, with C. M. Sublette (Bobbs-Merrill, 1943)
Rogue's Company (Bobbs-Merrill, 1943)
Waters Over the Dam (Bobbs-Merrill, 1944)
Fury in the Earth (Bobbs-Merrill, 1945)
Their Ancient Grudge (Bobbs-Merrill, 1946)
Darker Grows the Valley (Bobbs-Merrill, 1947)
Lost Homecoming (Coward-McCann, 1950)
The Long Quest (Westminster, 1954)
Summer Gold (Westminster, 1955)
The Smoldering Fire (Ace, 1955)
My Heart's In the Hills (Westminster, 1956)
For Chloe With Love (Lothrop, Lee & Shepard, 1958)
The Brazen Dream (Ace, 1961)
Riders in the Night (Univ. of Pennsylvania Press, 1965)
Bluegrass, Belles, and Bourbon (Thomas Yoseloff, 1967)
Mounds in the Mist, with Mildred Payne (A. S. Barnes & Co., 1969)

NEVER BEEN RICH

The Life and Work of a Southern Ruralist Writer, Harry Harrison Kroll

Richard L. Saunders

The University of Tennessee Press • Knoxville

First Edition.

The paper in this book meets the requirements of American National Standards Institute / National Information Standards Organization specification Z39.48-1992 (Permanence of Paper). It contains 30 percent post-consumer waste and is certified by the Forest Stewardship Council.

Library of Congress Cataloging-in-Publication Data

Saunders, Richard L., 1963–
Never been rich: the life and work of a southern ruralist writer,
Harry Harrison Kroll / Richard L. Saunders.
p. cm.
Includes bibliographical references and index.
ISBN-13: 978-1-57233-825-8 (hardcover)
ISBN-10: 1-57233-825-3 (hardcover)
1. Kroll, Harry Harrison, 1888–1967—Criticism and interpretation.
2. Authors, American—20th century—Biography.
3. American literature—Appalachian Region—History and criticism.
4. Appalachian Region—Intellectual life.
I. Title.

PS3521.R566Z88 2011
813'.54—dc23
[B]
2011021559

I have never been rich. There have been times when I needed money desperately. One never, I suppose, achieves the success he could have wished. Yet, in another way, I have got further along in the writing racket than I had dared to dream.

Looking Back, 1947

CONTENTS

ILLUSTRATIONS

ACKNOWLEDGMENTS

No book produces itself and no author writes biography or history alone. I must, simply must, thank the Kroll family and close friends, all of whom have been both kind and generous throughout this process: Harry Jr. and Nelle Kroll, Robert T. and Edith Kroll, and Claudia Hicks. Each has contributed materially to the Kroll collections at the University of Tennessee at Martin, answered many questions, and provided hours of pleasant conversation and exchanges of correspondence. Unless credited otherwise, all photographs appear by the courtesy of the late Robert T. Kroll. Acknowledgement for direct assistance or support is made to the late Steve Rogers, former Paul Meek Library director; Ed Frank, Special Collections librarian at the Univ. of Memphis; and Jimmie Corbitt, whose generous foresight established an endowment at my institution without which I never would have been induced (or been able) to acquire Kroll material for the collection.

Particular thanks are due my fellow library professionals, those who indulged me as I leafed through dozens of dusty bound volumes (sometimes as the first person ever to do so) or who ironed out research queries in collections I could not examine personally for this project: particularly Leanne Garland, former archivist and special collections librarian at Lincoln Memorial University and now at Nashville Public Library, together with Sandra Bates of the Bodleian Library, Oxford University, England; Moreen Blader from the Library and Archives of Canada; Carolyn Davis of Syracuse University Library; Sheila Frey of Cook Communications Ministries; Peter DePuydt at Elizabethtown College; Michelle Ganz, Lincoln Memorial University; Stephen Gateley and the library staff of Dargan Library at LifeWay Inc., Nashville; Sara Harwell, Disciples of Christ Historical Society library, Nashville; Jennifer Nace, Syracuse University Special Collections; Karl Schneider, National Agriculture Library; Jennifer Woodruff Tait, Methodism Librarian at Drew University; Wilfredo Tangunan, Drew University; Phillip B. Tucker of Vanderbilt University; as well as the reference staffs of the Library of Congress and British Library, clerks in a dozen county courthouses across Alabama, Mississippi, and Tennessee, and an equal number of nameless librarians and volunteers in small public libraries who offered help and suggestions with their local history and its sources. Thanks also to Chris Green of Marshall University, who organized a session on Kroll and his Lincoln Memorial University atelier at the 2006 Appalachian Studies Association conference, where I was fortunate to cross paths with fellow presenters James Lorance (Don West's biographer) and Carol Boggess (James Still's biographer). Charles Bradshaw of University of Tennessee at Martin, Thomas E. Douglas of East Carolina University, and Elizabeth Lamont of Lincoln Memorial University, read and commented on the manuscript. Liz was involved almost from the ground floor. She not only read, but her criticism and encouragement made this biography relevant. She has been in my corner throughout the project.

Many others helped by supplying details or other services incident to research or writing, including Peggy D. Downing, and the ever-cheerful Kathleen Smith at Vanderbilt University Archives. I also encountered, without introduction or warning, goodly souls whose spontaneous kindnesses provided answers, leads, and context at various places across small Tennessee towns, rural Mississippi, and south Alabama: Tracy W. Latham, Dr. Steven Petcher, Dorothy Quimby, Willie and Frank Thornton, Elizabeth P. Henderson, and Joy Nored are among those I can name, but there were many other helpful acquaintances of a moment whose names I have either forgotten or never knew. Editorial folks are not ignored. Scot Danforth took the risk on bringing Harry before the public in printed form. Joanna Juzwik McDonald conducted the heroic battle for verb agreement, sentence structure, continuity, and slew the run-on sentences.

As usual, the family made the sacrifices and provided the greatest support. Thank you, dear; thank you AnnMarie, Stephen, Heidi, and now David, who have fledged and flown, and thank you to those still in the nest: Pinkie, Dan, Missy, and Nathan as well. Writing may make life fun, but all y'all make it worthwhile.

INTRODUCTION

Readership is fickle and reputation fleeting for the vast majority of writers. Interest in a writer's work rarely transcends generations. Who today, other than the most focused academic specialist, reads or even remembers the work of Ellen Glasgow, Arthur Machen, Robert Nathan, or Elinor Wylie? Paul Leicester Ford was one of the most popular American writers of the first decade of the twentieth century, yet his work remains memorable and collectible chiefly because of his publisher's book designer, who created splendid artistic bindings that cased his work, rather than for his widely popular stories. One must wonder what sort of literary legacy will come from the best-selling work of John Grisham, Anne Rice, Tom Clancy, or Danielle Steele in another fifty years.

Occasionally an author's work is rediscovered by a later generation of readers or scholars. Herman Melville was one such resurrectee, whose work was largely ignored during his lifetime and judged relevant only long after his passing. For those who are not literary giants, like Melville, scholarly interest often grows, if sparked at all, because of the attention of book collectors or an institutional library. With luck, one or more of those collectors will be sufficiently impassioned and well informed to begin compiling a checklist. With very good luck enough of the author's and publishers' manuscripts and papers survive to document the writing, production, manufacturing, and distribution of an author's work. With extraordinary good luck, someone will join the descriptions to the source material to produce either a bibliography or biography. Because they are so labor intensive, compilation of a descriptive bibliography typically stands as the symbol that an author has taken a seat among the demigods of literature—only rarely is a writer's importance to scholarship so great that researchers are interested in the minute details about not only the texts but also the forms in which those texts appeared before the public. Descriptive bibliographies focus on the publications themselves as the measure of a prominent author's career.

Once it is laid before the collective public, production of a bibliography also generates interest in an author's literary career, provides a platform for future study, and insures that the author's work will at least not be lost to comparative scholarship. Unfortunately, most authors that are publicly read during their lifetimes are never studied bibliographically. Later generations of scholars are often left to study those whom other scholars have already studied. This self-perpetuating cycle emphasizes the work of a comparative few authors from any given period at the expense of a great many more. Many of these writers genuinely interested the public during their career but have fallen out of notice.

None of this discursion, however, really explains why the book you have in hand is about Harry Kroll, for which there are several reasons.

First, Kroll interests me as a practicing writer. The man's output is astounding. He wrote constantly. The still-growing list of his work I have kept runs to nearly 30 books, over 900 short stories and essays, more than 100 illustrations, and about as many poems. Still, Kroll produced at least twice and perhaps as three times as many more manuscripts than appears on his list of mere publications. I write a lot myself, but his volume of work is simply remarkable, and telling the story of such an active writer is important.

A second reason for my interest is, that Kroll is much more typical of the vast majority of popular writers than literary figures like Eudora Welty, William Faulkner, and the like, who arrived at a point of having publishers falling over themselves seeking their work. A widely recognized author eventually reaches a point at which their work becomes acceptable because it *is* their work, irrespective of its quality. This is not to accuse well-respected writers of producing drivel; it is merely an acknowledgement that their status is no longer that of the vast, struggling body of writers. Despite his respectable volume of published output, Harry Kroll never really made the transition from writer to literary figure. I won't argue here that he was or wasn't good enough, just that despite his strenuous effort it never happened.

So if he wasn't an important literary figure, why is Kroll important to literary scholarship and why have I lavished time and attention on this biographical project? Well, for several reasons:

First, Kroll spent much of his career as a well-respected and enormously popular professor of literature and composition at the institution where I work. When a story about him was run in the campus alumni magazine in 2004 we had alumni coming out of the proverbial woodwork to share their "Mr. Kroll stories" with us. We began building a collection of his work partly in response to alumni interest, a process which has broadened into this project. Only later did he come into focus as the teacher of seminal figures, credited with an important but neglected contribution to modern Appalachian literature, a decade before he arrived begrudgingly at our little school. Indeed, this point may be the only thing many academic readers will find interesting or important (or at least arguable) about Harry Harrison Kroll.

Second, he ranks by numbers alone—and by quite a respectable distance—as Tennessee's most-published author of the twentieth century, yet he is virtually unremembered. Only T. S. Stribling comes close in matching output. That is a curious mix of significance and insignificance.

Third, Kroll's work is so typical of popular writing of the period that it is virtually anonymous. Popular literature may be common in the pejorative sense, but it is also common in the social sense. Because it is common, popular literature provides a window into the time and a culture to which it appeals. Kroll published in venues that most of practitioners of "high literature"—literature spelled with a capital letter—would (and did) consider beneath them, but as a result, he was undoubtedly more widely read across the country than the much-better-remembered Agrarians, whom he knew. Harry Kroll was a populist and regionalist on a national stage, the rural poor white Southern kid who got literate and whose work bridges generations.

The fourth point is related to the third, in that his writing career breaks across two of the three sea changes in American reading culture from the twentieth century, and not many writers managed to do that. The first change was the decline of the popular story magazine following both the rise of commercial radio in the mid 1920s and then the introduction of sound to motion pictures in 1927. The second change is the dramatic upswing in the importance of commercial non-fiction following the Second World War. What happened to Kroll's career as a writer is emblematic of the same affect on the world of popular literature at large. I enjoyed a brief career in the production side of American book publishing, and that caught my attention.

Fifth and finally, frankly, is to do my part in encouraging scholarship to pay attention to the "everyone else" in the world of letters, not merely the pantheon of writers in the canon of literature. This is my driving motivation. We are losing too much of the world's writing as graduate schools train scholars by studying the masters that every other graduate school seems to focus on as well, leaving the scholarly understanding of the rest limited or nonexistent. As I illustrated in the opening paragraphs, the vast majority of popular writers are never studied, their work falls out of fashion and is never read, yet they contribute to the social milieu of a time (and often a place, as well) in ways that *belle lettres* never does. In that sense I am being literarily democratic with a small *d*. There will always be a place for studying giants of literature, but let us remember to include those of the second or third ranks of importance as well. "Spheres of influence" tend to come in all sizes and colors in this kaleidoscope we call literature.

A couple of disclaimers. First, because of personal experience I am sensitive about Nettie Kroll's place, or lack of a place, in the text. This omission stems mostly from a dearth of source material. I hasten to say that Nettie contributed materially to her husband's writing process, and the sum of her influence can be glimpsed in the discussion of one specific book of his discussed in the third chapter. The problem is that what we have of Kroll's private writing focuses solely on him and his work. There is next to nothing from or about her, although her willingness to subsume her personal interests to maintain their home and allow him to write was probably a major reason he was able to pursue the career he did. Had not Harry had a supportive wife, whether ignored, diffident, submissive, or dominated, he would not have had the sort of temporal and social platform that allowed him to write as he did.

Second, and in the vein of temporal and social platforms, some modern literary scholars may find this study to be inadequately literary. This is intentional. As an historian, I tend to harbor at best a wary suspicion of the premises of literary criticism, particularly postmodernism, which, though its grasp is weakening somewhat, still holds a grip over many approaches to literature. Postmodern views tend to privilege language and perceived meaning in its approach. The viewpoint can be useful—if tethered firmly to the factual realities around a writer, but when cut from their moorings, postmodern interpretations tend to read present sensibilities, themes, ideas, and priorities onto the past. That sort of teleological thinking is unfair to the subject, because it may assert motivations or influences an individual simply did not have.

My scholarship tends toward historicism, with its emphasis on the events of the past in their own context of time, place, and culture. This book is about Kroll, the business of his writing, and his times, not really about his literature. With the exception of an important juxtaposition against his contemporaries, the Nashville Agrarians, I do not attempt to put Kroll into much of a Southern or American literary context beyond the skimmed surfaces you will find here. I am a librarian trained in history with topical practice the U.S. of the twentieth century, the American West, and printing history. This biography is written from those perspectives (well, some of them); I do not aspire to the role of textual critic or literary scholar and simply don't have the training to tackle the mechanics of comparative literary criticism (although I do plunge in like a tyro in spots). More attention is paid to the market for popular writing of the period. My criticisms are limited primarily to narration and observation. I measure Kroll's work and his choice of subjects against literary contemporaries only rarely. This work is primarily to provide a foundation and contextual outline for Harry Kroll as a writer of popular literature and the forces during the twentieth century that made him. I will leave to other scholars the job of putting him into a broader literary context.

CHAPTER 1

A Poor-Man's Boy, 1888–1921

A factual picture of Harry Kroll's early life is obscured by the shading and stories he redrew about himself and his family in later years.[1] To his three sons he was as honest as any parent is about his upbringing, but throughout his "autobiographical" writing Kroll consistently spun the story that his parents were less-than-successful Southern sharecroppers, led by an idealistic but unambitious father and superstitious, passively aggressive mother. Where and how he grew up provided twentieth-century Tennessee novelist and short-story writer Harry Harrison Kroll with a broad, fertile field to plough for his crop of stories.

Harry once described his father, Darius Wesley Kroll as "a smallish man, dark from weather and open sunlight and hard work; his hair, jet black, was beginning to [streak] with gray; . . . his expression was placid and without meaning." Though the description sounds harsh or unfeeling, it was a solid compliment paid by Harry to his father. His son consistently portrayed Darius Kroll as one who understood and accepted bone-hard work as an inalienable right; but Harry also painted his father as a man harboring a broad streak of dreamy, impotent idealism that impelled him to hunt ceaselessly for the sure-thing opportunity, or the place where "fried pigeons would fly into his mouth." Despite the picture of a work-faded dreamer he presents, Harry Kroll's nostalgic affection for his father suffuses his writing about him, even when it seems uncomplimentary. Darius—pronounced with the emphasis on the second syllable—hailed from Indiana. Though official notices of him must exist in scattered public records, he left none of his own. The eleventh federal census taken in 1900 records him as born in October 1857. Virtually nothing is known of his early life and training. His youngest daughter, Natalie, recalled in the late 1970s that her father had worked as a machinist in Muncie, Indiana, before his marriage.[2] Given Darius's later documented work history this position was probably as a semi-skilled assistant rather than as a tradesman, a reflection of the industrializing but still heavily human state of technology in the mid- to late nineteenth century.

The picture Harry Kroll draws of his mother, Caroline or Carolina Cripe, is much less flattering but probably more accurate. Where Harry described his father's physical characteristics and hardly ever his mannerisms, his glimpses of his mother are exactly opposite. Kroll rarely described her physically beyond being "a thick-bodied, unbeautiful woman," with a sweat-stained stamina and nearly limitless capacity for hard physical work. The few photographs in which she appears show a tight-lipped woman with the beginnings of jowls on either side of her face. There is little question from which side of the family Harry inherited his own. More often he portrays her through her actions or speech, allowing her constant seeking for signs and portents, the demands she made of her children's affections, and other unflattering glimpses of personality to speak for themselves. She was furious with the picture of her Harry created in his writing, which she reviled for making her appear low and uncultured; his portrayals clearly reflect the long-held anger Harry felt toward her. Family tradition traces her Anabaptist origins indeterminately to the northwest corner of Indiana, between Indianapolis and Chicago. No precise record of her birth to John C. Cripe Jr. and Rachel Ann Fouts Cripe has been located, but the 1900 census enumeration dates it to November, 1862.[3]

Darius and Caroline Kroll were nominally a Dunkard family (more properly, German Baptist Brethren). The Dunkard sect rose in Germany in the early eighteenth century. Their identity comes from the German term for baptism, *tunken,* which assumed an initial *d* when spelled in the United States. Their distinctive practice of baptism distinguished Dunkards from other sects, even from other Protestants: only adults were baptized and the candidate was immersed face down three times while invoking the names of the Father, Son, and Holy Ghost. Two mass migrations from Germany in 1719 and 1729 brought virtually the entire sect to Philadelphia among the early waves of German immigrants to the New World. From there sect members multiplied quickly and began migrating: into mountainous Maryland, Virginia, and North Carolina by the Revolution, and a generation later into the upper Midwest. Those in the mountains were swept up in the Second Great Awakening of the 1820s and integrated into the fire-eating Baptists widely described in Appalachian communities. Those who had moved to the Midwest maintained a tightly knit, pietistic group for another generation. They remained or re-created a cohesive social organization until the first years of the 1880s. Then in a major cultural paradigm shift, the sect stepped into the mainstream of American Protestantism by establishing Sunday Schools, adopting the practice of a paid clergy, and creating a religious revival tradition. These measures split the denomination into three groups at almost exactly the same time that Darius and Caroline Kroll began their family.[4]

That Darius Kroll and Caroline Cripe met and married is a foregone fact, but the circumstances of how and where they met do not survive in a written account, even among their son's writing or in family tradition. Their 1880 marriage is likewise lost in a dim county record somewhere; Darius married in his early twenties, Caroline in her late teens. According to their youngest daughter's memory, about two years later Caroline delivered a baby boy, who is remembered only as Jimmy, and in 1885 another boy, Charles Blaine. Jimmy died while Charlie was still a baby, leaving the younger boy as the oldest child in the family. Harry Harrison was born to the couple at Hartford City, Indiana, on February 18 or 19, 1888. Years later he decided the eighteenth was fine with him and cited it as his birth date. A little more than a year after Harry's birth, a daughter, Mildred Catherine (Millie), was born (May 1889). Finally in March 1897, around the time they determined to move south, a second daughter, Natalie (almost always called Nattie), was born.[5]

About 1890 the family sat for a group portrait. Like many portraits it presents a study of personality and circumstance. Darius and Caroline are bookends of the group, sitting at opposite ends of the family. She sits at the left of the picture in a collarless, plain, dark work dress with Mildred on her lap, eyes caught by the camera flicking down to check Millie. A neutrality on her face comes across as forced,

The Caroline and Darius Kroll family, ca. 1890: the children, *left to right,* are Mildred (six to nine months), Charles Blaine ("Soddy," six), and Harry Harrison (two, still in skirts). Natalie (Nattie, or "Hatch") would not be born for another six to eight years.

leaving the slightest sign of a tight-lipped frown as the image was taken. Charlie stands between his parents—a meek, round-faced five- or six-year-old with close-cropped hair—wearing a sack coat over his shirt, the loose fist of his right hand holding on uncertainly to two fingers of his left. As far away from his wife as photographic convenience will allow, Darius sits with legs crossed on a wooden kitchen chair, a violin stood upright on one knee with his elbow on a table beside the chair and the bow set casually across his lap. He has a rather weak chin, which he has offset with a broad but rather thin mustache. His hair is short without being cropped, but is shaped or styled only by leaving an unruly or at least ill-combed length on the crown. Darius's eyes glance off to a place beside the camera in an ill-timed, momentary distraction—symbolically, perhaps, it may appear as if he is distracted from the richness of the present by looking for some better, golden chance elsewhere. His bow hand rests on the left shoulder of his youngest son, Harry, who stands closely beside his father in a pattern-print dress. Such attire was the common lot of young boys until they could make it regularly to the outhouse on their own. Harry looks like a typical child, until after a moment an inconsistency in the picture resolves to visual awareness: Harry's left arm is noticeably smaller than is his right. It is not a trick of light; as an infant Harry contracted a mild case of polio. The disease spared his lungs and legs but deadened many of the nerves in one shoulder and upper arm. While he had effective use of his fingers and some rudimentary mobility in the arm itself throughout his life, his left arm was essentially a deadweight. In photographs taken late in life he is often seen with his strong right hand cradling its twin protectively in front of him, or with the left hand hidden by convenient nonchalance in a trouser pocket.

Like so many rural, nineteenth-century Americans, virtually nothing about the Krolls exists in records of any sort. By the late 1890s, the family had moved south to Vincennes, Indiana. With family homes two hundred miles north, why they went to Vincennes, when they arrived, and if they remained long enough for the two girls to be born there as well is a mystery (all the census enumerator recorded on his sheets in 1900 for anyone's place of birth was "Indiana"). Beyond this, nothing at all about the Krolls' early family life is known beyond a few pet names. Darius seemed to have been addressed by his first name by all his children, though Caroline was "Ma." As he was learning to speak, before the girls were born, Harry seemed unable to pronounce the consonantal *ch* and *l* sounds in Charlie's name, which became "Soddy" in his immature speech. Among the family the name stuck. Even sixty years later when he wrote his siblings, Charles still neatly signed his name "Soddy." Millie became "Murdy." Nattie acquired the nickname "Hatch" from her oldest brother since he teased her mercilessly about being hatched under a rock rather than born. As the years passed, however, her brother's teasing took on an affectionate tone between them. On the other hand, Mildred despised her nickname with passion.[6]

In Indiana, the Krolls were among thousands of rural families uprooting from settled American farming communities, pressured from several directions. After the economic expansion of the 1880s, the panic of 1893 rippled outward from the collapse of railroad stocks into the rest of the economy, upsetting credit markets, trade cycles, and farm prices. At the same time a series of droughts in the early1890s left farmers without incomes. Drought debts fueled a round of farm consolidations at the same time that unclaimed arable property in the Midwest was becoming scarce and land prices were increasing. Family holdings of first- and second-generation immigrants were being divided among heirs in parcels too small to sustain them. The average size of land holdings was growing, as smaller parcels were consolidated in the hands of more successful farmers who, thanks to mechanization, could operate on a larger scale. Developments in agricultural implements which made farm consolidation possible also provided for the breaking and cultivation of new land in the huge open spaces of the treeless western plains. Midwesterners—particularly the Brethren, and often as entire communities—responded to territorial land promotions on the high plains of the Dakotas and flocked westward to open the last homesteads of the century. Creating the larger market-responsive farms of the Midwest and new settlement on the Great Plains was possible only through mechanization, which required capital.

A stronger draw, however, pulled rural Americans toward the growing number of manufacturing jobs in burgeoning cities. The U.S. population had gravitated toward the cities as the country industrialized after the Civil War, but even as late as the 1890s a substantial percentage of the country's population was still rural, particularly in the South. Being of German Baptist extraction, Darius and Caroline Kroll were undoubtedly aware of the general dispersal among the sect's fourth- and fifth-generation families. Though some congregations began affecting the standardized costumes that later distinguished Amish and Hutterite sects, most did not. The Dunkard communities were assimilating quickly.

For those who remained on small family holdings, self-sustaining diversification on individual prairie-state farms was shrinking. Older, traditional hand- and animal-powered agriculture was dying quickly. To maintain a working hold on traditional non-mechanical, family based agriculture, a crop succession was required, away from cereal grains to grocery crops. With the new land of the Great Plains unsuited for this type of agriculture, some of the Brethren looked southward to the newly cleared lands of the Southern Pine Belt.

Farm mechanization was slower in the South since the region retained a large, essentially captive labor force. Two races could be played against each other to control labor costs, with a third wildcard—the threat of foreign immigrants—that could be played at will by property and industrial owners if the first two did not cooperate. All three groups could be bound down by the shackles of debt and the inverted economy of scale that family labor represented. Southern farms, tied not to high-yield grains, but to labor-intensive row crops like sweet potatoes, cotton, tobacco, and corn, tended to be divided into small operations under sharecropping or tenancy arrangements, or worked as a smallholding. Working for shares or as tenants against a line of credit, extended and accounted only by the landowner, virtually guaranteed that laborers could never progress up the "agricultural tenure ladder"—sharecropper to tenant, tenant to land-owning smallholder, smallholder to labor-contracting planter. In the 1880 census a large percentage of Alabama's white population had been smallholders, but land ownership consolidation had occurred in this section too. By 1890 most rural whites across the Deep South had sold or defaulted on their land and become tenants. By the turn of the twentieth century the vast majority of Alabama landowners never actually worked on the land they owned. A large percentage of the state's populace—often off-season farm laborers—also worked for wages in the extensive Southern pinewoods extracting railroad ties, softwood lumber, and turpentine. Still more worked in the coal mines of extreme southern Appalachia, and in the steel and cotton mills that later sprang up.[7] Life in the Deep South for virtually all blacks and most whites, native or immigrant, was a ceaseless round of hard, unremitting work and frequent migration.

Of course, promoters emphasized the opportunities inherent in the South's snowless climate and heavy forests. Nearly eighty years after the fact, the Kroll's youngest daughter recalled—or perhaps speculated—about the motivation that brought the family from Indiana to Alabama, a strange contravention to the general westward exodus of the Brethren at the time. "My dad heard that everything was wonderful down South," she said. "Somebody had made a trip to Alabama and [reported that] everything was wonderful down there, they lived in big houses like a king and queen. Then my dad decided to come to Alabama. That's where they were headed for." If Nattie's memory accurately reflects her parents' motivation, it is tempting to wonder just what Darius and Caroline Kroll had been told. It would be a guess, but a coincident German Baptist venture based in Alabama provides a tempting foundation upon which to speculate.

Among the Midwestern German Baptist Brethren communities was an undercurrent that flowed south, against the general emigration tides to the north and west. Around 1895 one branch of the Brethren had bought large parcels of public land in west Alabama and was developing it specifically for their northern kin and fellow believers. Given the timing of the Krolls' move, 1896, it is very likely that Darius and Caroline had seen or were at least aware of James M. Neff's baldly promotional *Southern Almanac and Hand Book,* published by a development company specifically to attract other Brethren families to a swath of yellow pine forest in the southwest corner of the state. In 1894 Neff had been a teacher at Mt. Morris College in

Illinois, and moonlighted at the Brethren's Publishing Company. Neff approached another educator, N. R. Baker from Mobile County, Alabama, about the possibility of establishing an educational and colonial enterprise somewhere in the sparsely settled areas of the South. In October 1895 the Brethren's School Company was incorporated. Funded with several gifts of unoccupied land, which was to be sold to finance the school operations, a primary school was established in Fruitdale. The Deer Park Academy was acquired in a town of the same name, and Citronelle College was founded in a two-story frame building there. The Brethren School Company was officially a private educational organization, yet the firm and its directors were closely tied to the Alabama Land and Development Company. The latter was actively engaged in enticing colonists south, promoting southern migration among the families of German Baptist extraction in more settled Midwestern areas across Iowa, Illinois, and Indiana. The Krolls were almost certainly among those who elected to try their luck among the sandy pines, but they managed to get to Alabama only after a ten-year delay.[8]

Natalie was only an infant when the family left Indiana, but she claimed that around 1896 Darius loaded the family and their possessions into a wagon and headed for Alabama. Her information is faulty (she was born in Indiana herself the next year, so she was obviously off a bit). Seventy years or so later she recalled to one of Harry's sons that their family had managed to get as far as Dyersburg, Tennessee, before the team wore out and their wagon broke irreparably. Harry opened his 1936 book *I Was a Share-Cropper* with the same story: his narrative begins autobiographically as the weary and travel-worn family crosses the Mississippi River and pulls into West Tennessee. If the accounts are correct (and the accuracy of Natalie's memory and Harry's book are both somewhat suspect), then the family probably crossed the Wabash River and the southern tip of Illinois heading for the bridge at Cape Girardeau, Missouri. Turning south, they would have trailed through the cotton lands of the Missouri bootheel and ferried the Mississippi River about where Interstate 55 now bridges the river. Natalie, as noted above, was an infant at the time; Harry would have been eight.

Frankly, there are problems with both versions of the story. The route is hardly a direct road between Indiana and Alabama. Harry's "memoir" as a whole was essentially fanciful, based only loosely on fact, and Natalie's old-age reminiscence—the only other account of the family's early life—is suspect because it parrots her brother's book in so many details. A skeptic could speculate that because *Share-Cropper* was so prominent in family politics it is possible that the whole story about limping into Dyersburg was simply invented by Harry and unwittingly assumed to be accurate by his youngest sister because their mother hated his book so badly. Yet if Natalie's version is not accepted at face value (she was, after all, an infant at the point she describes) it must at least be considered. So both Harry and Nattie say the family limped into Dyersburg.

The Brethren's School Company land, however, straddled the southern stretch of the Mobile & Ohio Railroad main line, which reached northward from the Gulf port at Mobile, Alabama, to St. Louis, Missouri. At Cairo, Illinois, the M&O connected with the Terra Haute & Indianapolis Railroad (Vandalia Line), which passed straight through Vincennes, Indiana. Under an arrangement with the School Company, the M&O was offering free transportation to Brethren moving to the Alabama settlements. Given the preeminence of rail over roads for interstate travel in the late nineteenth century, it is positively curious why the Krolls did not take the train. Perhaps they did, but Harry later decided that riding the train hardly met with the idea of a poor white sharecropper on the move, and wrote it out of his story. Perhaps they had money enough only for passage part of the way. We do not know. But irrespective of how the family arrived in Tennessee, they did, and the facts of the family's landing there and their reasons for settling there are probably an irrecoverable detail.[9]

The family settled into Dyersburg, the seat of Dyer County. In 1895 Dyersburg was a town of about 2,800, good-sized by nineteenth century standards. The town sits about fifteen miles inland from the Mississippi, almost exactly parallel with the bottom of the Missouri bootheel. It was a regional cotton depot, its fields and gins producing baled cotton by the trainload, destined for the Memphis cotton market. By Natalie's account, Darius found work in the municipal electric plant and the family settled into a large house "of eight or nine rooms" about a mile from town. Her account presents a far different picture than the accommodation Harry later portrayed as a ramshackle sharecropper's cabin in *I Was a Share-Cropper.* Around Dyersburg young Harry may have observed firsthand the rock-hard existence of cotton sharecropping, but the family circumstance was probably not what Harry Kroll later described. He may have worked a garden plot for family provender, and he and the other children may have done fieldwork on a seasonal basis. If Natalie's memory is accurate and Darius worked for the city, he did not remain there long. The 1900 census lists his occupation not as a city worker but as "dairy man," and notes that his house was rented, not owned, so he was likely working as herdsman or milker for another landholder. Thirty years later in the typesetter's manuscript for *Share-Cropper,* the publisher uniformly changed the name of George W. Pierce—who may have been Darius Kroll's employer—to George Washington "Wash" Kinsey.[10]

Though the Krolls remained in Dyersburg for nearly a decade, they avoided notice in virtually every public record: they neither bought nor sold land, were neither sued for non-payment of their debts nor resorted to the law to collect what was owed them. No one in the family was born, died, was declared incompetent, or became a ward of the courts. Darius never a served as witness or juror, was charged with no breach of law, evidently paid their debts, and owned no personal property of sufficient value to tax. They did no business that required a pledge of assets against a contract, which was common in what was still largely a cash, barter, and private-credit society. The only Dyer County or Dyersburg city record in which a family member actually appears is the county tax assessment record. Darius was annually assessed a $2 poll tax. Since the poll book columns were never marked "paid," he never voted in an election, either. By 1900, when he reached an age sufficient to be exempted from the poll tax, the entire family had already vanished into complete legal anonymity.[11]

In his publishers' advertising material and while teaching college courses years later, Harry was fond of claiming that he had never been to school. The claim must be taken at face value since no contemporary records exist to confirm or disprove it, but there are historical problems with Kroll's claim. The chief problem is that his major piece of "autobiographical" writing is largely fiction, but it is virtually the only comment on his early life and the closest thing to source material that exists. Both parents were literate, and Darius was said to read music as well. The couple demonstrated some commitment to education. Thirty years later, in one of the few passages more likely to be autobiographically accurate in *Share-Cropper,* Kroll discussed his introduction to literature in listening to his mother and older brother read from the reading material common to the working class of the day—story papers, delivered weekly. The two girls made a daily rail trip to and from school after the family moved further south. Soddy became a respected architectural draftsman and later a chemical-plant worker for Monsanto, which requires specialized training, Harry's earliest publications reveal a fairly sophisticated familiarity with writing that his claim does not support.

Even if he *was* natively bright and a quick study, it is exceedingly unlikely that Harry Kroll would have developed into the sort of writer that he became, strictly on his own. The Krolls were a family with some attainments, however limited; but while the two boys were young they worked for wages instead of attending school. It would not have raised many eyebrows. "Poor whites feared the loss of wages," notes Alabama historian J. Wayne Flynt, "but also resented the way compulsory school attendance laws meddled with their children's lives."[12] Yet the family also probably realized that literacy was a means of social improvement. Harry Kroll frequently invoked a theme of "I cannot remember a time when I could not read" as evidence of individual effort when impressing someone with his rise-from-rural-poverty upbringing. What broader literacy Harry gained came from natural talent as a reader, listening to the stories read from story papers on the porch in the evenings, and whatever infrequent efforts Caroline (or more likely Darius) made in educating the children at home; but it came hard won, primarily by self-driven study. Unless he was flatly lying about never attending school, literacy and education became a lodestone for Harry Kroll quite early in life. At twelve Harry secured a subscription to *Cosmopolitan,* which was then a literary magazine, by saving three hundred discarded tobacco-sack tags and gum wrappers.[13] Literacy became important to him.

The American working class of the Gilded Age (1869–1896), both urban and rural, read almost as avidly as the middle and upper classes, though their literature differed from the magazines and books more likely to be preserved and remembered in libraries. Most of it came in the form of cheap serials, either bought in newsstands, at drug store and tobacconists' counters, or by subscription through the mail. America's mainstream publishing industry shifted generationally in the 1880s, and its three market segments—books, newspapers, and magazines—underwent a paradigm shift as well. The popularity of sophisticated literary of writers like Oliver Wendell Holmes, William Dean Howells, Louisa May Alcott, and Henry James declined overall in favor of what literary historian Christopher Wilson has called "popular naturalism," stemming from the Progressive views of individuals like editors Edward Bok and Samuel S. McClure. A social conscience crept quietly into mainstream American fiction and magazine culture, one that saw its highest expression in the Muckraking journalists of the 1880s and 1890s. Concern for actual conditions over abstract ideals, sparked by endemic industrial exploitation, seeped broadly into popular writing just at the time that Harry Kroll was discovering American letters. Of course, Harry Kroll and most of the rest of working America did not read within the literary mainstream. He read the "common" or "casual literature" of the day: cheap weekly publications like the four- and eight-page story papers published by Sunday School organizations, and the children's columns of farm-life family publications like *Our Country Home* or *Progressive Farmer.* Delivered by mail and passed from hand to hand, both genres had broad rural followings. Virtually every publication available included short fiction in its pages—windows into worlds of adventure and invitations to moral development—that would have supplemented the standard education of the day.[14] For Harry Kroll, reading and rereading casual literature substituted for an education.

Even during the late nineteenth and early twentieth centuries it would have been common for a poor rural kid, particularly in the South, to have little or no formal education at all, for several reasons. First, schools were pinned to specific locations in a community but attracted children from rural families thinly dispersed over large areas. Grandparents' and great-grandparents' stories of walking miles to school, at which later generations rolled their eyes, were not necessarily exaggerations, since non-work transportation was severely limited or nonexistent. Second, from the time they were large enough to swing a hoe or pull a cotton boll, children's labor often represented a substantial labor asset for a poor family. Working the land or earning wages at a factory was common in childhood until child labor laws were enforced in the 1920s.

In his upbringing Harry Kroll did indeed learn how to work and to work hard. As he grew, work opportunities shifted and changed. For a few years as an early teen, Harry was a delivery boy for Portillio's Meat Market, a circumstance he worked into a memorable short story, "My Mother," which appeared in the *Atlantic* and was adapted for inclusion in *Share-Cropper*.[15] During his mid-teens he served as a message runner for the Dyersburg Western Union telegraph office on east Court Street for awhile. In Harry's late teens Darius is said to have bought into the novelty of early motion pictures. He secured a projector and record player, and bought or rented a few short reels which could be secured through the mail from commercial film distributors. Charlie and Harry hit the road with a traveling movie show, hauling their equipment between schoolhouses, working the Dyersburg area as theatre operators. Harry's capacity for hard work over long hours as a youth paid off in later life when he focused on producing typed manuscripts by the ream.

While they lived in Tennessee, Darius and Caroline continued to look southward and had not lost sight of the temperate climate and agricultural ease that Alabama promised. At some point late in the summer of 1906 the couple recalled their itinerant sons from travels with the projector, moved out of their home in Dyersburg, and landed temporarily in Meridian, Mississippi. Charlie and Harry were happy to come, since they were losing movie business to a competitor with better equipment. Seventy years later Natalie remembered making the trip by wagon; more likely they went by rail. By November the family settled into a rented forty-acre parcel in the tiny west Alabama sawmill town of Yellow Pine. With merely a hundred residents in 1918, it was little beyond a log-loading rail stop. Yellow Pine, named for the company that processed the trees of the same name, was a lumber and turpentine town along the Mobile & Ohio Railroad line between Mobile and Meridian, Mississippi, virtually on the state line. A family photo dated November 1906 shows the family standing outside what is most probably their new residence. It is a painted (or whitewashed) two-story affair with a decent front porch, suggesting that the family's income was at least sufficient enough to provide better-than-average accommodations. Why they were attracted to such a small community is not adequately explained by Natalie's memory of land-agent platitudes. It is much more likely that they were still drawn by the decade-old promotional promises of the Brethren's School Company brochures. Caroline at least had grown up in the Brethren religious tradition.[16]

For a century, Alabama's cheap land had attracted a huge population of immigrants (mostly Scots-Irish) who became the state's white rural poor. These were not jobless families, but rather individuals who worked assets they did not own or who, despite their work, could not realize economic gain.[17] Alabama was a public-lands state. Creek Indian lands in Alabama had been preempted by white European squatters before 1818 and were parceled out to legal settlers thereafter, even though most could not meet even the minimal federal payments of $1.25 per acre on the land they occupied. Undisturbed, the thin soil may have been ideal for pine trees but was inadequate for virtually every other crop. Stripped of its trees and the fallen needles that carpeted the forest floor, the loose soil eroded almost willfully, leaving leering orange gashes in the landscape. Soil loss worsened as greater and greater areas were cleared. Most settler families quickly declined into subsistence agriculture, and a bare subsistence at that. By 1845 even the federal land commissioner was petitioning for easier payment schedules. Only with the widespread introduction of cotton, a readily marketable cash crop, in the 1850s was there a genuine bettering of economic conditions, until by 1860 roughly 80 percent of white cotton farmers owned the land they worked. This, the only real period of reasonably general prosperity in Alabama's history, was coincident with the Civil War.[18] Cotton brought prosperity to land owners, but only if they could also collect and hold onto the labor needed to work the crop. Cotton became an economy of scale in which those of limited means could not meaningfully compete. Alabama's cotton culture had the equal and opposite reaction of Newton's first law of motion: within a generation or two, farm work stripped assets, evaporated personal economic power, and bound almost inextricably those whose primary asset was their manual labor, whether black (as slaves or as freedmen) or white.

While the Deep South is culturally portrayed as a two-class, racially divided society, there were actually three separate, almost rigid, social classes. One was exclusively white, made up of those who controlled the vast percentage of wealth in the state (property and position, and the power that accompanied them). The second consisted of blacks, descendants of slaves, together with the offspring of racial miscegenation, which was always defined as black. The third class was the overwhelming majority of a Southern state's white population: poor white families working land, mill machinery, and mines. Scholars have long pointed out how closely related were the social and economic issues facing blacks and poor whites, but also how radically rigid racial divisions, stoked by the wealthy, kept both groups from making economic progress.[19]

After the war, with land holdings subject to Reconstruction, and the population to displacement and hunger, Alabama's economy turned to extractive industry of various sorts and basic processing: coal dug from the Appalachian hills fueled Birmingham's iron mills; timbering in the virgin pine-belt forests sawed lumber, hacked railroad ties, and bled pinesap for turpentine stills. Yellow Pine and a hundred other similar towns were cut into tiny clearings in the Southern woods, a seemingly limitless forest that spread like a broad smile across the chin of the continent from east Texas to the Georgia coast. The post-Civil War world began cutting into the rich forests. Machinery began bringing to market the old-growth logs of virgin timber, straight as an arrow, three and four and five feet thick. Isolated turpentine camps exploited the smaller trees, tapping and cooking the pungent pine sap for the strong solvent that was a staple of industrial production. This was the setting William Faulkner wrote about in his classic short story "The Bear." By 1905 the silent long-leaf and yellow pine woods were already cut through with loggers' drag-trails—the stillness broken by the echoing knock of distant axes; the chain rattles of shuffling ox teams tugging at their loads; the sharp whine of saws licking through logs in rickety, open-sided shacks; and by the steamy chuff and shriek from dozens of small steam railroads. The woods were being cleared and a second generation was being invited in to turn the sandy grey and orange soils of south Alabama into the country's agricultural garden spot.

There were still huge tracts of open, unclaimed federal land in Alabama up until the early twentieth century, which made the state a focus of development schemes. James Neff was a major figure in the group that established Fruitdale and Citronelle, about sixty miles north of Mobile in the yellow pine forest. Neff's *Southern Almanac* touted the suitability of the climate and land, once cleared, for rotated-crop produce farming. It was filled with testimonials, photos, and suggestions of the comparative ease with which wealth could be won. His brochure was identical to scores of similar promotional items that described virtually the entire continent in strikingly similar terms. Such promotional stuff was a magnetic attraction to the landless, like the

The Kroll home in Yellow Pine, Alabama, 1906. Darius, Natalie, Caroline, Mildred, Harry, Charles (Soddy).

anxious sons and daughters of intensely agrarian but landlocked social cultures in the American midland, such as the German Baptists. What promoters like Neff and settlers like the Krolls overlooked or ignored were the wide variations in the state's quilt of economic prosperity. Despite the promises, the sandy, acidic soil—ideal for native pines—was not rich enough to support either most root crops or the grass needed for intensive grazing. The garden produce familiar to families who were used to rich, black-loam midwestern prairies simply could not be grown in Alabama, despite the more temperate climate.

For their part, the German Baptists came late to the region. Yellow Pine was a wye junction where the Washington & Choctaw Railway, ran north from the M&O tracks. It was initially a ten-mile dummyline spur built by the timber company, which originally dead-ended in a town ignominiously named Fail. A few years later the line was extended north to connect with the Alabama, Tennessee & Northern Railroad the line Bolinger. When the Kroll family arrived, Nattie remembered, Soddy and Harry landed jobs in a local mill, despite Harry's obvious physical handicap, most probably the E. W. Gates Lumber Company. Their father, she remembered, worked in the railroad station until someone realized that he had experience as a machinist and induced him to work in a repair shop. By then the family's two girls were of school age. "The girls went to private school down there," Nattie remembered years later. "My dad decided to enroll Millie and I in the Springhill school down there. We rode the work train which left at six o'clock in the morning. . . . At six o'clock in the evening we rode back to Yellow Pine."[20]

The family soon moved a few miles down the tracks to Fruitdale. They remained there while Charles and Harry worked at various occupations as opportunity permitted. Harry may have loved or hated the work, but familiarity with logging camps, railroads, and field work later allowed him to draw upon his work experience for realistic story settings.

Out in the World

By 1908 Harry was nineteen and had had enough of the family's redneck existence.[21] Stoking his discontent with youthful ambition, he began aspiring to something more suited to his physical disability and temperament. Sometime that year, he and Charles ordered a camera outfit from the Sears and Roebuck catalogue and decided to set up "a little studio" twenty miles south across the Mobile County line in the larger town of Citronelle, Alabama. Exactly what the arrangements were and how long Charles and Harry lasted as storefront businessmen isn't known, but evidently the trade wasn't good enough to stay fixed in one place. At some point in 1908 or early 1909 the pair closed their door in town and took to the road as itinerant photographers. Until 1910 the two brothers tramped about the rural southwest corner of Alabama with their cameras, a canvas tent, and a portable darkroom laboratory. Photography at this professional level was strictly a daylight business, which left nineteen-year-old Harry evenings beside the campfire and slack times to read and to chase whatever unattached young women were in the neighborhood.

The quickest, easiest transportation around the countryside was by rail. The pair drifted down the M&O tracks from Citronelle toward Mobile, then turned north again, closely following the line of the old Alabama Great Southern, which had become the Southern Railway a decade earlier. More than fifty years later, Soddy reminisced to his younger brother, "I have cherished recollections of our piney wood days when we struck out together in the little studio at Citronelle, to hit the road with stopping off stands at Homer Turner's sawmill; near Oak Grove; Mount Vernon [barely a dozen miles due east of Citronelle]; Carson Station across the Tombigbee from Jackson; . . . We were very close in the times of our early venture."

In December 1909 the pair landed in the neighborhood of Fulton, Alabama, dominated by the large Scotch Lumber Company sawmill, and planted themselves to work the territory in an older, less successful settlement named Alameda. On their first night in town Charles and Harry boarded with a school trustee named Danzey whose family also boarded the local schoolteacher, a Miss Annette Heard. A day or two later the photographers set up their tent in an open space between the railroad tracks and some abandoned shacks, and went into business. Their informal introduction to the school system paid off. Harry shot a negative of the local school; Miss Annette ordered a dozen prints from the photographers. He and Soddy ate well for a week on that $3.50 commission.

Coming as they did just before Christmas, Charles and Harry were drawn into the local holiday celebration. The schoolteacher had a Christmas tree in her school and thoughtfully hung an orange on it for each of the tramp photographers. "To show the perfidy of the young male animal in his early courting stages," wrote Harry years later, "I was also walking evenings with a . . . pineywoods girl named Cynthia Kelly, and she was sitting with me at that tree. . . ." Harry gave her half of the orange, an event Nettie sometimes mentioned strategically in later years.

The local school teacher in Fulton was Hattie Annette ("Nettie") Heard, daughter of Robert C. Heard of Grove Hill, Alabama, the Clarke County seat a few miles south of Fulton. R. C. Heard served as superintendent of education in Clarke County between 1896 and 1909, but in its social order he was insufficiently notable to be featured with other former local officials in the county history a few years later.[22] The Heards were a family of schoolteachers, well-educated people by rural Alabama standards, but the family did not possess land holdings and therefore either the economic or social standing to qualify as gentry. Annette had grown up above the rural, dirt-poor poverty that Harry had, but not far above it. Following the family business, she had aspired to a teaching career and attended Alabama Normal College in Livingston (now the University of West Alabama) during the 1906–07 school year. Harry recalled to their son after her death that "she found a greater fulfillment in going to school at Livingston than maybe anything she ever did." She was bitterly disappointed when her father's recurrent problem with alcohol, and the family's poverty required her to quit school and return home to help provide for them. Withdrawal from school at Livingston ended her formal education and prevented her from earning a college degree.[23] Harry, however, remembered her as an excellent schoolteacher who could read and write Latin fluently.

Harry Kroll's previous romances of convenience had been with young women of similar social and economic background. Annette Heard and her family, however, were "reading people." When spinning the story of his upbringing to later audiences, Harry claimed that he had married the local schoolteacher, who agreed to his proposal only on the condition that he get an education. It may be a romantic story but is almost certainly a fabrication. It is more likely that the shy, vaguely pretty schoolteacher was a lodestar whose attention in return finally gave direction and drive to his private aspirations. Nettie's position as a teacher represented a type of social authority to which Harry, with his background as a redneck dirt farmer and laborer, had glimpsed only occasionally, and then only from the outside and below. Certainly, courting Nettie Heard prompted him toward making a social climb toward formal literacy, writing, and the cultural refinement that they implied. This change of perspective, brought about by his acquaintance and budding romance in a muddy south Alabama townlet, became perhaps the watershed moment in his existence.

Harry quickly dropped his attentions to other young women, and he and Miss Heard kept each other's company through the spring. Within a few weeks the teacher began meeting him at church, and then walking there and back with the picture maker, much to the disapproval of the school board. "It was kind of an unwritten law in those parts that no teacher was human enough to have a boy friend," Kroll later noted. "We drifted toward an understanding in the spontaneous way of those who neglect the formalism of human affairs, and want love quite terribly." Perhaps their mutual longing for stability grew out of each of them having a family that remained together but exacted a high emotional price from its members. Alcoholism seems to have defined Nettie's family and shaped her future since she shaped her ambitions to its stresses. Similarly, the demanding emotional domination Harry's mother exhibited appears to have been a caricature of affection between family members. Surely these challenges, coupled to poverty but fueled by moderate ambition, drew the two emotionally hungry young people together.

Eventually the photographers had worked through the Alameda/Fulton area thoroughly. Before the Kroll boys left town, Harry visited his girl and bumbled out an informal proposal to Miss Heard. "'Some of these times, well—er—.' And she understood and nodded and that was it. Nothing like a formal declaration of love," he confessed decades later to their children, "indeed I wonder if I knew what love was—or did she. But it was an understanding. So we were engaged to marry at some indefinite time in the future not stated, or even discussed."[24] Their troth plighted, the couple parted a few days later. Harry and Soddy followed the country railroad line north and east about twenty miles to the little crossroads settlement at Pine Hill. After her Fulton contract closed, Annette turned south toward home at Grove Hill. Following a short stay there, Annette's father sent her to board with his sister a few miles away at Gosport to complete two months of another teacher's school contract. Perhaps she had let it be known she had a suitor and her father intended this arrangement to put as much distance as possible between his daughter and the white-trash upstart photographer. The distance was not great enough to matter. On one occasion, while Soddy was out drumming business on the road, Harry caught a train from Pine Hill south through Grove Hill to Whatley and then hiked the remaining seven miles to Gosport. On a whim at Suggsville he bought a pair of snappy patent-leather shoes and planned to arrive in style. "I carried along a spare collar in the camera's hollow body. I remember that beautiful walk," he remembered years later to his sons.

> I toted my coat and hit the long trail. Everywhere the niggers were breaking cotton land. They'd wave as I passed and call, "Mornin' boss." I would call back and we'd exchange smiles and I clocked off the miles in my patent leathers, my feet burning. Yet the transparency of the day, the sappy youth in my bones, the joy of being alive, of being in love, they all remain strangely nostalgic in my memory.[25]

He spent the weekend with Nettie, her Aunt Ibbie, and Uncle Bob Brewer. Other than Nettie, the rest of the dour household were not thrilled with their niece's visitor. Before he left, the couple made a visit to the river landing and shot a roll of photographs of themselves.

For awhile in the late winter or early spring of 1910 the two photographers worked fruitlessly around Pine Hill but eventually gave up, riding the dummyline Alabama and North West Railroad west into the south end of Marengo County. There the pair landed at Dixons Mills, just over the Clarke County line, about a hundred miles almost due north of Mobile and roughly sixty from their parents' home. There they made arrangements to board with William A. Dixon for ten cents a meal, which included permission to pitch their canvas residence/business establishment in his orchard. There the census enumerator located them in mid-April 1910, and enrolled them as boarders with Dixon and his wife Dollie, their son Elmore, and Dixon's eighty-two-year-old mother, Tilda Dixon.[26] Though Harry did not know it, Dixons Mills would be an on-again, off-again home for nearly another decade.

The orchard represented a metamorphosis for Harry Kroll, the way a cocoon marks a change from caterpillar to adult. It was his circumstance and location for making the sorts of life-changing choices made in youth. When they had struck out on their enterprise a year or so earlier, Harry had cut a deal with Soddy that had given him a large part of the day to loaf or chase local girls wherever they camped. Soddy did the photographic legwork, traveling the road with a straw boater hat and broad smile, making contacts and taking the portraits, while Harry remained in camp to do darkroom developing and printing, the housekeeping, and lay on meals. No more.

Meeting Annette and making their tenuous engagement seem to have galvanized Harry's ambition—no more laying about the tent. He grabbed a camera and set out on the road as well. Using the Dixon orchard as a base, the brothers separated, working the territory in opposite directions with their cameras. Harry was losing interest in the business, however, and wanted a way out. "This time I was working hard to get a stake so as to knock off and study and later go to school," he remembered. "It was the idea that Soddy and I had been talking around the fringes of for a long while. It recommended itself to us as the handiest avenue of escape from the blind alley of picture-making. It was the prospect of marriage that made me touch the plan with decision, to start putting it into action."[27] With a few weeks of hard selling, Harry managed to save $60, part of which he promptly invested in a stack of state-approved schoolbooks. Back in the tent, having kept enough money to scrimp by temporarily while Soddy continued to "smoke pi'tures," Harry fell to studying. Through the late fall of 1909, just as Jack London had done a decade earlier, Kroll held himself to a strict, self-imposed study regimen, eight to ten hours daily, an hour or so working the schoolbook problems on each subject, taking time every few weeks to walk the tracks twenty miles to visit Annette.

It was also during this period of feverish change and personal development that Harry was gripped with the urge to create, and wrote his first novel. In a reminiscent letter written to his two surviving sons in 1962—a year after their mother's death and barely three months after their youngest brother Dan's passing—Harry related the beginning of his writing career, but with slightly different details than his other accounts. His first story, he told his sons, had been written longhand in a fit of romantic literary excitement. "I did it in pencil on a scratch tablet, 10 pages to the chapter, 20 chapters to the book. I wrote a chapter a day. It was my first experience of sitting still and writing and I remember how tired I got. But I finished the book."[28] In *I Was a*

Share-Cropper (1937), the story of his first story was worked into the narrative, again with some variation: "Twenty sheets of scratch paper to the chapter and twenty chapters to the book," he remembered. "I was . . . going forward . . . [with a] boy and girl and making their story, conventionally leaving them when they were married. I wrote because I loved it. Nothing could have been more remote from my mind than any hope that someday I would be a writer. I had never seen a writer." [29]

Harry's early attempt may have been an immature effort, but its writing seems to have fixed the tone and topic for his perspective of what constituted "literature." The conception of romantic boy-meets-girl fiction, born of his youthful experience with juvenile popular literature and themes, and probably flavored at the time by his own budding romance, formed the thematic core of Kroll's literary ventures for the rest of his life. Virtually every book of his, with the exception of his late-life nonfiction, revolves around romantic relationships—usually troubled, and always passionate. Harry was excited to have written something of his own, but quickly tossed it away. Other than himself, Charles and perhaps Nettie were the only souls who might have seen it. This story may have been little more than untrained ramblings, but it was the beginning of a lifelong creative process.

Kroll had developed as a reader and came to writing at the historical point in which Victorian Romanticism had been essentially replaced by what historian Christopher Wilson calls the "popular naturalism" of the Progressive period. Wilson identifies several, often contradictory elements in this broad style of writing. First is the tradition of a central character, adopted from Romanticism, and blended with a journalistic use of specific facts, direct purpose, and straightforward narrative. It was a style, Wilson notes, that refused to give up the tropes of romance, but attempted to bring journalistic accuracy and social focus into the realm of literature. Second is a strongly self-referential, almost narcissistic voice, one that employed forward-moving fact and purpose over the being and feeling of Romanticism. Kroll reflected this by writing much of his short work and at least two novels using first-person voice, and telling most of his stories from the viewpoint of one narrator. Third, popular naturalism appreciated technical skill and ability, an element that reflects the influence of industrialism. During the Progressive Era (1890s to the 1920s), writing for publication also changed. It became a genuine market, shifting from a mostly informal, avocational process to a professional basis, where writers expected to make a living from the sale of their manuscripts to publishers. Also writing in these years, Samuel Clemens never entirely gave up the "lyceum" or public-lecture circuit, but publication became an increasingly larger segment of his income as the twentieth century crept closer. Finally, the popular naturalism approach attempted to illustrate life as it was really lived, sometimes idealized, but always believable. Fantastic literature would come, but popular literature prior to the Great War attempted to draw and paint believable characters and settings in "real" terms.[30] This was the approach to literature that fueled most writers read by the young photographer, studying in a tent amid a southern Alabama orchard.

Later that winter (1909–10) Harry Kroll had had enough of self instruction and enrolled for a single term at the local school in Dixons Mills to at least experience formal education. He was twenty-one. Kroll had mastered his schoolbook collection well enough to place with the seventh- through ninth-year classes in various subjects. That was something of an accomplishment in itself. Marengo County boasted 109 schools (63 of them for white students) for its official population of 2,742 white and 10,060 colored children between the ages six and twenty-one. About 80 percent of white children, but barely a third of black, were enrolled in school at some point that year, even though white school sessions averaged less than six months of the year. Only nine schools in the county were organized to the point of dividing students into actual grades. The county claimed a high school at Thomaston but failed to provide its educational statistics to the state superintendent.[31] Along with the vast majority of students, Harry Kroll pursued what education he could get in an ungraded school, where students might or might not remain until they managed to work through the contents of the state textbooks and graduate. Despite the blatant age and size disparity between him and his classmates, Kroll was intent on his goal and did not recollect being self-conscious in class. The children, two-thirds his age and younger, called him "Mist' Harry" with the deference of Southern social convention, but otherwise treated him as one of their own.

When that school session ended in March or April of 1910 (in time for the planting season), Kroll got word that teachers in Thomasville, about a dozen miles away in Clarke County, were organizing a six-week remedial session for students needing additional help. Thomasville also halved the distance between Harry and Annette, and he enrolled. At some point Harry returned to the orchard tent and discussed matters with Soddy. This discussion and their parting became a poignant vignette in his fictionalized autobiography.

> We stood at the gate of the house where we had spent the night, and waited for the rig to come along. It was a day in deep summer, going into the autumn. Cottonlands crept to the skirts of the village, came into the village itself. They were green, but would not be much longer now, for they must soon be white. Directly I would be going up the country to be married. I remember how Soddy stood there leaning against the picket fence in the shade, a tall dark mature person, his hard irregular teeth forming a narrow smile across his brown tender face. I remember how I felt—mute, touched, yet thinking too that presently I would have a wife, and that would temper the grief of this parting.

> The buggy was coming along the road, over the brow of the low hill. Soddy stooped and picked up his camera and bag of clothes and outfit.
>
> "Well, Harry," he said, "good-bye."
>
> He put the stuff down and we shook hands, then he took it up again. I said:
>
> "Good-bye, Soddy."
>
> The rig came up and stopped. Soddy got in, and looked at me and smiled. Then the buggy went away, and disappeared along the sunny road. There was an abrupt silence and emptiness for me.[32]

Charles Blaine Kroll eventually drifted to Birmingham, where he became first an architectural draftsman and later a chemical technician for Monsanto. The brothers met

Harry and Annette shortly before their marriage, ca. 1910. Harry holds a thread to trip the camera shutter.

only rarely in their adult lives after parting in the spring of 1910, but between them the elder remained "Soddy" forever after.

The class in Thomasville not only brought Harry closer to Annette, but allowed him to make final preparations for taking the Alabama Teachers Examinations later that summer. Over three sweltering July days in the Clarke County courthouse, Harry wrote for the examination and qualified for his entry-level credential, a third-grade Alabama teachers certificate. This permitted him to teach in the state's primary schools. Under pressure from the state, Clarke County was already raising the base requirements for teachers, so Kroll grabbed at a hunch and walked back to Dixons Mills, where he had ended his photographic career to pick up education a year earlier, and engaged to teach school there through the 1910–11 school year. The personal effects he brought with him would not have been substantial, but included at least one important addition since leaving the year before—a typewriter. It was secondhand, probably a little worse for the wear, but it allowed him to compose his story manuscripts much more quickly than writing longhand. Though his handwriting was decent, the typewriter resulted in a cleaner, simply more professional page. Now back in Dixons Mills, with no one and nothing other than class work to distract him, Harry threw himself into first learning to type, and then tailoring his mental capacity for direct keyboard composition. In a short while his native capacity for hard work, his careful studies in English grammar and literature, and his passion for stories and popular writing allowed him to set down stories at a fast clip on the typewriter, almost stream-of-consciousness, and needing only fairly light corrections. "I wrote many long pointless tales, of love and adventure," he recalled. With the typewriter at hand he began writing in earnest. Between 1911 and 1919 he remembers having knocked out eight or nine complete novel manuscripts on that first in a series of secondhand manual typewriters, "though how many others I started, and only half finished, or stopped when a third done or three-quarters done, I don't recall; but they were many." As proud as he was of his creativity, Kroll recognized these early works were little more than trial pieces and discarded them all. While they may have been stylistic workouts, the process by which he created them also helped him fix in practice the idea of writing as a process of regular effort and dogged work composing at the typewriter, a routine that became standard habit throughout his career.[33]

Fixed as Harry Kroll was on becoming a schoolteacher, personal writing merely represented a creative outlet hinting at literacy, sophistication, and attainment, but it did not pay bills—not yet, at least. He determined to become a teacher at almost precisely the same time that the country was beginning a push to improve public education and professionalize schools. Alabama was not alone in enacting its first major school reform during the opening decade of the twentieth century. Eighty-one percent of Alabama's school-age children lived outside incorporated communities, which were the only non-legislative public entities with statutory authority to levy local taxes to fund schools. Thousands of local or "district" schools taught Alabama's rural schoolchildren and were essentially private schools, paid for by the tuition of whoever could attend. After decades of outright neglect the legislature passed the Educational Code of 1907. This law was the first statewide effort to introduce structure and organization to what had effectively been a private system at the local level. For the first time in state history, the educational system was divided into elementary and secondary divisions. High schools (grades above seventh) were established with specific requirements for advancement. Even a year after passage of the act, one county superintendent, R. C. Heard of Clarke County, noted with some optimism that the levels of education and teacher preparation were improving. "It is becoming more difficult each year for inexperienced or third grade teachers to secure a school at all. The custom of securing a low grade certificate to teach summer schools as a stepping stone to something else will soon be a thing of the past," he noted. The act also provided the first state funding for school repair and construction, teacher salaries, and equipment and minor supplies, creating the first stable base for rural education in Alabama history. While the state superintendent of education later complained that some sections of the law effectively cancelled each other, it was at least a first major step toward creating a system of equitable public education.

Though the county administrators and many school districts supported the change, there was still strong general opposition among the state's mill and mine owners, who based business on the cheap-wage labor force that children represented. The legislature allowed a compulsory school attendance bill to die without consideration as late as 1911. "How we are to become an educated people when only about three-fourths of the white people are in school and they average only four months in attendance is a difficult problem to solve," complained the state superintendent. For all its faults, with the Code of 1907 Alabama was at least (and at last) moving toward modern education. Oversights, like the act's failure to provide a legal structure for enacting local school taxation, were fixed in later years, but imposing educational reform was hard going. Many of the legislative "fixes" merely cancelled out effective but unpopular parts of the initial comprehensive law or failed to address anything at all. As late as 1914 the state superintendent accurately observed that "educational progress in Alabama at present is impeded much more by the need of progressive legislation and by constitutional inhibition than by a lagging public sentiment or a lack of effort on the part of those engaged in educational work."[34]

While Harry settled into the rigors of teaching in his first year at Dixons Mills, he and Annette wrote to each other frequently, though no letter between them survives; they probably shared occasional visits as well. They married at the Heards' home in Grove Hill on May 23, 1911, at the conclusion of the school term and on the same day that they applied for a marriage license. That same day, "immediately following the ceremony," in fact, the couple returned to Dixons Mills and moved to a rented cabin three miles out of town, one of a loose clutch of houses known locally as the Etheridge settlement. Here they spent the summer living on their combined savings, learning about married life and each other. In later years Harry wrote with fondness one story about that honeymoon summer, but within two weeks of their marriage they experienced their first fight and Harry learned that his quiet bride could also inspire in him a flashing temper.[35]

After their sons struck out on their own, Darius and Caroline Kroll moved once again, around 1910, from Fruitdale another ten or fifteen miles down the track and across the Mobile County line to the larger Brethren settlement at Citronelle. Here, his daughter remembered, Darius bought a camera and also became a photographer; Caroline developed film and printed both for him and occasional tourists. Natalie recalled that her father specialized in rural and pastoral images, and sold prints to a Chicago calendar company. If she was remembering correctly, his foray into photography may have been a necessity. By now his breath was coming more laboriously; he was weakening physically to the point that he could not work in the field, mill, or machine shop as he once had. Wracking coughs were more and more frequent. Something was wrong.

Annette and Harry outside their first residence near Dixons Mills, Alabama, 1911.

Despite land promoters' nearly miraculous claims regarding health and the vigor encouraged by the climate, Alabama's rural poor were plagued well into the twentieth century by a host of virulent infectious diseases. Disease spread easily due to poor health habits and nearly nonexistent sanitation. The health situation was worsened by chronic malnutrition at virtually all ages and across classes. Typhoid blazed through neighborhoods; hookworm infections ranged as high as 60 percent of study populations; and malaria and nutritional deficiency resulting in pellagra afflicted the state's population indiscriminately. All these diseases claimed victims, but none so effectively as did the grey death of tuberculosis. With nearly a 90 percent *annual* mortality rate among those diagnosed, tuberculosis reaped grimly in the South. It was such an effective killer that in 1910 the president of Alabama's medical association called the disease the greatest public health menace in the state—even above endemic rural malnutrition. Darius Kroll became a data point in these statistics when he was diagnosed with tuberculosis in the late summer of 1910.

Charles was becoming established as an architectural draftsman in Birmingham by this time, and suggested that the family gather there. Darius, Caroline, Milly, and Nattie sold what they owned in Citronelle and took the train to Birmingham. Darius moved to one of the city's sanitariums on their arrival but the disease had progressed savagely through his system. Darius Kroll died in June 1911, a few weeks after arriving and barely ten months after his diagnosis. Harry learned of his father's death by mail and felt the loss. "I remember how I walked to the gate and stood in the summer sunlight and wept," he recalled in plain words. His father's death affected him deeply, but the poignant picture that concludes *I Was a Share-Cropper*, in which Harry visits the country road which has been cut heedlessly across his father's backwoods burial site, is pure invention. Darius Wesley Kroll is buried not under a rural West Tennessee road but outside Birmingham, Alabama, in the East Lake Cemetery.[36] Harry's wife Nettie probably never met her father-in-law.

When the 1911–12 school season opened that fall, Harry and Nettie discovered that they had overlooked one obvious implication of marriage on their career arrangements, and the couple ended up spending the school year apart. Harry taught in northern Clarke County at a newly built, 140-student school in Thomasville, while Nettie occupied a position across the Alabama River in Wilcox County and stayed with her Aunt Lou. He would have made around $350 annually; she would have made almost as much, since Wilcox paid better on average, but the state pay rates were lower for female teachers.[37] Other than occasional weekend and holiday trysts, they were not reunited until the end of the school year and were thereafter more careful about accepting teaching contracts. Their prospects would have been limited.

According to the state superintendent of education, less than a quarter of the schools for Alabama's white children—1,079 of 4,570 schools in the state in 1913—

had more than a single teacher for all grades.[38] Though the rates of teacher improvement toward the first-grade teaching certificate were increasing, many teachers were minimally qualified, barely out of school themselves. The only credential required for an individual to teach school was the ability to pass the state qualifying exam, just as Harry Kroll had. In 1912 Harry qualified for a second-grade certificate, and the following year reached the highest pinnacle of personal ambition he could imagine at the time, qualifying for a first-grade Alabama state teacher's certificate.[39] Other successes would come later, but this second major achievement exemplified the strength of his internal drive for social self-improvement.

Education in Alabama was overwhelmingly a rural issue through the entire first half of the twentieth century. The 1910 federal census summary placed 82 percent of the state's population in unincorporated areas or communities that did not meet the 2,500-resident definition of urban. Even if the benchmark for "urban" was lowered to towns with a 1,000-resident population, more than two-thirds of the state population still remained rural. Since one-teacher schools were the rule among rural-district schools in Alabama, the Krolls could not be too choosy about where they worked. The years of their early married life were characterized by rotating between annual appointments in a succession of country schools. For the 1912–13 year they moved to Goodwater, southeast of Birmingham, followed by another one-year stint back across the state at Shiloh School, near Sulligent in Lamar County. In 1914 the Krolls managed to move south again, back to Marengo County, where they accepted positions as probably the entire faculty at the Wesley Chapel School, a mile or two east of Dixons Mills. Finally, in the summer of 1917 the couple accepted positions in a two-room rural school in Dixons Mills, where Harry had begun his teaching career.

For two-hundred sixty dollars, in September 1913 the couple bought a six-acre parcel out of a larger farm along Beaver Creek, on which sat a small cabin. Now moving back, Harry devoted the summer to dressing up the accommodations, tearing off the rough plank siding and installing sawn finish siding. The interior he finished entirely with four-inch tongue-and-groove yellow pine flooring, a commodity which could be secured inexpensively from local sawmills. "For that day it was a cozy dwelling for a pair of country school teachers. I had a garden and a cow and chickens and no end of firewood on the place," he recalled fondly.[40] Married six years and with a house and property of their own, they enjoyed a stability and financial security Harry had never known growing up.

That winter, snow fell heavily in Memphis on December 7; by Christmas a cold front had inched its way toward the Gulf Coast, dropping temperatures and snow on the ill-prepared South. When it reached southern Alabama, Harry stoked the cabin's fireplace into an inferno as the temperature dropped, futilely trying to burn enough

The Kroll home in Dixons Mills, Alabama, ca.1917.

wood to beat back the cold. The couple eventually gave up, covered the small windows with blankets, stoked another fire in the kitchen cook stove, and finally went to bed, hoping to stay warm. About midnight they awakened to flames licking up the walls surrounding the fireplace. Racing barefoot across the flint-hard frozen ground, shuttling slopping pails of icy water between the backyard well and the house, they managed to douse the fire. Robbed of a heat source in their living space, they spent successive nights shuddering in the kitchen until the weather broke a week later. Digging out the damaged section to replace the charred timbers, they discovered that the brick hearth and fireplace were merely laid over the cabin's wooden support timbers, insulated only by a thin bed of sand spread over the planking. The all-day stoking had heated the bricks enough to ignite a slow fire in the wood, which spread outward through the floor and eventually up the walls.[41]

While their teaching work in rural schools seemed a relatively secure life for the moment, there were pressures on the Krolls that must have concerned them. Teaching school certainly represented a more stable and fulfilling existence than sharecropping or tramping as a photographer, but it also suggested that life would be little more than a succession of short-term contracts without opportunity for further improvement. Harry needed only to consider the situation of his alcoholic father-in-law to realize that school teaching or even administration in Alabama appeared to be a dead end career.

The importance of academic credentials was beginning to color school-district hiring practices. School consolidation, mandated by the state in 1912, had two effects. First, it slowly reduced the number of schools with teaching contracts available. Second, consolidation began weeding out the less qualified instructors, with preference given to those who were formally trained. In 1914 the state legislature was shocked into mandating some level of at least secondary education for its teachers when it was discovered that 1,200 of the 1,500 third-grade certificates granted by the state had been issued to individuals with *no* professional training at all. "The reason for this . . . appeared to be that our certification law in Alabama made no difference in the requirements for the issuance of certificates in the case of the elementary school graduate, the high school graduate, the normal [school] graduate, the university graduate—all alike had to go through the same mill, being graded solely upon their ability to pass a uniform test." Before that gate closed, anyone well informed enough to pass the exam at even a minimal level was qualified as a teacher. Harry Kroll had been one of those. Had he postponed his early career effort even five years Kroll would never have gotten the start in life that the school system offered. Even so, without the trump card of formal education in his hand, the future presented little outlook beyond the classroom, and even the attainment of a county school superintendency was becoming more remote a likelihood.[42]

Circumstances were slowly but certainly squeezing Harry Kroll in a new direction. Uninterested in changing careers, certainly more ambitious than other teachers, and realizing that he was handicapped without collegiate experience, Kroll determined to bull his way into college just as he had into teaching. There were many teacher training or "normal" schools across the country that could have given him basic qualifications within two years. He could have attended any, including Alabama Normal College reasonably close in Livingston, as Nettie had. Looking beyond a normal degree to the point where states might require an actual college degree of their teachers, and supremely confident of his ability to study hard and retain effectively, Harry applied to the biggest school he knew. His target was the South's premier teacher training institution, the George Peabody College for Teachers, situated in Nashville across the street from Vanderbilt University. Trusting his own abilities, with merely a term of formal schooling to his credit and therefore no school grades of his own, Kroll sat for qualifying college examinations at his own school in Dixons Mills in the spring of 1919. His highest marks were in English. Of the twenty-two credits or "units" for which he qualified by examination, English ranked the highest with four. The couple sold their house and acreage in Dixons Mills to raise four-hundred dollars. On the strength of those scores, and probably expecting to find work in the city, Harry Kroll was admitted to Peabody College for the summer session of 1919, the year he turned thirty. In later years Nettie would take their children to her parents during summer vacations, but in 1919 the couple were alone and she may have accompanied him when he moved to Nashville.[43]

Though it was a year-round institution, the George Peabody College for Teachers was less than a decade old and served primarily as a training and credentialing entity for practicing educators from across the South. The school was a great experiment that exemplified the Progressive Era. Its best chronicle notes that the school was grounded in the practice of socially-oriented education. Therefore, in becoming

Harry Kroll, ca. 1917.

a Peabody student Kroll was broadening his own mission of bootstrap personal improvement. "Students felt this, gained confidence from it, and carried it with them as they went back to what amounted to their mission field—a benighted South [with 80 percent of its population still rural and intensely agricultural], awaiting the redemption that depended on dedication and commitment, on a type of learning that was fully integrated into all aspects of daily life." The student population at Peabody was a moderately small body of full-time students during the traditional September-to-May school year; it swelled dramatically during the two summer sessions as public school teachers flocked in to pursue their degrees during the long mid-year holiday. Most Southern states, not just Alabama, were consolidating, professionalizing, and upgrading their public education systems. In 1919 Kroll joined several thousand summer students from all over the South upon arrival at Peabody—working teachers like himself—who were supplementing their state credentials by completing professional degrees in education.[44]

Admittance to college was a tremendous personal step, but rather than being an accomplishment in itself, taking that step plunged Harry into a new set of problems. One challenge was making the leap from rural to urban life. Related to that was his and Nettie's need to sustain themselves while he attended school. Money—or rather, the lack of it—was an issue. With both of them teaching at home in Alabama, he and Annette could feed themselves from a garden and barnyard animals while saving salary money during the year, but a term at college, on a city lot without garden or barnyard animals to rely on, swallowed savings quickly. His teaching career itself presented another problem: if he were to attend college only during summer sessions, his education would be a piecemeal proposition, drawn out over years. If he pursued it full-time he would have to leave off teaching but sustain the family somehow. Going back to photography, farming, or millwork offered no adequate solutions. How he would solve the problem was still a mystery even as he arrived to begin his education on savings and faith in himself.

During his first term at Peabody in 1919 Harry took the Agricultural Journalism course. He had been writing for a decade already. On a series of battered used machines, he had beaten out eight or nine complete novel manuscripts, each of which (along with all the false starts) was duly discarded as merely a stake in his practical education as a writer. Undoubtedly in class he was introduced to the market for freelance magazine and newspaper writing, and regional publications specifically. In the early twentieth century Nashville was the South's central point for publications. Firms such as the *Southern Agriculturist,* which distributed across the Southeast, and the R. L Polk directory publisher operated from Nashville. Most publishers in the city, however, were sectarian, focusing on church curriculum materials and juvenile devotional and story magazines. It was not an idle boast the business directory made when it noted that the city "is the center of the printing industry of the South. In volume of business, investment and number of employees in this industry, Nashville is larger than any two cities in the South combined." As early as 1880 publishing had become the leading industry in the city. There were plenty of possible venues for an enterprising new writer.[45]

It must have been with some nervous excitement that Kroll either posted or delivered a few pieces to a publisher who catered to the world he knew. On the first day of September, only a few weeks after the Peabody summer term closed, Harry Harrison Kroll's name appeared in print for the first time over a story, "John Jones and His Hired Men," in the *Southern Agriculturist.* In the story, a farmer describes to an acquaintance the economic and labor issues involved behind motivating agricultural workers on his rural smallholding. Two weeks later the same magazine published Kroll's first piece of nonfiction, a practical description of a chicken-brooding arrangement called trap nesting. Both pieces had most likely been written in his Agricultural Journalism course. Harry Kroll's first published writing demonstrates that he had attained a surprising degree of sophistication as an essentially self-taught writer.[46]

Perhaps flush with his small success, he determined to complete the one novel manuscript on which he was working and take the risk with a publisher. The manuscript, which he referred to later only as "Clementina," was perhaps the first Kroll regarded as substantial enough—and had courage enough—to submit to a publisher. Nothing at all is known about the book's setting, characters, or plot, nor of the ultimate fate the manuscript faced, other than that it was never published. Through 1919 and perhaps as late as 1921 "that sister," he recalled years later,

> interested a Philadelphia book publisher, poor as it was; he even had me rewrite it and let him see it again. He had the sound judgment to turn it down. I can see that now, but it nearly killed me then. Well, I sent "Clementina" around to several publishers. In most cases the publishers took time off to comment on it. Harper's actually said it was very interesting material, and not badly written. The Penn Publishing Company said there were so many things the matter with it they didn't know where to start telling how rotten it was (or words to that effect); but suggested that in case I cared to attempt rewriting it I might produce a real book, in which case they would be glad to see it again.[47]

This one comment and one other sidelong mention provide the only record of the manuscript and its short, unhappy life. Though it is named, no manuscript survives of this or any earlier work.

While Harry Kroll's juvenilia, the half-score of novel manuscripts produced between 1910 and 1919, fixed the nature and subject of his writing around romantic situations, his experience with "Clementina" marked a critical development in his idea of markets, which not only set the stage but also dictated the action for his later career as a practicing writer. He seems to have taken three lessons from his decade of writing practice and first tentative success with selling his work. First, he learned that the excitement of having someone look at his work seriously was never trumped by requests for revisions. Once his work began selling, he considered income (an outright purchase or advance against royalties) more significant than the further step of publication. Kroll was willing to change details, language, or story to get his work in print; artistic integrity was always a distantly second consideration. Second, the failure to get the "Clementina" manuscript accepted, despite revisions, underscored the lesson he had learned with his previous manuscripts: that writing was work and not entirely a natural activity. Harry knew how to work, and writing became a process of effort at least as intensive as chopping cotton or feeding the licking steel tongue of a mule-engine sawmill. Third, the widely different responses he notes between these two publishers seems to have emphasized for him the inherent fickleness of the marketplace, and he concluded that a market existed—somewhere—for virtually every piece of writing of decent quality. If a piece was kept in circulation, good writing would eventually be picked up. These core principles were critically important to what he presented to writing students in his later career as a college professor.

When Peabody's 1919 summer session closed, Harry returned to school teaching in Alabama. He did not take any courses between the 1919 summer session and the summer of 1921. He had accepted a professional position as school superintendent in Columbia, a town at the southeastern point of the state, on the Chattahoochee River dividing Alabama from Georgia, only a few miles north of the Florida line. The Krolls boarded with the Widow Campbell, her two children, and another young couple, the Domineys.[48] After eight years of marriage Nettie became pregnant between Christmas and New Year's Day 1920. The need to provide stability for her was probably why Harry did not return to Peabody for the 1920 summer session. A few months later, just before her confinement and terribly fearful of possible complications, a very pregnant Nettie determinedly crossed the state to be with her parents in Mobile. They had moved south from Clarke County after Robert C. Heard's retirement from the school system. The city provided the sort of genuine medical care rural southeast Alabama lacked entirely. As the late summer heat prickled across the landscape and just as school was beginning, Harry Jr., whom Harry usually called "Son," was born at Mobile's Providence Infirmary on Commerce Street on September 7, 1920.[49] Both 31, Harry and Nettie Kroll became parents, with all the weight, uncertainty, and pleasures of a young family. Certainly Harry made a trip to Mobile to see his new son, but he would have then returned to Columbia with his wife and baby boy to finish out the school session and his contract, and probably a new novel manuscript as well.

While little is known about "Clementina," even less is known about a contemporary second novel manuscript, whose existence was given nothing beyond ordinal notice in the same article. Calculating the chronology from what snippets of information Harry dropped incidentally, we may conclude that this manuscript was complete by late 1920 or early 1921. Possibly hoping that income from a book publication would help lift the added financial weight of a new baby, Harry submitted this second novel manuscript to an unnamed publisher during that same period. The sliver of a clue he gives suggests that working on either or both books might have been how he occupied his free time while superintending the public schools in Columbia, and apart from his wife, while she was delivering Harry Jr. in Mobile. Of this submission Kroll said merely that it was "the one that W. W. Jacobs almost took in 1921, and I wept when it came back after 10 months with the publisher." Other than his juvenile scrap-paper attempts at writing in the Dixons Mills orchard camp, this note provides a bracket date for his professional interest in the novel form. He described it in terms of a beginning author proud of what had been produced: "The manuscripts were perfectly typed, the spelling was accurate, the paragraphing, English, sentence structure, punctuation, all were right. I wrote in scenes, in character, and plot. The plot was not particularly good. The characters were not particularly well realized. But everything was there except the skill that came ten years later." Kroll held onto the typed pages until at least 1947, when he mentioned both this and the "Clementina" manuscript with obvious fondness in a personal nonfiction article about being a writer. Presumably he held onto both early manuscripts as keepsakes, but for how long he never said.[50]

Eleven years of both effort and chance had taken Harry Kroll in a dramatically different direction since landing in Dixons' south-Alabama orchard. He was a proud new papa and was becoming a determined writer, one that was also planning a major move. By the end of the 1920–21 school year, their boy was old enough, Annette well enough, and Harry had scraped together money enough, to take the risk on education. Having sold the house and acreage in Dixons Mills two years earlier, Harry borrowed a thousand dollars from J. J. Harry's bank in Gulfport, Mississippi. It was a stake that allowed him to move the family several hundred miles from south Alabama to a small house on Division Street in Nashville, three blocks north of the Peabody campus, just in time to allow him to attend classes full-time for the 1921 summer term. The Krolls never returned to Alabama.

CHAPTER 2

More than One Kind of Education, 1921–1935

In 1921, Nashville was one of the South's largest urban metropolises, and the only major city in the triangle between New Orleans, Louisville, and Atlanta. With a population of nearly 120,000, the city's hilly streets were beginning to chuff and chug with automobiles, some of them produced in the Marathon Automobile plant a mile southwest of downtown. Too far from the cotton factors west and south in Memphis and beyond the pale of the tobacco culture in the rim of northern counties bordering Kentucky, Nashville held onto existence as a regional light-manufacturing and river-rail transshipment center.

The American Expeditionary Force had returned triumphantly from France as the earliest bluegrass musicians were beginning to drift out of the Appalachian hills to entertain at county fairs. Nashville was not yet the self-proclaimed Music City; radio station WSM had yet to make its first broadcasts of "country" music, and the Ryman Auditorium still hosted more church meetings than music dates. Steam engines shrieked smokily while train cars crashed and jostled as travelers loaded and unloaded beneath the iron-riveted umbrella sheds of Union Station's passenger yard, adjacent to downtown. Electric street lights pushed back the dim shadows at night. Houses were crowded together, putting neighbors, even in quiet neighborhoods, in much closer proximity than country folk like Harry and Nettie Kroll were used to. Nashville was in the midst of an urbanization boom, one nexus of the inexorable depopulation of the rural countryside and growth of American cities. The city gorged and fattened on a steady diet of humanity. Thousands of former farm families, tired of the scratch and toil on farms, were looking to urban Nashville for jobs in the city's grain silos and flour mills, its rank and red-tinged stockyards and abattoirs, clanging foundries and casting shops, rambling wholesale warehouses, and the jumble of stores and businesses that catered either to black or to white customers.[1]

Harry had already spent the summer of 1919 in Nashville. Now with his wife and infant son with him two years later, he faced a different situation. Life in the big city must have been a culture shock for Nettie. Without family for comfort or the security of a garden to generate provender, she was left to raise her young son in a close, unnaturally noisy environment, with her husband gone all day. For his part, Harry threw himself into his studies with the same energetic singleness of purpose that he had demonstrated a few years before in the Dixon's orchard. Among his classes he took English 1A during the 1921 fall term at Peabody, a course in composition, which he then repeated twice in succeeding terms (as 1B and 1C). Meanwhile, as he ground through his coursework he kept up his writing practice.

At the same time that Kroll was struggling to shape a native talent into a marketable skill, Nashville was also seeing publication of the first issue of the *Fugitive,* a literary magazine with a locus in a neighborhood merely half a mile away on the other side of campus. It was the product of a collection of Vanderbilt students and professors acutely aware of the social changes occurring across the South and fired by an interest in creating a new literature, particularly poetry. While Kroll was beginning school across the street, these sixteen or so friends were meeting on Saturday evenings a few blocks south of campus to read and critique each other's writing. Donald Davidson reminisced in his *Southern Writers in the Modern World* about the way in which the Fugitives perceived their work.

> We gave strict attention, from the beginning, to the *form* of poetry. . . . Even the best poems might exhibit some imperfection in the first draft. It was understood that our examination would be skeptical. A poem has to prove its strength, if possible its perfection, in all its parts. The better the poem, the greater the need for a perfect finish. Any inequality in technical performance was sure to be detected. It was not enough for a poem to be impressive in a general way. Poems that were merely pleasant, or conventional, or mediocre did not attract much attention.[2]

Given how cosmically close Kroll was to the circle of writers that became first the Fugitives and later the core of the Agrarians, it is entertaining to wonder how he might have responded to an invitation to join them, and how the association might have shaped his future as a writer, but the exercise is purely speculative. Kroll was one of hundreds of students between the two campuses. The chances are remote that he would have even passed one of the private literary group on the sidewalk. Harry Kroll and the Fugitives also adopted fundamentally opposite approaches to their writing. Allen Tate, Donald Davidson, Robert Penn Warren, and their fellows were interested in writing as Literature, the social enterprise with its own capital letter—high literature.

Though the Fugitives were actively meeting and publishing their journal at the same time Kroll attended school (1922–25), he would have been disinterested in their brand of authorship, learning, and criticism. Jesse Stuart later observed that he "found out The Fugitives was a closed corporation. A stranger and an ambitious unknown couldn't just go to Vanderbilt and join them."[3] Two decades after leaving Peabody College, Kroll opined to Jesse Stuart on "the Vanderbilt bunch" with a caustic note that he was "itching to burn their tails off with a novel built around a combination of yours and my experiences in writing. We as realists have done far more than they, and still that batch of snoots go around assuming they're the bog knots on the rails. I'd like to hew them down to size."[4] As desperately as Harry worked to improve his craft, had Kroll known about the Fugitives while at Peabody—quite literally across the street from their Vanderbilt (Twenty-First Avenue, to be specific)—he would likely have dismissed them, as he would later, as over-literary blowhards. Though Kroll appreciated the high Literature of the past, he was one of the writers trying to make his way up from the soil. Kroll's chosen workplace was in the literature of the present. He was driven by publication, by writing as commodity, the marketplace rather than the salon. He was much more comfortable in literature without a capital letter—popular literature. Pointing out this difference is not to imply that the worlds of high literature and publishing were separate—they were not, but rather that the targets at which the writers aimed were very different. At first glance, Harry Kroll could be assumed to have the better chance.

Writers of the 1920s perched atop a century-long, up-trending slope of technical and stylistic development. Fueled by technical advances in mechanized paper production and printing presses between 1800 and 1837, newspaper and magazine publishing in Europe and North America had exploded. Following the Civil War, the expansion of public education was transforming the social place of literacy in the population, from a hard-won privilege to a common right, even among rural laborers like Harry Kroll. As a result, the expansion in the number of readers resulted in dramatic flowering of diversified reading matter as well, whose roots reached deeply into the American population. New markets for "sensational literature" or "workingmen's literature" challenged the traditional place that Literature occupied. In the 1870s American publishing exploded, flooding the populace with cheap paperback books and magazines. "As a result," literary scholar Sarah Wadsworth reminds us, "many people no longer perceived the world of book as the exclusive province of the educated, the privileged, and the intellectually refined. It had expanded to embrace, in its entirety, the literate—a category nearly as diverse and as various as the nation itself."[5] Serviced mostly by hack writers and formula fiction from the presses of firms like Street and Smith, and Beadle and Adams, these new markets were dominated by plebian popular literature widely despised by the "polite" or high-literary establishment of the 1910s.

The divide between high and common literature was neither absolute nor unbridgeable, and readers from all economic and social classes wandered easily between the camps. As a writer, Mark Twain had done the same thing admirably a generation earlier. Richard Lowery observes that by the end of Twain's career—just as Kroll was beginning to write and the Fugitive group was beginning to coalesce—the market was "shaped more or less [as] a hierarchical pyramid, with an elite form of literature occupying both the top of the structure and the smallest proportion of the market, and the penny press and dime novels serving as the base. In between lay a vast array of fiction, journalism, essays, textbooks, advice books, general interest magazines, and trade journals."[6] In their general approach to writing, the Fugitives occupied and defended a position on the heights of high literature. Kroll and the literature he knew from youth assaulted from far below. Their differing views of literature were reinforced by forces as far removed from publishing as the colleges each group attended. Beyond personal antagonism on Kroll's part, there were fundamental differences why the cerebral Fugitives (who became the conservative idealists of the Southern rural myth, the Agrarians) and deeply reflective writers like James Still were likely to have come from Vanderbilt, and the earthier "realists" like Kroll, Jesse Stuart, and Don West were much more likely to lean a different direction. The difference was fundamental, grounded in the curricula of the schools themselves and is worth some study.

The requirements under which Harry Kroll matriculated at Peabody College were flexible. The Bachelor of Science degree requirements included eight hours of psychology, eight more in educational topics suited to the interest of the student, one hundred hours from one of six optional course groups, and five additional hours in unrestricted electives: a total of 186 hours divided into twelve-week quarters. Most notably for Kroll, all Peabody students were required to take twenty hours of English.[7] His earliest class, taken in the first summer term of 1919, was Agriculture 160, Agricultural Journalism, a straightforward composition class with broad application: "Course adapted to needs of teachers, county agents, community leaders and to prospective journalists." It was a practical tutorial on how to write—specifically, how to write for common publication venues. When he returned to Peabody as a full-time student in 1921, Harry launched into the English 1 series with the component numbered 1A, Composition: "The especial concern of this course is the practical mastery of speech and writing for everyday needs, and greater breadth and enjoyment in general literature, with the heavy emphasis on composition. The work consists of frequent papers and oral reports, class criticism and discussion, individual and group conferences with the instructor, accompanied by assigned and voluntary readings in standard and current literature. The basal texts are Brown and Barnes's *The Art of Writing English;* Duncan, Beck, and Graves' *Prose Specimens,* and Palmer's *Self-Cultivation in English.*" This was not high Literature, nor were his subsequent classes.

During the summer of 1922 Harry came under Frank Leavell's tutelage for a Race Relations series numbered 11A ("Topics: The special article, community achievements as subject matter, types, writing the article, the beginning: illustrations; marketing the article") and 2 ("Topics: Case-histories, crisis, adjustments; leaders, their formative experiences, personal traits, methods; community self-study; community advertising"). Leavell later provided him with an important literary connection. In the fall of 1922 Harry enrolled in English 172, Teaching High School Composition, under Dr. Charles S. Pendleton. "After a review of the principles of composition this course will deal with such topics as the following: A definite and reasonable aim in teaching composition; composition as a means to an end—discovering possibilities and developing the expressional powers of the individual; life needs as the controlling standard in composition; life experiences and activities as the basis of composition material; stimulating assignments, models; relation of composition to literature; practice and drill in oral and written expression."[8]

All of these courses were, in substance, practicums in straightforward, efficient writing, closer in style and substance to journalism than to creative writing or literature. Where was the canon of English literature that fired the Vanderbilt Fugitives? Not at the George Peabody College for Teachers. The very best that could be said of a Peabody literary education was that students were oriented toward the high points of English literature they would in turn later introduce to students, and were instructed in the practicalities of effective composition.

Conversely, the Vanderbilt catalogue was explicit about its educational expectations: "Students making a specialty of . . . Practical Arts should not matriculate to Vanderbilt, but should arrange to take the full course of four years in the Peabody College. The nature of this work, its practical and special character, renders a combined course inadvisable for the student."[9] In fact, Vanderbilt University offered only two composition courses. One was English 2, which the catalogue described as "The elements of writing, *based upon direct study of selected authors,* with training in composition. Frequent themes" (italics added). The focus at Vanderbilt was literary criticism. English 2 was a team-taught, two-hour course, of which one hour was a straightforward literature class under John Crowe Ransom, Donald Davidson, or William Preston Moss. The only other composition course available was English 9, Advanced Composition, described in the catalogue as "A practical course in writing prose, including newspaper writing and the short story, and *accompanied by extensive reading of current periodicals.* Open only to students who are already proficient in the fundamentals of writing" (italics added). Also taught by Ransom, it still relied heavily on the study of literature. Everything else the university offered was traditional studies in the masterworks of literature. In short, Vanderbilt's approach to teaching fell within the time-honored traditional approach: expose students to the best examples of the form that can be located, teach them *why* it was good and what made good writing, and then have them practice mimicking it and commenting upon it. The

Vanderbilt English Department's curriculum focused on great books and writers, not on writing great books, and its most notable figures tended to be critics who wrote. This approach would have been the one encountered by James Still when he attended in the 1929 school year, and which challenged Jesse Stuart during his second attempt at a graduate education two years later.[10]

In the broadest sense, the two schools differed in the way they approached the culture of books and writing. Vanderbilt University had been founded as a vehicle to replicate a cultural elite, where students were expected to become appreciative receivers of an iconic (and thoroughly accepted) culture whose value was already firmly established—the measuring rod for later-comers. Peabody College for Teachers, on the other hand, was effectively a white-collar trade school. Situated on the east side of Twenty-First Avenue, Peabody students expected to become English mechanics themselves in order to help youth tinkering with language in their own classrooms. Across the street, on the west side of Twenty-First Avenue, students came to ascend to learning. The difference between the two approaches is related by one figure with feet in both worlds. Reflecting on his own experience about a decade after Harry Kroll attended Peabody (and after Stuart had twice been Kroll's student), Jesse Stuart wrote of his encounter with the two approaches in his autobiography. He recalled taking Robert Penn Warren's course on the novel, along with two students who confidently asserted they would be the ones to write the great American novel. A decade and a half later, in 1940, Stuart met one of the pair at a party in New York on the release of *Trees of Heaven*, his first novel. His former classmate, "one who had a private plane at Vanderbilt," had not yet written anything. "Being his Vanderbilt classmate and hearing him talk, an A student, I thought he would have been the one from our class to have written a novel. I have since learned it's not the grades that count. I received a B or less in The Novel. But I've been the one from that class who has written them."[11] Studying Stuart's poetry as a textual critic, J. R. LeMaster asserts that Stuart's poetic effort was shaped or at least strongly influenced by the Vanderbilt Agrarians. His year at Vanderbilt was certainly influential, but Stuart was already developing as a writer and brought something with him to Vanderbilt that educational experience there only polished. Considering the volume of Stuart's work produced as an undergraduate at Lincoln Memorial University and his recollection of Kroll's advice, LeMaster's conclusion is less supportable.[12] James Still's gentle and somewhat naïve lyricism was almost a stylistic rejection of hard-edged Fugitive literary sophistication. Both Still and Stuart celebrated the elegance of rusticity in their writing. Both returned to Appalachia without advocating Agrarianism as socially redemptive. It seems that Vanderbilt and its former Fugitives could produce writers with the energy and caliber and nature of Jesse Stuart and James Still mostly because the two students had already made fundamental decisions about writing careers, and about their subjects and the mechanics of voice and style, before coming to Nashville. They were writers long before arriving at Vanderbilt.

Interestingly enough, the output of either Kroll's or Stuart's writing alone would come close to equaling the volume of original creative work produced by all members of the Vanderbilt Fugitive circle combined. Volume, of course, does not translate directly into significance or influence. Willa Cather generated fewer than seventy-five short stories and a dozen novels, some short enough to be novellas. Stephen Crane died at twenty-nine without fifty stories and only four novels over his name. Besides his poetry and criticism, Allen Tate wrote merely one minor novel. Yet all three are seen as major literary figures. The essential difference of influence is not measured adequately by word count. Vanderbilt's cadre continues to be recognized because their writing is perceived to be on the plane of high culture. In truth, no clear line exists between high and popular culture in America. Scholars seem to invoke the subject without clearly defining it, as if it were clearly defined. The division occurs neither along the line between regional and national publication venues, nor between writing shaped around specific cultural themes.

The best working definition for modern American writing that I can generate for the first three-quarters of the twentieth century divides publications into unequal thirds along class lines. The best practical measuring stick whether a magazine was a high or popular venue may be the subject and appeal of the advertising it includes. For books, the publisher's list would suggest whether they tended to publish popular works or high literature. Publishers with editorial offices in New York and Boston would more likely be high culture venues, and publishers headquartered elsewhere (despite aspirations) might not be. Since the 1970s telecommunications and desktop publishing have blurred those lines somewhat, but in the 1930s, breaking in to the New York circle was critical. Therefore William Faulkner, despite his rural and Southern themes, is a writer of high culture.

The most important difference between high and popular literature as represented by the Fugitives and Harry Kroll, is that the group formulated a theoretical framework for their social criticism which Kroll utterly lacked. This study is not about their work, but their work exists as an important contemporary counterpoint to Kroll's populist approach to the world of writing. High literature also tends to illustrate or employ broad universal themes; it advocates change or understanding or exemplifies conflict, rather than standing as a straightforward diversion. Another major difference between these contemporaries is thematic. Harry Kroll's writing reflected a gritty idealism about rural existence, evident in his choice of settings, his style, and the publication venues that attracted his attention—clearly different than the Agrarians who he dismissed as aesthetes. Kroll was a popular writer who drew on the world he knew best as inspiration for his work. Having come up from the earth, Harry Kroll was more comfortable with genres where writing was more natural, more descriptive, and less representational or cerebral: namely, in popular literature. Though he captured much less acclaim than the high culture Fugitives/Agrarians, he became an excellent example of the overwhelming majority of actual American writers of the time.[13]

"Genre" typically represents a type of writing, but it also relates to habits of reading. Readers expect certain things from various genres. "Far from inhibiting the author, genres are a positive support," Alastair Fowler reminds. "They offer room, as one might say, for him to write in . . . a proportioned mental space."[14] Divisions between genres are not impenetrable. Kroll was capable of high literature when he "said something" with his work. The realism of Kroll and Stuart was the result of a different approach to writing and literature, borne partly of social and economic class. Eudora Welty would shortly thereafter use Southern realism as a basis for her work. With Donald Davidson's help, Stuart finally saw that he was aiming too low for his talent and crossed into the world (and market) of high literature. Kroll, however, could never really transcend his viewpoint about writing in the context of the markets he knew. The two groups of high culture and popular writers will not likely be remembered or studied by the same students until, like Stuart's writing, the latter become regarded as acceptably cultural. Harry, at least, was much more interested in what writing would earn than in expressive writing for its own sake. Although Stuart would transcend the view, hints of the same attitude may be seen throughout his career as well.

At Peabody College, Kroll carried a heavy course load, trying to get through school as quickly as possible. That process, however, left him little opportunity for wage work. No longer teaching in order to attend school, the couple managed for a time on savings, occasional loans, and living frugally, but still needed an income. Harry Jr. recalled that his father conducted Nashville streetcars for a time, but Harry himself never comments on it.[15] By the spring of 1922, less than a year into his college education, family finances ebbed to the point that Harry was forced either to quit school or to figure out how to otherwise provide for the family. "Here I was," Harry Kroll wrote of the time, "with a family on my hands, an unfinished formal education to cope with, inflexible requirements to be met; and my funds on the verge of exhaustion. It was a chronic adult situation. . . ." He could not get through school without an income, and he could not work for wages or on a salary without compromising his school schedule.

Thus, while he pursued a formal education in Nashville, circumstances necessarily changed what writing represented to Harry. As a young man in an Alabama orchard, writing was merely an outlet or diversion that met his hunger for self-expression in the world. A decade later in Nashville, Harry came to see writing as a tool for meeting the domestic needs of a family. Rather than having the luxury of idleness or studies filling his days while Soddy provided a moderate income, Harry himself needed to house, clothe, and feed his wife and son as well as himself. Writing provided an income, but it was a spare one. From these efforts he collected often less than a dollar apiece for his trouble.[16] It may have been rewarding for a self-taught former sharecropper to see his name in print occasionally, but the glow was a dissociated pleasure from the primary attraction of being paid to produce salable writing. Producing stories and articles with his battered typewriter became a market-driven enterprise for Harry, rewarded when his work sold to a publisher. So long as he was paid for the manuscript, it really did not matter to him whether the editor chose to publish the piece or not. Having sold a few pieces of student writing to local publishers during his first year of school, Harry determined to broaden his submissions and see if the downtown publishers would take anything else. It was something, at least. During the school year on off-hours, weekends, and holidays, Harry wrote dozens of "squibs"—short, nonfiction articles—for agricultural publications. The stock- and farm-related subjects appeared under his name and the housekeeping subjects appeared under his wife's maiden name, Annette Heard. It was not enough. If he were to support himself and family with writing while at school, Harry had to have a continuously fresh stock to offer editors.

The inventions of the paper machine, stereotype, and mechanized printing presses in the mid-nineteenth century fueled a dramatic rise in literacy. During the late Victorian and Edwardian periods (1887–1910) the vast majority of American recreational readers were entertained less by the likes of serious writers studied today, such as Rudyard Kipling, Joseph Conrad, or Stephen Crane, than by the thrilling and improbable tales of characters Frank Merriwell, Buffalo Bill, and Dick Turpin, written up in story papers and yellow-back dime novels. Serial fiction, newspapers, and magazines presented readers with fiction of all types. By 1907 the *Atlantic Monthly* could publish with a straight face Charles M. Harvey's eulogy on the passing of serious literature.[17] The same period saw the rise of the cheap-paper story magazines, or "pulps." These niche productions distributed scores of story magazines like *Sports Story* and *Fame and Fortune.* By the time Harry Kroll began hawking his work to magazines in the early 1920s, popular reading culture in the U.S. had shifted from the story papers of a generation earlier to popular series-fiction novels and novellas.[18]

The popular story publications were available across the country on rail-station newsstands, at drug stores, and through the post. New York was the center of the national fiction market. Fortunately for Harry Kroll, Nashville was the center of a separate publishing industry. Over a dozen publishing houses, many of them sectarian or associated with religious denominations, had offices within a few miles of the Kroll residence on Fourteenth Street South. Besides two daily newspapers in the city, the monthly *Southern Agriculturist* had an office on Broadway, but it was denominational publishing that was the industry's life-blood. The Cumberland Presbyterian and Southern Baptists had large publishing concerns in town, and the Pentecostal Mission Publishing, the National Baptist Publishing Board for black Baptist churches, the Publishing House for the Methodist Episcopal Church (South), the Seventh Day Adventist's Southern Publishing Arm, the Tennessee Book and Bible House (which would become a branch of Scottish firm Thomas Nelson & Sons) all busily cranked out blizzards of tracts, lesson materials, commentaries, devotional works, and most importantly to Harry Kroll, age-graded newspapers to entertain and encourage young Christians. Most of these published one or more pieces of short fiction in each issue. At the time, for instance, the Southern Baptist Convention publication office alone produced *Kind Words* for young children, *Boy's Weekly* and *Girl's Weekly* for preteen readers, *The Sentinel* for early teens, *Try* for late-teenage readers, and half a score of focused-interest adult magazines. Though centrally administered, each title published its own material—a dozen potential buyers within just one publisher.

Kroll realized that the sectarian publications and agricultural papers may not have distributed nationally, but they still published frequently, typically monthly, biweekly, or weekly. Though he did not expect to build a career writing for sectarian weeklies, if nothing else, he could use their markets as practice for honing his skill as a writer. Nashville's sectarian sheets consumed huge amounts of freelance writing in addition to regular columnar articles and advertising. They were not unique, either. Sectarian publishers farther afield than Nashville's Broadway, Demonbreun, and Charlotte Avenues generated similar serial titles and were also eager for suitable moral and/or uplifting material. Nationally, the Board of Christian Publication for the Disciples of Christ in St. Louis, the David C. Cook Company in Illinois, the Presbyterian Union in Philadelphia, and presses for still other denominations such as the Lutherans, Catholics, and the Northern Baptist denominations catered to other congregations. As an emerging writer of juvenile moral fiction Harry Kroll was flatly ecumenical—any press that would buy his work got more of it until the purchases fell off from saturation or shifting editorial interests. This was the world with which Harry Harrison Kroll became intimately familiar during his writing career.

Unfortunately, the very spontaneity of the writing market was its greatest weakness as well. Ready markets may have existed for fiction and illustrations, but sales were neither predictable nor reliable. One month he might sell a score of stories, the next only half a dozen. The income from each sale varied as well. An author with first one child, then two, after Robert Torrey was born in September 1922, gratefully took what an editor offered, without negotiation. Together the illustrations and stories generated during his off-hours from school brought in enough income to allow Kroll to remain a student. "The last year," he later claimed of the 1922–23 terms, "I earned my whole way, making nearly as much money on the side with Sunday-school stories, drawings, poems with ethical and nature themes, and farm articles, as I had made the last year I taught school." Occasionally he might pull in some prize money—for example, a badly needed $25 cash prize in winning the *Peabody Reflector*'s essay contest late that fall—but that sort of quick income was nothing dependable.[19] When he was not studying or doing coursework, Harry flung himself into freelance writing and drawing and began cultivating a writing habit that would become his practice for over thirty years.

Kroll also began looking further afield for help developing his writing ability. After taking English 1A, his first practical training in written composition, and confident in his reinforced writing ability, he was hungry for a chance to place a book after coming so close with "Clementina" three years earlier. During the 1922 fall term he requested help from Race Relations professor Robert H. "Frank" Leavell of the Peabody faculty. Leavell seems to have had a personal acquaintance with New York journalist Viola Roseboro, a Tennessee native and doyen of Gilded Age writing, who has been called one of the formative influences on public literature of her age. She had arrived in New York as an aspiring actress from her family home in Tennessee the year before Harry Kroll was born. Since the 1890s she had been the chief reader, and thus a major editorial figure, for the McClure Syndicate. An enormously well-regarded writer and noted conversationalist, her passion for discovering as-yet unrecognized literary genius offset the hard work of reading manuscripts. Her biographer notes that she read literally everything submitted to the magazine, whether typewritten or manuscript. "It was this that convinced J. S. Phillips, S. S. McClure's partner, that their publishing house missed nothing of value submitted to them as long as manuscripts passed through Miss Roseboro's hands." It was partly because of Miss Roseboro that Samuel S. McClure enjoyed a reputation as one of the major figures of American letters and a champion of new writers. Her focus on identifying and encouraging young talent, and her ability to perceive literary significance, gave her an enviable track record. Edwin Markham was one such discovery, as were William Sydney Porter (better known by his pen name, O. Henry) and Booth Tarkington, among others.

Besides its significance as a literary venue, *McClure's* was a respected national publication that built its reputation and readership on its support for the "muckrakers," a group of investigative journalists and critics of American business in the 1890s through the 1900s. By the late 1910s the magazine was in decline. Willa Cather departed from her position as the magazine's managing editor the year Harry arrived at Peabody, and the magazine even suspended publication briefly after its senior staff gave the mercurial McClure an ultimatum about office operations as the ebullient 1920s opened. When it resumed publication, *McClure's* was no longer the literary powerhouse it had been and Roseboro was no longer an employee, but her earlier advice remained influential and the magazine was a natural attraction for Kroll's socially conscious writing on behalf of rural producers. Even with its reputation dimmed somewhat, *McClure's* remained one of the few national magazines willing to publish fictional social criticism of the sort that Harry Kroll favored early in his career. It was then no accident that Kroll's first major work of short fiction would eventually appear in the pages of the reborn *McClure's*. Leavell's connection to Roseboro and *McClure's* provided Kroll with perhaps the best chance he would ever have of being discovered as an American writer.[20]

Kroll's practice in shaping his approach to writing benefited directly from one specific editorial comment, borne of Roseboro's lengthy experience. "His strength is in his own experience and convictions," she suggested in response to Leavell's query. "I have thought about Ks problem very carefully, and I can see nothing that solves it as would a volume of genuine personal reminiscences focused on this matter of country schools. . . . Let him begin with something of his childhood, if as I infer the hints here are really autobiographical."[21] The manuscript on which she was commenting in 1922 was probably one of the ten novels Kroll had written and discarded before 1928, but her comment could be a response to a general query on writing about his own experience with education in the rural South. Her advice seems to have provided a catalyst, settling in Kroll the idea that personal experience held an infinite store of experience which could serve as plot. Kroll was introduced in a formal way to the same practice used by writers with the stature of William Faulkner, Willa Cather, Henry James, and Wallace Stegner: on the strength of the old saw that "truth is stranger than fiction," build a fictional character from the traits and foibles of a real person or situation. What Kroll missed or ignored was her suggestion to meld his technical writing ability and perceptiveness with nonfiction as well. His writing did not have to consist exclusively of one or the other. As a result, he missed a sterling chance for relevance and entrée into the national literature of social criticism and improvement during the 1920s. Instead, Harry lashed himself to the excitement and potential of fiction—which he was learning to spill out almost at will—and determined to plunge into the hurly-burly of the literary marketplace.

Roseboro's critique of Kroll's writing reveals something of the degree of sophistication at which he was writing early in his career. The manuscript is known only from the few clues mentioned in her response letter, but obviously the manuscript's subject concerned rural people, as did all his work. Drawing from the Race Relations coursework under Leavell, Kroll also produced a story manuscript that contrasted nationwide public interest in Negro education with a coincident lack of concern about educating poor white children in the rural South. Roseboro's professional critique returned to the hopeful Nashville author in the late summer or early autumn of 1922

She encouraged Kroll to grasp the difference between writing in English colloquial dialect, what she called "jargon," and over-processed sentences dense with correct English word order and placement. He needed to loosen up and make his sentences more "clear and direct." Responding to Leavell as the submitter, Roseboro pointed out that "grammer [*sic*] is the only thing he knows how to look out for." Abraham Lincoln was a careful and self-taught grammarian; Kroll was the same, but his medium was not intended for the erudite courtroom bench. Rather, Harry wanted to present himself to the casual reader in the sitting-room armchair. Roseboro encouraged Kroll to write about what he knew. The idea of a genuinely autobiographical work, however, only saw publication almost fifteen years after the critic's letter arrived.[22]

As he began submitting more and more work to magazines and papers, somewhere along the line Harry realized that his personal experience represented a broad but finite pool of ideas. He decided to carry Miss Roseboro's advice a step further. Though he had a store of his own varied experiences, he began listening carefully to students around him as they talked about home, their families, and work. To help him maintain his thoughts he began keeping a notebook in which he recorded folk sayings and story ideas. It became almost a trademark. One of the clearest things his former students recall years later about their teacher, beyond his plaguing them about what they had been doing recently and how it felt, was a small black pocketbook into which he might jot notes even in the middle of a conversation. Perhaps in the same notebook he also began recording a trophy list of sales to publishers. That practice probably had practical roots, as publishers often accepted work for which the author was paid only later, sometimes very much later. Having a list of what had been accepted and the purchase price was good business sense on his part. Keeping a notebook in his pocket, then, became something of a portable office, at once a source of ideas and a record of his business success as a writer. Until at least the 1950s he would maintain a long succession of similar pocket volumes. The jottings and half-told personal stories, caught in casual conversation or overheard between his students, became increasingly important as he aged and the zestful wine of youth was drained and dried by middle age.

Harry's drive to acquire personal stories involved him with common people at a rate that was unusual among writers of high literature. By drawing upon others' triumphs and tragedies he gained a limitless supply of potential material. It gave him a tremendous thematic range across which to write. Most of his fellow students at Peabody were raised rurally as he had been, and his later students were often of similarly rural backgrounds. Unsurprisingly Kroll wrote about the worlds he and his informants knew best: high school students; yellow-pine logging camps; rural kids self-made by dint of effort, careful thought, or education; plucky young clerks; mountain railroads; and schoolteachers. What he heard (or overheard) from others he adapted into whatever settings, descriptions, characters, or narratives he felt best put across a story. Accuracy to the original event was immaterial since the firsthand experience was merely a catalyst which sparked a story: he was *writing*, not reporting.

Though it would be a few more years before Kroll's work as a novelist resulted in a published novel manuscript, Roseboro's advice shaped the direction he was moving, toward becoming a popular writer. Structurally, Roseboro's opinion of his story was that the work was not quite a novel and not quite an educational treatise. Her suggestion that he produce "a volume of genuine personal reminiscences" probably did not interest him, because he did not see who would buy such a thing. He had already published one essay on racial issues (not a particularly sympathetic one), and this type of essay writing probably did not appeal to the budding writer, especially one looking for a platform to proclaim his social criticism. A revision to the manuscript she had seen was probably never written, but her advice may have provided a stylistic footing on which Kroll would base *Cabin in the Cotton* a few years later.[23]

Roseboro's advice was critical to Harry's development and education as a writer but did nothing to produce immediate income. Unfortunately, even the fairly steady sale of his writing alone was not enough to make ends meet; the pay rates were simply too low. By 1922 the family's financial reserve had dwindled, freelance writing alone wasn't paying sufficiently well, and he still could spare no time for regular employment. He needed something that had a higher time-to-income ratio than a flat wage offered. Harry didn't have to look far. The children's papers also bought illustrated work, often poems, which paid substantially better than stories and fiction. Never one to be intimidated by a literary challenge, Kroll dived in to see what he could do with illustration. Typically, he did not let the fact that he had no training and had never actually done illustration deter him.

> I had been drawing cabins in cotton fields all through a dull course of English composition; some were in pencil, others in ink. I sat down one Saturday, using a drawing-board borrowed from the art department, and by working that day and the Sunday following, I had several pen-and-ink sketches, and examples of hand-lettering, to use as samples. On Monday I called among the editors of the Sunday-School publishers in Nashville, saying that I was an illustrator, and would like to have poems or stories to illustrate.[24]

His first work was not particularly successful, but the sale of one or two pieces was encouragement enough, and the potential income that illustration offered was incentive. Illustrations that could be laid out in pencil and then carefully inked in with a pen across two evenings, netted between five and ten dollars apiece, roughly equivalent to a week's wages at other employment.[25] Harry Kroll's first published illustrative work, a panel for Katherine Atherton Grimes's poem "The Oldest Girl," appeared in the *Southern Agriculturist* during the summer of 1922—as a cover illustration, no less—immediately after the spring term in which he completed his last mandatory composition class. It was a fairly amateurish production but done well enough to suggest artistic potential. Encouraged by his sales, Kroll began producing illustrations for several city publishers, few of which (if they were actually published) have been located, but publishers regularly bought more work than they actually printed, or held it until there was an issue into which it fit thematically or was needed to fill column inches. "I had taken no art," Harry later remembered, "though by this time I might sell as much as fifty dollars' work of stories and drawings in a month: now I made it one of my minors."[26]

By the time his first illustration actually appeared in print Harry had already enrolled in a "Drawing and Design" course: Fine Art 2, taken the first summer session of 1922, followed by the advanced section Fine Art 102A during the next session, and then repeated the course yet again in fall term of 1922. Kroll may have discovered at least a modest native talent for pen-and-ink illustration as he sat in composition, but it was this real training that made his work salable. The formal classwork in drawing undoubtedly helped him apply the design elements of line weight, visual balance, form, and layout to his doodling. "By the close of the year [1922] I was doing as good work as I would ever do; and in those imaginative child drawings, where no necessity existed for realistic handling of the human figure, I often achieved results that had some beauty." A ready market existed for all sorts of drawings. Technologically, line drawings were much simpler (and cheaper) for a printer to reproduce than halftone photograph reductions. Line illustrations, either technical or fanciful, added visual interest to the pages of virtually every publication in every subject. This was the era not only of Kate Greenaway's classic children's illustrations, but also the work of scores of lesser artists and specialty illustrators who drew catalogue illustrations, page borders, vignettes, and technical drawings by the millions. Piece for piece, illustration paid better than writing. Harry's coursework in art was evidently worth the investment. By 1924 his work, both stories and illustrations, was appearing in many of the juvenile sectarian publications that flooded out weekly from Nashville.

While he was pursuing his education in Nashville, Kroll's existence was crowded with demands on his time. By carrying a heavy course load between 1921 and the end of spring term of 1923, he compiled enough credit units to qualify for his baccalaureate degree. Even before graduation he sat for graduate entrance exams in May and dived directly into graduate work a few weeks later in the succeeding summer term. Harry Kroll's Bachelor of Science degree in English was awarded at the commencement exercises following the school's busy summer session, on August 31, 1923. Never one to miss an opportunity, Harry picked up a few extra dollars by lettering names on the year's diplomas.

An Educated Man

By the time Harry Kroll was again turned loose on the public educational system, much had changed across the South. With the ink still drying on his diploma, in the summer of 1923 Kroll contracted to teach English in Woodburn, Kentucky, where he held the position of principal as well.[27] Woodburn was a small community of 350 situated a few miles south of Bowling Green along the Nashville road. Simply to make the move he was forced to borrow $15 from a sympathetic faculty member, Dr. Mary Torrey Roudebush. It was probably while teaching at Woodburn that Kroll was introduced to basketball. Kentucky had adopted basketball as a girls' high school sport

A thirty-something Harry on the steps of Kissam Hall at Vanderbilt University, ca.1923–25.

in the 1890s and its popularity spread quickly through the state. The first state girls' championship was played in 1921. Despite its small size, Woodburn High School fielded one of the state's five most successful female teams, coached by a woman as well, Audrey Peterson, who would have been a member of Kroll's staff. Though Harry Kroll remained at Woodburn only a year, the girls' basketball team went to the state tournament five times in a row in the 1920s and finally took back-to-back championships in 1931 and 1932.[28] The drama of on-court action provided Kroll with yet another subject for his fiction. In the long run, however, Woodburn was possibly too small for Kroll's ambition and he had no intention of accepting a position there permanently. He resigned the appointment after the 1923–24 school year closed, sent his wife and boys to live with his wife's parents in Mobile for the summer, and went back alone to Peabody to again pursue a summer's worth of intense graduate work.

Kroll's installment of graduate education lasted merely through the summer of 1924, including half a dozen classes and seminars in English topics or English education. This too was merely a stop along the road. In the late summer of 1924, with his incomplete graduate degree on hold, Harry again left Nashville to accept a split principalship and teaching appointment at the Lula-Rich Consolidated School, in a corner pocket of the billiard-table landscape that was the Mississippi cotton delta. From Nashville he wrote Nettie at her parents' home in Mobile to collect the boys and be ready to move. He drove from Nashville to southern Alabama, where the family reunited, and then from Mobile north and west across Mississippi to arrive in time for school to begin.

Lula, Mississippi, sits sixty miles below Memphis in the northern point of the Mississippi Delta country, a few miles north of the Coahoma County seat of Clarksdale. The rich bottomland region had been cleared and farmed beginning before the Civil War. The Yazoo-Mississippi Delta, or simply "the delta" as it is known there, is not a delta in the literal sense of the term. Properly defined, a delta is a fan-shaped alluvial plain at the mouth of a river. The Yazoo-Mississippi Delta, however, lies in the northwest portion of the state of Mississippi, bounded by the river of the same name and with its southernmost extent located some 230 miles north of the Gulf of Mexico. More precisely, the Yazoo-Mississippi Delta is the floodplain that lies between the Mississippi and Yazoo rivers. The Mississippi River forms the western boundary of the region, and the loess bluffs near the Yazoo River form the region's eastern boundary. The delta is shaped like a lozenge, or long ovular leaf, with Memphis, Tennessee, near the northern tip and Vicksburg, Mississippi, in the south.

The Mississippi Delta region, once densely covered with native hardwoods, had been cleared during the nineteenth century and the rich, black land planed smooth for expansive cotton fields. The land is almost perfectly level, varying only by inches across miles of territory. Many cane brakes and bayous, like the Yazoo Pass (a long channel linking the Mississippi River to Moon Lake and the Coldwater River), still meandered back from the river while the Krolls lived in the area. Intensive agriculture developed later in the Mississippi Delta than it did in other parts of the American South. At the time of the Civil War, only 10 percent of the region was in cultivation. By 1900, two-thirds of the Delta still lay in old-growth hardwood forest. Dense vegetation, numerous swamps, the perception of malarial and yellow fever infestation, and frequent flooding conspired to impede agricultural expansion in this region of rich soil. After 1865, the construction of railroads in the delta helped increase settlement.[29]

Forty years after its founding, Lula boasted a population of about 425, with several hundred more, black and white, scattered in little constellations of sharecropper cabins orbiting the plantation houses and barns outside the town boundaries. Highway 61 ran alongside the railroad tracks straight through town. Busses stopped four times a day, two running between Memphis and Clarksdale, and two moving to and from the river landings a few miles to the west. Lula had a movie house, several stores, and a bank. Two cotton gins competed for processing the local crop. The open-topped automobiles of small farmers rattled into town, passing the mule-drawn wagons of sharecroppers. Rich, two miles east, was not nearly so pretentious, merely a clutch of residences and agricultural structures standing idly around a country store and fill-

Looking southeast toward downtown Lula, Mississippi, from the railroad, 1924 or 1925. Photograph by W. L. Barbee, courtesy of Bill Barbee.

ing station. Though Harry Kroll and his family remained in the delta town less than a full calendar year, this position became a watershed point in his writing career.

Like Alabama, Mississippi had begun to modernize its school system in the opening years of the twentieth century by consolidating small schools into larger but more centralized districts. County schools for Coahoma's white students had begun consolidating in the late 1910s. Located at the north of the county, far enough to make riding to and from Clarksdale prohibitive, several rural and community schools around Lula and Rich were mandated to combine into one district around 1918. Since the small rural schools had been successfully and closely controlled for years by various individuals and cliques, combining them into a single district accomplished little more than to set interest groups—wealthy planters, local churches, and the residents of the two communities—against each other in a battle for dominance on the new unified school board. The towns of Lula and Rich wrangled fiercely over a site for years until the communities finally agreed to split the difference and build a new school between them on donated property. The two-story, four-class brick edifice had been finished in 1921, along with a separate house or "teacherage" for the principal. Though its public school building may have been solid and distinguished, partisanship continued well after its opening and was probably the reason that Harry Kroll was the fourth principal at the school in as many years. When he accepted the appointment he was almost certainly unaware of the communities' political situation. Kroll's post was a split position, as both principal and upper grades instructor in the four-teacher faculty, but the job essentially made him manager of virtually the entire facility. A large gasoline storage tank beside his house's detached garage filled several jittery school busses that shuddered around country roads. Driven by older students, the busses may have been a convenience but were evidently haphazardly maintained. They transported mostly the poor students from outlying areas who either could not walk to school or did not have their own transportation.

Also similar to Alabama, Mississippi's school system was rigidly segregated by racial division, with only token support for schools serving the huge numbers of nonwhite students. Black students, those who were educated, attended school on barely half the annual schedule as white students, in a ramshackle building a mile south and west of Lula. At the Lula-Rich Consolidated School, Kroll and three other teachers taught children whose racial identity bound them together in a setting of economic dominance that even wealth and poverty could not effectively divide. Because they were not black, white sharecroppers' children sat in the same classes with children from wealthy planter families. Once that division had been made, however, the social classes quickly stratified within the schoolrooms.

By the time Kroll arrived, the plantation system, broken up under Reconstruction, had reconstituted under many of the same land-owning families. Tenants, who rented land outright, and sharecroppers, who labored for a percentage of what they grew in a season, worked the land. Effective farm mechanization for the soft black soil was still a decade off and the expansive fields were worked by mule-drawn wagon and hand-swung hoe. Like other crops in the days before mechanization, cotton cultivation was a labor-intensive operation, requiring the work of hundreds of farm hands. Agriculture was conducted in bursts of effort—planting, thinning, weeding, harvesting—leaving weeks idle between them. This "laying-by time" was any time the crop did not demand attention. When there was work to be done, children as young as ten could "chop cotton," wielding a hoe taller than they were down the long, shadeless field rows to control weeds. In the fall, even a five-year-old could pull the soft white bolls from the dried, saw-edged petioles. Laboring families, black and white, lived for every fraction of an ounce of white fluff that a field could produce.

Tens of thousands of laboring delta families, black and white, were held in thrall by a credit system that favored landowners, who advanced their workers goods from private stores against the value of crops at harvest. It was a system easily exploited by those who both measured and maintained the records of crop and credit, and it kept illiterate workers lashed firmly to a plantation owner by debt. The fundamental corruption of the system, which exploited the poor and enriched the idle, Harry Kroll illustrated in his 1931 novel *Cabin in the Cotton.* There was plenty to illustrate. During the mid-1920s cotton was selling at solid prices. Those who owned the land and extended and exploited the local credit system were drowning in luxury. At school in Lula, most of the older students from affluent planter families flew recklessly around the county's unpaved roads in early roadsters, while their parents' economic hold on black and white sharecroppers to protect their fortunes tightened from a mere grip to a stranglehold. A decade later in his semi-autobiographical account, Harry related the sentiment of one school board member that dominated the delta fields—perhaps fictionalized, perhaps not—"If I don't skin these niggers and peckerwoods some other planter will. Anyway, they expect it. I long ago figured out the ethics of the business—if I don't take what they make, they'll throw it away. So what the hell?"[30] As someone who had scratched his way up from poverty, Harry smoldered over the careless exploitation, but also knowing the character of some of those in the cotton cabins he could understand both sides. In perhaps no other place in his life was Harry Kroll so deeply buried in the South's time-honored rural economic system, and it honed his sense of socioeconomic injustice to a keen edge.

Besides being principal of the Lula-Rich school, Kroll taught the upper grades—or attempted to teach them. "I found my students coming to school in their own cars—those who did not use the school busses. Many of these were powerful machines, built for the rich. Arrogant, difficult fellows the young men were; and equally difficult, in their way, were the girls. Both boys and girls declined none too politely to have traffic with the course of study." The careless lack of personal drive that privilege had given some of his students galled a man who had scraped dirt for every opportunity he had found. "I realized, in desperation," he remembered, "that nothing in my courses of education helped me much to cope with a sophistication I could not imitate and did not understand." Harry Kroll placed faith in the gospel of work, sweat, and the ability to think and create. Seeing his privileged students carelessly tossing away whatever did not entertain them drove him to distraction. Above him the school board continued their partisan wrangling, motivated less by differing educational policies or goals than a constant jockeying for domination by churches or personalities in town. "It wasn't long before I saw that my job was simply to hang on with as little friction as possible, finish the session, and get out. I would, and gladly."[31]

Attempting to keep a low profile in Lula and avoid being caught between the warring parties, Kroll poured himself into his typewriter, producing story after story for the distant magazine publishers in New York and Chicago. Having already been introduced to the sectarian story papers while he was in school, Harry began to covet the larger venues of national detective and adventure pulp magazines, which paid dramatically better. He learned to generate stories quickly and completely in a single sitting, making little effort at revision. Most of the stories he wrote did not sell, but the ceaseless practice provided him real life experience producing marketable writing. After school dismissed in the afternoon, if he didn't have an idea for a story, Harry would occasionally wander between the tenant and sharecropper cabins, visiting his poorer students' accommodations. "Don't loaf and invite inspiration," wrote Jack London as early as 1903, "light out after it with a club, and if you don't get it you will nonetheless get something that looks remarkably like it."[32] Tucked in among the weathered shacks and beaten-dirt yards Harry quickly found a wealth of conflicts, problems, and relationships that easily provided plots and story lines he could turn into marketable tales. "In the afternoons when school was dismissed I would walk out on the plantations and sit on the wooden steps of the cabins and talk with the croppers," he later wrote. "The wage tenants were Negroes. There was a scattering of white tenants, and these usually were typical share-croppers. Some owned their own mules and implements, but mostly they cropped on halves, the planter supplying rations, seeds and fertilizers, mules and implements, and the cropper furnishing the labor. I visited white and black cabins alike. Sometimes I talked with planters." Kroll sat on door stoops, swapped stories, listened to words stewed in the fluid drawl of the delta, making mental notes. Through the school year, as he taught school, dealt with the community leaders, and visited with the students and their parents, Kroll gleaned stories, jotted notes. These stories formed the core of material that after a number of revisions were eventually combined into the single larger work.[33] Slowly Harry came to see that it was not merely rural poverty that was the greatest challenge to stability in the school, but the landowners' willful adoption and careful manipulation of poverty as a tool to maintain control of the cotton economy.[34]

The inequities under which he had grown up in Tennessee blazed into sharp relief as Kroll taught in the Mississippi Delta. He continued teaching in Lula while seething indignantly over the inequalities that the cotton sharecropping economy created. His impotent disdain also sharpened his awareness of what was going on immediately around him. "There was a boy in school who might have been myself—a lean fellow, quiet, sometimes hungry looking, who did his lessons mutely, and only occasionally looked enviously at the planters' sons, or with another sort of hunger at the smooth, shapely girls. There was one girl in particular who was a rich, glowing, she-creature. She came to school with a pad of blank tenant contracts upon which she did her algebra. After a while these contracts, [the girl] herself, the boy, a news item about how a gang of cotton thieves had been bagged, and the first-hand account of a lynching one night in the swamps from one of my seniors, began to jell in my mind."[35] A justice story of another sort, "The Law and the Evidence," had already been submitted to *McClure's* and was accepted for publication in December 1924. While it was under

"Rows of young cotton around tenant houses. Mississippi Delta." This image exemplifies the physical setting of cotton sharecropping around Lula and Rich in the mid-1920s, which stirred Kroll. Photograph by Marion Wolcott, FSA, March 1940, Prints & Photographs Division, FSA/OWI Collection, Library of Congress.

consideration and with Roseboro's earlier advice firmly in mind, it did not take long before Harry slammed out a long short story on his typewriter in the Lula-Rich teacherage and fired it off to Roseboro. He followed up this with two more closely related short stories about ambition and poor white sharecroppers trying to make ends meet as they sweated in the cotton lands of the Mississippi Delta. "I wrote my Mississippi material in fury," he remembered later. They were each bundled off to the magazine as well.

These three stories do not survive in separately identifiable forms, but each one addressed different aspects of the cotton sharecropping society, based on Kroll's impressions and circumstances, all related by place and time. Roseboro critiqued one of the three manuscripts carefully but held the first back from publisher Samuel McClure until Kroll improved it.[36] Kroll's sharecropping stories, inspired by his time in Lula, ultimately never appeared, since *McClure's Magazine* ceased publication permanently in early 1926. Harry was left with three related stories that he had written from the blood-tinged sweat of the delta's soul. Life in Lula awoke in Harry a deep yearning to swing a newly sharpened sword of righteous indignation through the economic inequalities of the Southern planter system; but following rigid social conventions of the time, that same sword conveniently and perhaps inevitably cut off black neighbors and sharecroppers from his sympathies. Perhaps not a conscious racist, Kroll simply accepted the status quo as unchangeable reality, and therefore creating as sympathetic a picture of the hopes and dreams of Southern blacks as his fellow poor whites would simply have been an idealistic affectation that flew against his tendencies toward literary realism. As he developed into a Southern writer, Harry Kroll's writing consigned his few African-American characters to the lot he knew from experience, where they were always subservient, tangential figures. Kroll's writing universally allotted them the separate, segregated existence and casual but uneasy interaction around the lower edges of his Anglo-Saxon world.

If school at Peabody College in Nashville provided Kroll's introduction and earliest training in writing, it was his writing while holding down the teaching job in Lula that provided his writer's apprenticeship. In many ways, the lessons he learned while in Nashville shaped his perspective on the literary marketplace, but it was Lula that fixed his thematic topics and helped him establish a regimen for exercising his craft. It was also in Lula that he realized the struggle of being a rural participant in what was essentially a strongly localized urban industry. Cut off from the dominantly Eastern editorial marketplace except by mail, Harry Kroll sought for some means of remaining connected, getting current information, and bettering his work. During the year he became acquainted with the *Editor,* a small-circulation magazine published out of Highland Falls, New York, which encouraged the development of would-be writers.[37] The *Editor* served as a venue for sharing technique and sales tips between readers, provided running lists of publishers buying all sorts of written material, and advertised professional assistance: editorial services, reviewers, and books and materials useful to writers. Since Peabody College taught journalism and writing, Harry probably encountered the magazine at the campus library. By the time he moved the family to Mississippi he certainly had subscribed to the publication. While teaching in Lula he contributed a pair of articles to its pages as well. Though he left no real clues about what he read himself, it is evident that the magazine was an inspiration. "There is a place somewhere for every good manuscript," was the *Editor*'s motto. Harry Kroll adopted the saying as his own, and it encapsulates his seemingly heedless drive to place his manuscripts with publishers. By the time he left school in 1925 he was confident that he was a good writer, therefore he assumed that breaking into the publication process involved merely being patient enough to submit, and resubmit, and resubmit again, until a manuscript encountered "the right place." To take a lesson from his upbringing, tobacco could not worm and sucker itself, cotton did not chop itself, corn did not hoe itself, and therefore manuscripts would not sell themselves. Sending a manuscript to a dozen publishers did not bother him a bit. Given the right publications, he was even a marketable writer. Kroll's practice was less like the carefully placed single bullet than it was like the repeated blasts of a shotgun. He swallowed rejections and submitted manuscripts undeterred until a piece either managed to land an acceptance or he decided not to bother further.

Ironically, it was just as Harry Kroll was fulminating his socially conscious critique of Southern cotton culture that a few of Vanderbilt's Fugitive circle were returning to Nashville. By 1928 they were reforming and extending themselves into a new group, a collection of conservative critics of modernization which came to be known as the Agrarians. J. A. Bryant Jr. points out that "The more perceptive among the Fugitives had begun to recognize the importance of the regional context that had produced them—one that for various reasons has been spared the worst aspects of the nation's advance toward an industrial economy which seemed destined to erase sectional individuality and render irrelevant the South's long-standing claim to distinctiveness."[38] Bryant is only partly correct. At their core, the new literary Agrarians were conservative, urban, and sophisticated Southern social philosophers. Searching for a means of insulating Southern culture from the acids of increasing economic interdependence and social complexity, the Agrarians assumed an anti-modern argument. "We believe," wrote Donald Davidson to the editor of the newspaper which published his weekly book column in Nashville, "that neither the Reconstruction nor the War, injurious as this wa[s], really destroyed the South. It is only now being finally menaced. . . ."[39] Their critique challenged the depersonalization of industrial development and the encroachment of urban industrialism by idealizing the South's historic status as an indefinably purer agrarian-dominated society. The anti-industrial assertions formed a social philosophy and ideological approach to past, present, and future, which constituted neither a social nor political movement. Even Allen Tate admitted that the Fugitives/Agrarians were literary philosophers "conservative in politics and agrarian in economics," who "weren't political and we didn't farm."[40] They asserted that reestablishing an agrarian economy was the sole method for moving the South forward without recreating the social failings of an industrial economy. It was not agriculture itself which lit their ideas, but the idea of an opposite and preferable social system to the dominating, depersonalizing force of modern industrial economy. Translated into practice, however, the writers variously addressed the redemptive virtues of both society and politics, emphasized "Southern tradition," idealized the plantation economy, and lionized selected Confederate figures while blithely ignoring the coercive labor and class structures which were the sole forces that had made possible the South's genteel "traditions" of "leisure, kindliness, and the enjoyment of a simple life, . . . virtues which thrive in an agrarian climate but do badly in an industrial."[41] Essentially ignorant of the harrowing uncertainties of crop cycles, weather, and the crushing weight of poverty among small farmers, and utterly ignoring the premise of racial exploitation, the Agrarian circle sang paeans to idealized rural life in the face of industrialism, economic change, and increasing heterogeneous social complexity. The high culture represented by the conservative Agrarians was a luxury of privilege, and the Agrarian movement was at its heart a callous invocation to strengthen class structures. The Agrarians wrote for readers who settled into an easy chair for an evening's reading, not for those who worked the fields from sun-up to sundown. In fact, those whose unremitting fieldwork made possible the genteel agrarian life might have resented the implications of Tate, Davidson, and Ransom's race- and class-borne idealism.

The Agrarian ideal mirrored precisely the sort of evocation of idealized "heritage" that women's memorial associations had championed during the late nineteenth century, and was being championed by newer organizations like the United Daughters of the Confederacy and the Sons of Confederate Veterans. As the publishing center of the South, Nashville in the 1920s was the throbbing heart of the Lost Cause mythology. The Agrarians, along with the national and local memorial associations, wanted to pick and choose elements of the region's history and reality which reinforced their own conceptions and which could serve as a tradition worth defending. In this sense, the Agrarian message was a literary reflection of dissatisfaction over the cultural deadweight of the inelegant parts of the Southern past.[42]

On the other hand, disgusted with the hopelessness of rural work and looking for any way to transcend it, Harry Kroll *had* farmed and was desperately trying to stay away from it. Though he grew more conservative as he aged, as a student at Peabody

College in his early thirties, Harry held strong Progressive and Democratic leanings. Those points set him apart from his more literary-leaning contemporaries across Twenty-First Avenue. Kroll was a decade older, less academic, and had behind him a much grittier life experience than most of those in the Fugitive and larger Agrarian circles.

Harry Kroll had been introduced to the juvenile weeklies and sectarian story markets while in school. By the time he reached Lula, and probably thanks to the marketing columns in the *Editor,* even while he began making decent money from juvenile sectarian papers, Harry began aspiring to transcend the $4 and $12 payments doled out by the sectarian publications. He set his sights on breaking into the much more lucrative national market for fiction—the "pulps," and later the upper-class "slicks," which could pay between $60 and $150 for a single story. Pulp magazines like *Munsey's, Argosy,* and *Everybody's* were sold by the hundreds of thousands at city newsstands, corner drug stores, and tobacconists everywhere across the country. They presented a vibrant world of vicarious action, heady romance, and heart-pounding adventure—worlds of escape from daily reality for millions of readers every week. Printed cheaply on soft, high-bulk, wood-pulp paper, the pulps bridged an enormous market gap between juvenile and young-adult nickel weeklies and the urbane, more expensive literary magazines like *Cosmopolitan,* the *Atlantic Monthly, Collier's,* and the *Saturday Evening Post.* Most pulps were niche publications, but broad ones. The titles and thematic contents of such magazines varied as much as the readers who curled up with them. Romance, westerns, crime, science fiction, fortune stories, adventure, and general story pulps were published by dozens of publishing firms. They consumed thousands of stories annually and represented a huge market for writers and would-be writers. Pulp story magazines were truly the country's first genuinely national literature. Antebellum story papers and their offspring, the yellow-back or dime novels, were wildly popular but circulated primarily in urban areas. Newspapers remained local niche publications, distributed almost exclusively to the cities and towns in which they appeared. Beginning in the 1890s sectional lines dividing American literature were dissolving as high-speed printing presses cranked out filler for the reading market, and new business structures and transportation homogenized the fictional material available in any given market. The national market for pulp fiction was enormous. There were hundreds of titles from dozens of publishers. Luck-and-pluck fortune stories; romance; westerns; adventure of all sorts in the air, on sea, and abroad; mysteries, detectives, and crooks—they were published with bright covers in monthly and often semimonthly issues, for a populace that had just been introduced to the wonders of radio, had not yet seen a talking movie show, and for whom television was yet a fantasy.

In formulating his own work, Kroll had stumbled upon a process similar to what earlier serialists had employed while writing for the national story papers. Edward Z. C. Judson, writing Buffalo Bill story serials (and a dozen others) as Ned Buntline, described his method: "I never lay out plots in advance. I wouldn't know how to do it, for how can I know what my people may take it into their heads to do? First I invent a title. When I hit on a good one, I consider the story about half finished. After I begin I push ahead as fast as I can write, never blotting out anything I have once written and never making a correction or modification. If a book does not suit me when I have finished it, I simply throw it into the fire, forget it, and start another." Horatio Alger Jr., Prentiss Ingraham, and scores of other writers did similar, nearly stream-of-consciousness storytelling day in and day out for years. Craft was not an issue; the tale was. Newspapers guzzled stories and spit out bundles of daily, weekly, semimonthly, and monthly issues filled with wildly improbable adventure, fortune, and eventually romantic tales. By the time Kroll began writing in the 1920s, fiction was an industry.[43]

Kroll's writing method was similar in speed and perspective, but his experience in the Mississippi Delta and in the Tennessee and Kentucky hills had demonstrated that life had a million stories surrounding him. Where Judson relied on a fertile imagination and not-too-discriminating readers, Harry Kroll listened to the people around him and kept notes of things he heard. Many of them would be worked into his manuscripts.[44] As time wore on and his practices developed into habits, then into reputation, drawing stories from people he met gave his writing an immediacy and personality that many writers lacked, but it also lashed him to the stories of the people and places with which he associated. His sources would thus prove factors that also limited his writing, but in the mid-1920s it was good enough. Though he had seen limited publication of his writing while in college, it was while working as a Mississippi schoolteacher that Kroll found his first genuine commercial success as a writer. "In the past thirty days," he wrote proudly to the *Editor* in December 1924, "I have sold $343 worth of fiction to McClure's, Weird Tales, Complete Story, Kind Words, and Young People"—one social journal, two pulp story magazines, and two sectarian papers.[45] It was a notable start, especially since he was making around the same figure on salary; but far below the $30,000 which Frederick Faust would glean about the same time for one serial novel in *Collier's* under the name Max Brand.[46]

The position in Lula-Rich was untenable, and Kroll was glad enough to find excuse to leave. Though his account in *Share-Cropper* suggests he left with ire on both sides, the published version is probably a literary device. More likely he bowed out of local school politics with some grace. The arrival of such a well-educated individual, a writer who had actually *published* stories, stirred the community's attention. Kroll pasted into his scrapbook several *Register* clippings about his accomplishments.[47]

Coahoma County society was probably loath to see him depart. A clipping from his scrapbook noted that the Lula-Rich principal was leaving to teach "English, the short story, and rural journalism" at Peabody for the 1925 summer session.[48] Mr. Kroll, the newspaper reported with awe, "is at present collaborating with Dr. [Kary C.] Davis [of Peabody College] in writing a text book on the teaching of English in southern rural schools." Whether this was a boast or an actual project has escaped documentation, but a book on the subject never appeared under those names. Though he had filled the school year by taking a series of correspondence courses toward his degree—Agriculture 147, Advanced Problems—Harry ultimately left Lula for Nashville to complete the coursework for his master's degree in English. Because they owned no real property and remained in Lula less than a year, Harry Kroll and his family managed to avoid documentation in virtually every official record, other than the annual school accreditation report, which he filed with the state Department of Education as the principal. Mr. Kroll graduated his students of the 1924–25 school year that spring. Within a few days or weeks Harry dusted his feet of the delta soil, piled his family into the Dodge Runabout, and turned his back on the Mississippi cotton lands, heading back to Nashville. The Krolls left Lula just as his former students began forming up in long lines to begin threading across the flat, black fields to "chop" cotton: thinning the season's cotton sprouts and weeding the fields for the first time. As they drove north and eastward on the long, dusty, and bumpy drive to Nashville, Harry was confidently and Nettie resignedly planning to exist and complete his education living off of Harry's writing.

Frank Leavell had successfully connected Kroll and Viola Roseboro by mail in 1922, and Kroll maintained contact with the literary champion during his stay in Mississippi, despite the cash it cost him for her service as a manuscript reviewer. After fleeing Lula and at her suggestion, he decided to pull together the three short Mississippi pieces, fill out the story, and draft an expanded version as a novel, one based on experience but not so heavily that the topic or location would limit its appeal. The manuscript was initially titled "Peckerwoods." This bit of slang was a biting contemporary insult, a term for a poor white farmer that carried the same amount of respect as "nigger" would if referring to blacks today. This new novel he sent to New York for a professional manuscript review as early as the late fall of 1925, just after the Krolls returned to Nashville for Harry to complete the Peabody summer term. H. M. Hamilton of the *Editor,* a reviewer and longtime associate of Roseboro's, suggested that Kroll eliminate complicated and sophisticated words to focus on straightforward, simple English. He also urged some character development, but on the whole was complimentary. "You've got the gift, man; . . . Keep to your heritage. It is the desire to complicate that leads to the faults I have marked." Both author and reviewer felt that even in its fairly rough draft the story development was essentially complete. Hamilton responded to Kroll's inquiry about a suitable publication venue with some practical skepticism. "Take a list, send to one after another, and (leaving out the Bonis and Knopfs [i.e., Boni and Liveright, and Alfred A. Knopf, both relatively new, successful publishers of American high literature]) just make the rounds. The new houses may do well with you; some writers say that a long list kills a book's chances."[49]

While the "Peckerwoods" manuscript was being read in New York, back in Nashville yet again for a few months, Kroll completed the Special Problems class series in agriculture and classes on the works of Tennyson and Browning. As he approached the number of required credits to complete his degree, the subject of a thesis naturally became a topic of concern. Kroll never pretended to scholarship; schooling was, for him, merely an unavoidably necessary step toward professional status. Lacking the interest or substance required for a comparative literary study or original research, Kroll chose a topic that fit neatly within his rural and democratic view of writing. The master's thesis he produced was a dictionary compilation of vernacular speech, essentially a list of idioms and slang, rather than the analytical study implied by the title: "A Comparative Study of Upper and Lower Southern Folk Speech." His introduction listed four general purposes for the compilation: (1) to record specific dialectical specimens, (2) to compare "several dialect districts in the upper and lower South," (3) to "arrive at the laws of the vernacular," and (4) to compile the findings in a usable dictionary form. It was a great statement. Though he either missed or failed to acknowledge it, the second and fourth purposes essentially worked against each other, and in completing the document Kroll eventually chose to emphasize structure over content, which was easier to produce. His resulting dictionary does represent a collection of regional speech, but contains just as many phonetic spellings of common word-pronunciations as it does genuine idioms. Two pages of conclusions at the end of the document present his analysis, brief comments on the anticipated disappearance of folk speech due to exposure to the correct spelling and grammar in newspapers, and to the diction and pronunciation available via radio broadcasting.[50]

To an informed reader it is immediately apparent that each of the fields he describes as study sites were places Kroll had lived or worked: in other words, he made no attempt at compiling a real study. The lower Southern dialect fields include Washington, Mobile, Clarke, and Marengo Counties in Alabama (all of these coincident with his eleven years as a mill worker, tramp photographer, and schoolteacher between 1906 and 1917); and Harrison and Coahoma Counties, Mississippi (the location of his year as a schoolteacher in Lula). The upper Southern folk speech is represented by Dyer County, Tennessee (where Kroll spent his boyhood and had not visited in twenty years); Davidson County, Tennessee (home to Nashville and Peabody); and Warren County, Kentucky (where he had taught a year in Woodburn). Though the academic rigor of theses in the 1920s was improving, it was still possible to produce and submit anything reasonably original as research. Impatient to be back in a paying job, Kroll plainly chose his topic to be one that looked good and could be most easily knocked out in short order.

In his one-page method statement, the author explains that he had maintained a notebook in which he recorded each expression and its usage, but fails to note anywhere that he had compiled this book during his years of self-education, before even coming to Peabody, and that his thesis represents a substantive transcription of these notes. The definitions were obviously edited and amended, and occasionally he inserted reminiscent observations. In fact, the composition suggests he did almost no research specifically for the paper and could well have recalled most or all of these entries straight from memory. He was certainly capable of doing so, as the slang and dialect he employed in *Their Ancient Grudge* demonstrated almost two decades later.

With his thesis completed, the final step in his graduate education, Harry Kroll's graduate degree was awarded at commencement at the end of the college's busy summer term, and he became "Harry Harrison Kroll, M.A."[52] With his newly minted graduate degree in hand, in the late summer of 1925 the Krolls moved about forty miles south of Nashville to settle in Unionville, a small town north west of the Bedford County seat at Shelbyville. Harry accepted the principalship in a newly established consolidated district with the uninspiring moniker "Community High School." The "community" designation came from the fact that the new structure consolidated students from ten rural districts; the "high school" was appended chiefly because it included students through grade 12. It was built after the Rover High School burned to the ground the previous year after merely a week of classes. The Community School was a six-classroom, frame building with a small auditorium (which probably also served as an activity room), a separate building for an agricultural program, and a dirt-paved outdoor basketball court that capped a low rise behind the building. Here, besides being principal, Harry taught English. It would be the last year he taught in graded schools. During his principalship at Community High School, Kroll renewed his acquaintance with girls' basketball by organizing and coaching the school team. His star player in 1925–26 was Cloy Thompson, who Kroll once observed "was the fastest thing on two legs I ever saw."[53] True to form, he devoted as much time as he could free from the classroom, ball court, and his growing boys, to continue his avocation as a writer. For awhile his short fiction and illustrations accepted for publication tended to reflect his interest in high school girls' sports, drawing on his familiarity with basketball for short story topics and settings. A dozen or more of his girls' basketball stories appeared in the Sunday School papers published in Nashville during the 1920s and early 1930s. "Some of the girls' names were changed," one community history recalled, "but most were near enough to the real names that they could be recognized."[54]

In his first teaching post since leaving Mississippi, and still smoldering with the memory of Lula's social inequalities, Harry adapted his evolving story of Danny Morgan and Nordie Lord into a play. It was produced at the school in the spring of 1926, perhaps under Harry's direction, with a cast of students and community members. Harry played the part of Dave Culbertson.[55]

In later years, reminiscing about living at Unionville, Harry Jr. contributed a curious story about his father's career. He is the only source for the story, which may be blended from a man's recall and a boy's misunderstanding. It went like this: shortly after arriving in Unionville, Harry Sr. is said to have attended a minstrel show by David "Uncle Dave" Harrison Macon. Macon was a well-known, flashy Nashville entertainer and a stellar banjo player. Since 1918 Macon had been barnstorming the rural South as a stage entertainer at county fairs and community frolics. He had cut his first album in a New York studio during the summer of 1924, and had returned the following April for another group of sessions. In December 1926 Dave Macon would begin performing for the earliest broadcasts of radio station WSM's Barn Dance, predecessor to the Grand Ole Opry. At Macon's performance, their shared middle name may have provided Harry an entrée to strike up a conversation, and Harry supposedly invited Macon home for supper. After some discussion they agreed to team up. Harry either owned or acquired a 35mm projector and a handful of silent-movie shorts, and joined the traveling band of Macon and fellow musician Sid Harkreader on weekend performances in local schoolhouses. According to Harry Jr., who would have been five or six, the pictures were interspersed with musical variety numbers by Macon and Harkreader during reel changes. Harry's part on the tour did not last long, for one or more of several reasons. The projectors operated with a hot-burning carbide lamp as illumination, and the nitrate-based film of that medium is extraordinarily flammable. Fires could flare up without warning and the buckets of sand needed to douse a fire (since nitrate continues to burn even when submerged in water) played havoc with projector gearing. Kroll also had a family to provide for and could not have traveled widely.[56] Harry Jr.'s memory could possibly have been faulty as well, blending his father's earlier travel with his later interest in early country music.

The Lincoln Memorial Idyll

Despite his school responsibilities in Unionville, extracurricular writing, and roadshow activities, Harry kept plugging applications and letters to colleges and schools, looking for an appointment that would get him out of graded schools entirely. In 1926 he was thirty-eight, with a pregnant wife and two small boys, yet he still had the strength and energy of his youth remained on tap—he still felt full of life's juices. Looking just at what is presently known of his work, the arrival in Unionville seems to represent a tipping point in Kroll's writing career. After leaving Mississippi he began writing seriously, not just occasionally or when an idea was at hand. Harry began sitting down to the typewriter regularly, like a hobby woodworker with a basement shop producing craft-fair merchandise. He already understood the Nashville sectarian markets. Selling there gave him the confidence to approach publishers further afield. The gamble paid off handsomely. He began producing (and selling) work in huge amounts. Fifty stories were published each year in 1925 and 1926. Because of the wide range of his submissions across the country, that number certainly cannot presume to include every publication. He sold probably another half again more than the fifty stories presently known, and certainly wrote two or three times more than actually sold. Most importantly, for the first time Harry was able to place work repeatedly (twenty times) in some of the great story publications of the day, including the semimonthly *Complete Story, Weird Tales,* and *Detective Story Magazine.*

Modern readers whose encounter with periodicals is limited to the slick magazines in grocery store aisles, ponderously laden with visually intense advertising, often find it difficult understanding the significance and breadth of magazine publishing to earlier generations. The decade of the 1920s had been widely touted as the Literary Decade, and while sophistication and experimentation were all the rage in some circles, books and magazines were the common occupiers of American's free time across all classes. The market was enormously broad and gulped written material in a frantic drive to fill its tens of thousands of pages weekly. A typical semi-monthly issue of *Complete Story Magazine* (a Street and Smith publication), for instance, included 144 pages of straight reading matter, usually consisting of a novelette or novella of around 50 pages, and five or six stories of 20 pages each, interspersed with poems and stubs (half-page articles used as space filler). Advertising was limited to four pages behind the front cover and four more before the back, or to a few back pages. The pulps printed work by hundreds of writers and sold by subscription nationally and by the issue in city street newsstands. Small-town drugstores carried racks of them for the third of Americans living outside the cities. Selling a fifteen-page manuscript story to *Kind Words* or *Boy's Weekly* might pay Harry six to twelve dollars, rarely more, but the pulps paid six to ten times that amount. They were an attractive, lucrative market for writers—but a frightfully uncertain one. Unlike a salary, irrespective of how long he wrote or how many story manuscripts he mailed, there was no guaranteed income as a freelance writer of short fiction. Relying on writing to provide a family income would have been tremendously stressful.

Finally his job search paid off. During the late summer of 1926 an offer arrived to join the faculty of Lincoln Memorial University, a small private college in Harrogate, Tennessee. LMU was on the Tennessee-Kentucky border, a stone's throw south of the Cumberland Gap, the historic pass through the Appalachian Mountains between Virginia and Kentucky. The school had been founded on the good intentions and condescending conservatism of 1890s Gilded Age wealth. Like many small colleges in poor areas it survived on the largess of the Northeast's upper crust, making the college essentially a *noblesse oblige* effort to civilize the last "pure Americans," Appalachia's mountain people. In practice, however, the faculty of Lincoln Memorial University was anything but elitist, fueled instead by the idealism of educating Appalachian laborers and farm kids—the common man. "Already the spark of ambition is aglow in the breast of the mountain youth," Harry may well have read in a 1926 issue of LMU's *Mountain Herald.* Who knew but what in some mountain cabin there dwelt another Shakespeare whose muse would "pass him by in the cloud of ignorance" because he had not been afforded the "Lincoln Advantage."[57] Discounting the occasionally maudlin rhetorical flourish, LMU was looking for teachers who were practitioners in their fields and not merely pedagogues. It was an ambitious school with an unaccredited educational program. Still, for a man who had thus far spent his career teaching in ungraded schools and rural high schools, and given the school's mission "to make the education . . . denied [Lincoln] possible for the children of the humble, common people of America," LMU was certainly a step up. The appointment was welcome but

The Krolls' faculty accommodations at Lincoln Memorial University, 1957.

complicated life tremendously. Nettie had become pregnant with their third child early in the year and was due imminently. In the first week or two of September 1926, while Harry crated their belongings in Unionville, Nettie packed the boys off once again to her parents' home in Mobile.[58]

While Nettie and the boys were visiting the Heards, Harry drove the family's Dodge Runabout from Unionville to Harrogate. He would have arranged with a local wagon owner to ferry the packing crates of family belongings from the small railroad station up the hill to their new faculty accommodations. The Krolls were housed in both sides of a small school-owned duplex on the road that ringed campus. With the goods settled, Harry drove to Mobile to pick up the family. For Nettie, eight and a half months pregnant, the drive back to Harrogate on ungraded roads in a suspension-spring, open-topped automobile must have been agony. A few weeks after they arrived, on October 3, 1926, Daniel Wesley Kroll was born just across the Cumberland Gap in the hospital in Middlesboro, Kentucky. Harry had been in classes and got word only after the blessed event. He drove the car the half-dozen miles north and arrived to have a son, their third, placed in his arms. "I had wanted a girl," he confessed to a professional group in a speech years later, "but when the nurse produced a small, wrinkled monkey-like creature and placed it in my arms with the triumphant report 'it's a boy,' I looked down at this fruit of my loins with a wonder I had not felt at the sight of my other two babies. He did not protest my strange embrace, and in that moment I knew all a man ever learns about the last born becoming the focus of his decaying powers of affection."[59] Dan became immediately and forever afterward his father's favorite. Harry lavished attention, indulgence, and confidence on his youngest boy that was dished out more sparingly to Harry Jr.—known to everyone in the family as "Son"—and Robert Torrey, who was called by his middle name until he was an adult.

Nettie's sisters Fannie and Evelyn had come in September to see her during the last difficult days of her pregnancy and Evelyn intended to stay for the confinement, but Harry's mother Caroline arrived soon afterward, ostensibly to see the new grandson. On the other hand, now that Harry had a solid income and position she may have been hoping to move in herself. More than the extra squeeze on already tight accommodations, Caroline's grating personality and constant demands for deference and attention created an intolerable situation in the house. She was positively acidic in the small college community. Nettie, ever reserved to begin with, shrank from conflict with her rawboned mother-in-law, withdrawing for emotional stability and security into the care for her new baby. Caroline's gauche curiosity and utter lack of social grace was so disruptive that Harry not only asked her to leave but virtually threw her out of the house.

While their baby brother bawled in the bedroom at home, at five and three, Son and Torrey had the run of the campus. The news that their father was not merely a teacher but an active and quite successful writer went through campus like a brushfire and earned his two boys the nicknames Big and Little Short Story. Both still too young to attend school themselves, they played on the steep hills that rose like theatrical backdrops behind the college and roamed at will, but they were terrified of a pair of savage and nearly wild German Shepherd dogs kept by the dour biology teacher and his wife, Frank C. and Iris Grannis.[60]

It was at LMU that Kroll finally formed some of his closest relationships. "Country folks are good folks, but their intellectual climate is far from stimulating," he admitted years later. "Now for the first time in my life I had close personal ties with men of my own intellectual level. They were my contemporaries—not the teacher-student relationships I found at Peabody, . . . but with me who belonged to me and I to them." Forrest Gaw of the Music Department, theatre/speech instructor Earl Hobson Smith, and the college dean, Charles Lewis, each became close friends in different ways. Kroll and Gaw shared an appreciation of music: classical, but also the new hillbilly records just beginning to be released and discovered in Nashville and New York. Kroll and Smith occasionally strolled up a road that rose behind campus to the ridgeline, to a spot overlooking some large poplars where they could talk and play the boyish game of pitching rocks at trees in the hollow beneath them. The relationship with Lewis

Lincoln Memorial University, ca.1932. Courtesy of University Archives of Lincoln Memorial University, Harrogate, Tennessee.

was different. A career of nearly continuous conflict in school teaching had developed in Harry a wariness of administrators, and Lewis was probably uncertain of how to approach his atypical new faculty member. "But presently all that changed, with no conscious effort on our parts; and we came to talk free, speak our minds, with no loss of standing because of the freedom."[61] Kroll's fellow faculty members and the intellectual climate at the school were less significant to him, however, than the mountain culture which suffused the school itself. Harry would draw on Appalachia for scores of story plots and characters, including what is arguably his best work, twenty years later—a fictional account of the Hatfield-McCoy feud entitled *Their Ancient Grudge.*

Harry Kroll's service at Lincoln Memorial University was crucially important for his development as a writer, but it was also here that he made his one notable contribution to Appalachian literature and the broader field of American letters. As a faculty member at Lincoln Memorial, Harry Kroll initially taught lower-division English classes in practical composition, focused on journalism and story writing. For his first year at LMU, 1926–27, Harry Kroll was the English Department. A second professor, Earl Hobson Smith, came the next year to teach speech and drama, but for a year Kroll taught every LMU underclassman.

Quite by chance, Harry Kroll's arrival at Lincoln Memorial intersected the early college careers of a remarkable number of talented and motivated students from the Kentucky, Tennessee, and Virginia hills. Infused with Kroll's energy, many wrote and marketed their work while they were students. His arrival on staff also put him in the position to serve as a catalyst in the development of several LMU students who would, in time, begin what has since been identified as modern Appalachian literature. Had he not been an instructor at LMU during the 1926–28 school years it is likely that these writers would have continued their development, but doubtful that the outcome would have been as formal or as widespread. While Kroll did not awaken the literary voices of his already-writing students, he was on hand to stand as a defining influence on such figures as Jesse Stuart, Don West, Roland Carter, James Still, Louise McCamy, and others who chose not to pursue careers in writing.[62] Harry Kroll exemplified a successful writer that did not operate within the "social uplift" mission which drove the chancellor and on which the school was grounded. Unfortunately, this difference, combined with the popularity of his approach, loose structure of his classes, and his informality, set Kroll at odds with the college administration.

Harry Kroll's importance to LMU's budding writers as an example of a practicing writer, his hands-off teaching style, and his liberal doses of raw praise, were defining forces for his students. LMU students had previously been subjected to rote teaching from the standard canon of European literature, an effort to lift them out of their Appalachian rural degradation. In his reminiscent *Beyond Dark Hills,* restated in *To Teach, To Love,* Jesse Stuart contrasted his English experience as a freshman with his sophomore year under Mr. Kroll. As a literary sergeant commanding the European literary canon, Kroll's predecessor, Kathryn Howard, had actively discouraged Stuart's nostalgic, naturalistic writing, suggesting he "get away from the sedge and muddy waters and the night wind. Write high, beautiful things like Shakespeare, Keats, Browning, and Longfellow. Don't waste your time on such low, vile things."[63] The following year Stuart's experience in sophomore English could not have been more different. Harry Kroll's outlook was a complete reversal of Miss Howard's literary principles. I don't mean to imply that Kroll alone created a literary salon at LMU. Elizabeth Lamont points out that "officials and faculty, all largely outsiders, viewed the advancement of literary culture among southern mountaineers as the most efficient means to attain their larger goal of 'educational uplift.'" LMU had fostered an atmosphere of literary attainment drawing upon the high literature of the West. Kroll's success and popularity as a teacher at LMU came partly from shifting the focus of study away from the traditional literary canon and toward the hills from which his students had come. Kroll had studied English literature in his own education, but he also viscerally understood students thirsting to transcend the farm—he had been one of them. Rather than hem in his students with the heady thoughts of what has since been dismissed as a culture of "dead white males," he urged them to write about what they knew, what they heard at home and on the stoops of country stores.

> Get that story on paper. . . . Write the wildest stories that ever happened in your community. You can't get them wild enough. Get all the old scandals. Let them kiss and love but no four-letter words. Be more skilled at writing than to use these. Do them by implication. Write between the lines. Get them down so they won't die! Write like you talk! Just tell the story! Get it on paper![64]

Original fiction and folk stories were not the only material he encouraged. Yet while encouraging his students to write was a key part of the education he gave them, it was not enough merely to get his students writing. Many of them—Still, Stuart, and West among them, certainly—were already committed to writing but looked for direction. Kroll's freewheeling style inspired and enabled the thematic exploration and creativity of his students in ways that traditional education did not. His contributions to the development of LMU's writers went much deeper than merely encouraging his students to submit their work. In retrospect, there seem to be five major factors behind Harry Kroll's catalytic importance as a literary figure at Lincoln Memorial University.

Probably the most significant contribution Kroll made to his LMU students was as an example of a practicing writer, not a literary icon, but someone who held down a job and still managed to write and publish. Here was someone who not only preached loudly about writing, he practiced what he preached openly and proudly.

For some of those aspiring writers the simple expedient of dropping hints about how often checks arrived in the mail would have been a dramatic lesson in itself. That some of those checks amounted to as much or more than a month's wages as a field hand . . . well, it was impressive. Stuart was stunned when the professor once showed him a check for a single short story. Kroll's *success* as a writer—at least fifty-four published stories identified thus far for his years at LMU (1926–27 and 1927–28)—demonstrated for the students at Lincoln Memorial University that writing need not only be appreciated in the abstract, or limited to developmental exercises in following the inspirational "uplift" model of study in literature.

Kroll's second contribution to his students as a literary motivator was his firm belief that neither the topic nor the form a writer chose needed to be "high" to be acceptable literature. He urged his students to pursue meaningful outlets for their productions. "Don't merely write, do something with it" was an important message. Writing was not merely self-expression, it could be treated as a practical craft like preserving food or auto mechanics. As he had done himself, Kroll encouraged students to focus on producing and submitting work to newspapers, magazines, and sectarian publications of all sorts. He taught them to allow the market to winnow out the good from the bad rather than worrying about self-criticism and endlessly polishing their creations. This encouragement steered them toward the popular literature that he knew best. Harry Kroll's encouragement to write for publications their families read was fertilizer for a clutch of mountain kids who shared his rurally defined worldview and weren't quite in a position to pursue "art for art's sake." Turning out a story or an article for a few bucks, however, was something they felt they could do and did. "One girl wrote an article on how to cook greens," Jesse Stuart recalled twenty years later. "Kroll told her to send it to a farm paper. The editor accepted it; she was paid one dollar. She received five hundred letters from housewives asking her more about the way she cooked greens."[65] Stuart himself was busily taking over the student magazine, the *Blue and Grey,* to be sure he had a local outlet for his work. He later wrote,

> Other pupils in Harry Harrison Kroll's creating-writing class—it became the best known class on the campus—started selling articles to farm journals, small magazines, and a few large magazines. There wasn't any let-up of spirit among its members. As time passed, they grew more and more ambitious, the fervor fanned into flame, for the little checks were something to the needy students. Seeing their names in magazines made them as proud as I had been to see my name in the college paper.[66]

Overall, Kroll's emphasis on the intrinsic rather than the merely expressive or personal value of writing proved an individually motivating lesson for many students, especially Stuart. Kroll's approach gave direction to two of Stuart's basic drives: it provided reasonable outlets for his creative urge, and it justified the time he spent writing by showing him that he could derive an income from it—in theory at least. Kroll's market-driven approach was an exact inversion of the strangulated perfectionism practiced by the Fugitive circle in Nashville. It also had real limits. Using the market to pass judgment on whatever one produced provided few stylistic models for writing and offered little help with improving one's work, except by implication from what did not sell. Kroll's model focused on generating work that was neither perfect, nor necessarily *good,* merely *good enough.* Harry's method fostered writers and not merely writing. It was well suited to students showing natural talent but served less well those who needed direct instruction and a familiarity with the larger written culture. As with virtually every other institution of higher education, the former were relatively few at LMU.

Kroll's third influential emphasis was advocating a market definition of quality for writing: if a piece was accepted for publication, it was good. This was a critical departure from the traditional curriculum and practice. The approach was a revelation for some students, like Jesse Stuart, and deeply disquieting to others, like James Still. Jesse Stuart, perhaps more effectively than any other of Kroll's students, learned that a cash value existed in the roughness of imagery and language as he fitted and sometimes repainted Appalachian scenes and language into respected literary forms. Stuart perceived in the market the validation of his creative fire, a point he desperately craved and single-mindedly pursued. It was no accident that Stuart later dedicated his privately published first book of poetry, *Harvest of Youth,* to Harry Harrison Kroll; Don West did the same with *Crab Grass.*[67] Admittedly, Kroll's loose-limbed educational methods were at odds with the traditional expectations of collegiate classroom instruction. James Still seems to have seen in Kroll's approach a crassness, commonness, and venal inelegance to turn against.

Despite his broad significance, Kroll's influence resulted in no systemic literary groundswell or firestorm around him. Kroll was fundamentally a teacher who merely approached the subject and the classroom somewhat differently than other instructors. It worked for some students and did not work for others. Though remembered by some students as stimulating and popular, Harry was not even the sole locus for literary creativity on campus. French language professor Dr. Lucia Danforth—the only Ph.D.-holding individual in the institution at the time—was the gravitational center of a distinctly rival literary clique grounded in the appreciation of and aspiration to the excellence of the European literary canon. The relation between the two groups has not yet been well studied but undoubtedly reflected the differing approaches to literature held by each professor. Rooted in the romance language and culture of French, which was still the dominant language of art and culture in the early twentieth century, Dr. Danforth was more attuned to traditional approaches to literature. James Still was in that circle and was her favorite. She remained in touch with Still for years after leaving LMU.[68]

Harry Kroll's rather populist approach to writing, the writing market, and literature was generally important to his students without yet being catalytic. It was his fourth contribution that tied together the other three into something genuinely substantive: his students may have come to school steeling themselves for lectures, but at LMU Harry Kroll taught his protégés to open their eyes and describe the culture, the language, and the world around them, and then to be unapologetic in writing about it. He already encouraged them to write about things they knew personally, but he also began interjecting examples of mountain culture as it gained broader popularity. In class he encouraged discussion and argumentation and might lug in his wind-up Victrola record player. On it he spun early albums of mountain folksongs for his students, to illustrate their own culture of poetry and ballad. His encouragement for the students to participate in their own vernacular culture as writers was perhaps Kroll's most significant accomplishment. It was his unapologetic emphasis on common expression at the time when Still, Stuart, and West were present to be influenced that makes Kroll's tenure at Lincoln Memorial University significant. Though he was merely being practical in encouraging students to write about the experience around them, Harry Kroll was effectively pushing his students toward participating in an indigenous literature, an Appalachian literature. Don West's biographer noted that Kroll "demonstrated for students the legitimacy of Appalachian culture as a source material for literary work." His example as a professional writer (i.e., one who sold his work) underscored the importance of his approach in a way that straightforward criticism or praise alone could not. Had Kroll not convinced students of the economic viability of their own written work it is doubtful that he could have convinced them to write about their world in their own language at all. Had they not encountered Kroll, his three later-notable students may have continued writing but might not have become writers. All LMU had to offer aspiring writers before Kroll came was the traditional approach of cultural uplift through mimicry of a foreign canon. Harry Kroll provided LMU students with a new model for writers and writing. If Jesse Stuart or Don West had gone straight from LMU's traditionalist approach to the equally traditional Vanderbilt, without first drawing upon Kroll's rural and proletarian inspiration or market savvy, it is unlikely they would have emerged with the cultural sense of direction in their writing that they did. Kathryn Howard and Lucia Danforth taught the appreciation of writers from the literary canon, Kroll encouraged his students to prove that writers existed among the Appalachian hills. This popular, organic, and essentially Romantic *völkisch* approach to literature and writing was something new, newer than even Kroll imagined. Elizabeth Lamont ties together LMU's literary package of the 1920s by observing that "the Kroll-Danforth rivalry provided LMU's aspiring writers with something even the best creative writing schools often fail to: diversity of literary theory and practice. As such, 1920s LMU could nurture both the aggressively market-driven ethos of Jesse Stuart and James Still's more high-brow aspirations.[69]

Kroll also contributed a fifth and final element to the new literary life at LMU. Harry Kroll's position and encouragement naturally winnowed the LMU student body for both the best natural writers and those willing to work hard to learn the craft. From this group, early in his career at LMU, Mr. Kroll began collecting talented or interested students for an informal literary discussion session. In an interview with Frank Leavell, Jr. about his part in Jesse Stuart's education, Kroll recalled that he arranged for evening use of a classroom to continue discussions of writing. Like the Nashville Fugitives, the subjects of this tiny Appalachian salon turned around their own creative efforts. It was open not only for his students, but any student who wished to come. "Our little group of so-called creative writers met two nights a week down at Avery Hall, presumably for an hour a session," Harry wrote years later.

> Actually we knew no hours. We'd read and talk and mutter and argue for two hours, or into half the night. Just talking, sitting in the classroom awhile and then going out lying on the campus grass under the elms and hackberries and stars, murmuring this and that, Stuart in his jerky Kentucky eloquence, Roland Carter in his measured ecclesiastical manner, Louise McCamy in her cultured voice . . . but the others were there, and they had charm and talent and enthusiasm.[70]

They knew they could write, if not yet exceedingly well. A large part of Kroll's influence as an LMU instructor was due to a principle learned in these informal exchanges: "we figured an amateur critic is about as bad as an amateur writer," he said with wisdom, "and I, a beginning professional, realized professional criticism is for professionals, not amateurs. Thus we made a pleasure of a task; and appreciation was the coin of the exchange." The open encouragement for what was good reinforced the best work, while substandard work was allowed to die on the vine. "Creative writing, under this teacher and in this little school, was like many a religious revival I had seen sweep my own mountain vicinity. Everybody was willing and eager since the spirit seemed to move him," Stuart recalled. "I have never in my life seen anything like it. Mr. Kroll told us if we had just a little talent and worked hard enough at it, we could become writers." Years later Harry admitted to an interviewer that he did not feel he had influenced the style of Jesse Stuart nor his other students. He felt his greatest contribution was that "he added enthusiasm to the aspiring writer and lent plausibility to his dreams of becoming a writer."[71]

Overall, Harry Kroll's authority as a Lincoln Memorial instructor and example as a writer himself simply pointed and unleashed the creative talents already extant in his students. Their excitement and his encouragement pushed them to disseminate their work. Taken together, the rustic energy of Kroll's classes and discussion groups created a vibrant, creative atmosphere on the LMU campus that seemed to hum for his skilled and highly motivated students. That four of Harry Kroll's students became writers in their own right and that at least two of them went on to play key roles in the rise of a rural proletarian Appalachian literature is important. Without Kroll, it is not certain that Don West would have ever started to think of himself as a writer at all; and Jesse Stuart's life as a young writer would certainly have been much more lonely, frustrating, and bitter than it was. Perhaps he might have ended up as male, Appalachian version of New England's Emily Dickinson, dying with her trunk full of unpublished material. Despite the polish which later experience under Edwin Mims and Donald Davidson at Vanderbilt might put to their craft, both Still's and Stuart's literary explorations of mountain culture were first legitimized by Harry Kroll. Stuart essentially replicated his first mentor's market-determined practices throughout his own career as a writer, though with ultimately better success. The Vanderbilt Agrarians perhaps refined his writing, but Stuart fitted himself into Harry Kroll's mold as a writer. Even James Still, by consciously dismissing Kroll's plebian view of writing for the popular press, nonetheless used his LMU English professor as a launching point for the direction of high literature championed by Lucia Danforth. But he still chose, like Stuart and West, to write within his culture. If nothing else, Still replicated the Kroll model of holding down full-time employment, as librarian at the Hindman Settlement School deep in the southeast Kentucky hills, while pursuing a writing career on the side. Stuart reflected on the spirit of Kroll's time in several instances during his own lengthy writing career. One important and largely overlooked account is a descriptive short story published a decade after his graduation in Esquire, titled "The Crazy Professor." In this piece, "Shan Powderjay" stands surrogate for Stuart himself as taught by an only slightly disguised "Larry Sholl." The piece recreates the atmosphere and inspirational splash Kroll made with the LMU students. It is certainly factual but somewhat idealized as well, which allowed Stuart to create less of an autobiography than an homage to the man he deeply respected.[72] A truer picture in words was painted by Don West as almost his last publication, in which he paid Kroll a high compliment: "An honest janitor rates as high with Kroll as the university president."[73]

Harry Kroll benefited from the creative interaction with his LMU students as well. Building on Viola Roseboro's advice, he tended to form his stories around snippets from

Faculty portrait, Lincoln Memorial University, 1926.

personal experiences, yet his own experience was necessarily limited. Extending the habit he had begun informally in Lula, at LMU he began applying the same advice he gave his students: he began pumping them for stories of their own experiences, wanting to hear their accounts of dates, siblings, barnyard animals, neighbors, challenges and shortcomings—anything that might generate a situation around which he could build a story. "I remember that, after I would have a date," Jesse Stuart later wrote,

> he would call me to one side—maybe some place on the campus. He would say with a twinkle in his eye, "Tell me about your date. Did you kiss her?"
>
> If I answered yes, then he would ask me a hundred questions. He would want to know all the conversation that led up to this. I would tell him all I remembered.
>
> "Why do you want this?" I often asked him.
>
> "To keep up with the young people," he said. "I am older than they. A lot of my youth has gone. But I must know." And like a big brown-faced man of the earth with the air of all outdoors about him he'd slowly walk away with a pen in one hand, a pad in the other. He'd walk away, making notes as he walked.[74]

Teaching at LMU stimulated Harry Kroll as a writer as much he stimulated his students, and his notebook filled with notes from overheard conversations, stories in class, and odd ideas from all over.

One of his story sources was the departmental secretary, Helen Hatfield, a scion of one side of the famous Hatfield-McCoy feud. Helen introduced Kroll to that story from the inside. With some gentle probing, other students (both McCoy and Hatfield relatives), corroborated and filled in details Helen did not have about "the troubles." On the strength of those and other research, after class and when the thought took him, Kroll began drafting story outlines for a Hatfield-McCoy book, telling the story as a straightforward account from the perspectives of the chief participants. He eventually became dissatisfied with the narrative, which declined into little more than a blood-and-thunder account that was suitably violent but lacked the human dimension necessary for effective fiction. Recognizing that the story was not yet ready to be written he shelved the incomplete project in favor of other work, though he eventually worked aspects of the Appalachian feud story into many short pieces of writing.[75]

Before his second year began in the fall of 1927, Kroll restructured the composition sections to create a focused creative writing series numbered English 41, 42, and 43. The series built on the success of his informal after-hours salon and undoubtedly bore his stamp as a freewheeling, practical-methods instructor. A composition class under Mr. Kroll was no lecture series on grammar, structure, and style; and not a critical salon, like the one established by the Fugitives. "Although this course is journalistic in nature," the course catalogue reads, "it is by no means formal. Students are permitted to employ any medium or method which their talents will allow. Students of unusual ability in writing, without reference to their year-standing, may be invited to enter. The purpose of the course is avowedly to give students an opportunity to do creative work in the Short Story, Special Article, Verse, and Illustration and Decorative Design."[76] It isn't difficult to see that the curriculum mirrored precisely Kroll's personal experience with the publication markets. His approach offered an invaluable counterbalance to the literary traditionalists, who killed many students' ambitions by insisting upon aesthetics and the imitation of literary touchstones from cultures alien to young writers. He wasn't even the only writer of his generation to attempt using the market to measure the worth of one's work. Walter F. Campbell, who wrote under the pen name Stanley Vestal, was employing the same process teaching students two decades later at the University of Oklahoma.[77] In the broadest context, Harry Kroll was making independent steps toward a genuine creative writing curriculum, predating the first recognized program established by Wilbur Schramm at the Iowa Writers' Workshop in 1936. In his small-group collection of interested writing students Kroll was experimenting with the writers' workshop format, solidified later in Iowa, and reproduced virtually everywhere thereafter.

Like any faculty member, instruction was only one segment of Kroll's responsibility. In addition to his teaching duties, Harry also sat on faculty committees and served with Lucia Danforth as assistant editor of the campus literary/arts/alumni magazine, the *Mountain Herald*. Right away he clashed with the strong-willed editor, Iris Grannis, the college librarian and wife of a strikingly handsome but callous and unpopular biology professor. The editor-in-chief, she noted archly in one issue, "gathers material, writes copy, interviews people, takes pictures, visits schools, churches, and meetings of all kinds, visits with old people in the country who have knowledge of the early days, and keeps in touch with the county school teachers. . . ." Her summation left the two assistant editors with only nominal responsibilities. Dr. Danforth was relegated to the role of proofreader. "Mr. Kroll, whose name appears as associate editor," the editor noted unsubtly, "is busy writing articles to sell, so he can only contribute something every now and then."[78] Years later Harry offered a description of Mrs. Grannis, but at least had the decency to do so in private. "If there ever was a woman eaten out with vanity and self importance," he confided in a 1953 letter to Jesse Stuart, "it was she."[79]

A striking, raven-haired, patrician woman, Iris Grannis's primary professional qualification seems to have been a skill at intrigue. Kroll swore she maintained a stranglehold over campus administration and politics. Fifteen years later, as he tried to land a position back at LMU, Kroll confided to his former student that "[Earl Hobson] Smith and I both decided if we had those years to go over we would between us have taken good care of Mrs. Grannis and tried to keep the lady cooled to some kind of livable temperature. Between us, we judged, we might afford some temporary relief, and in any case get Mrs. Grannis out of the hair of the other faculty women."[80] In the 1920s they did not, and her machinations contributed to his problems with the administration that were shortly to erupt.

In his reminiscent 1956 account to a professional conference, Kroll noted that "in the library stacks one day Iris let me know that I was acceptable to her as a man." In an earlier letter to Stuart, Kroll also suggested a private undercurrent that impossibly complicated any sort of working relationship. In it Harry claimed that "I could have had her. She practically gave me to know this one day in the library in the stacks when we were secret and alone. Mrs. Kroll says [Iris Grannis] hated me because I 'spurned' her. I didn't exactly spurn her, I simply didn't accept the invitation." Years later Harry Jr. repeated the rumor that his father had lost the job over an affair with the college librarian. An affair is very unlikely. Though Frank Grannis was reportedly offered a one-year appointment to the Yale program to complete his Ph.D. in the fall of 1928, which would have provided the opportunity for an affair (his wife was to remain at the library on campus), the motivation, if there was one, appears to have been entirely one-sided. That Kroll did not like the woman at all is reflected in virtually every written document, fictional and not, in which she is mentioned. However, he believed

Mrs. Grannis was a powerful figure on campus despite her lack of either faculty or administrative status, and it was within a few weeks of this announcement about her husband and perhaps Harry's cool rejection that Kroll's career at LMU endured its meltdown.[81]

At least Mrs. Grannis was correct that Kroll at LMU was busily writing. By 1927 Harry Kroll had been publishing essays, short fiction, and illustrations for nearly eight years; but it was while teaching at LMU that he gained the second seminal cultural experience in the Appalachian Mountains which was reflected so clearly in his work. At LMU Kroll absorbed the culture and lore of southern Appalachia in the same way he had a few years earlier among the cotton lands of the Mississippi Delta. Scores of short stories and several books resulted directly from material he gleaned living in the Appalachian hills, including *Three Brothers and Seven Daddies, Smoldering Fire,* and most importantly *Their Ancient Grudge.* However, it was while teaching at LMU that Kroll both wrote and published his first novel and first book, *The Mountainy Singer.* Characters and events pictured in this story can be traced to Kroll's time in Unionville and his own fertile imagination, but the story employed the mountain setting that surrounded him at Harrogate. Curiously, this greatest success at the college was the defining factor in his failure there as well.

After Harry's first year as a collegiate faculty member closed, and probably for the first time in their lives, during the late summer of 1927 Harry and Nettie Kroll took a genuine vacation. It was not a spectacular one; they simply drove the family to Mobile to visit her parents. "It was a long 500 miles from LMU," recalled Harry Jr. "The Dodge would run faster than 25 mph, but the road wouldn't let him." The trip in the open-topped jitney required four days, the first from Harrogate to Chattanooga, then to Birmingham, Alabama, where the family stopped to stay overnight with Soddy, and to visit one of Nettie's school friends. From Birmingham they took a two-day drive to Mobile, perhaps passing through Dixons Mills. The high point of the visit for the boys was a trip to a local amusement park.[82] Nettie and the boys stayed with her parents while Harry returned alone to the Tennessee hills just before the fall term started.

The last leg of the trip was the drive from Nashville, and as the car chugged and shuddered along, a new story began organizing in Harry's mind. He arrived home in Harrogate around 4 p.m., he recalled later. He parked the car in front of the house and himself in front of the typewriter and began to set down the story. By late evening he had generated the first chapter of a novel. "After that," he remembered, "it was simply a matter of putting the story down. It came without effort. In ten days I finished the last chapter." As the process unfolded, part of his writing process for this novel involved creating an atmosphere in which to work. "I wrote with deep emotional absorption. I would play hillbilly ballads on the victorla [*sic*], work myself into a fog of feeling, and then I'd write. In due season there was the book."[83] Over a two-week stretch he completed the text and made minor revisions. The resulting manuscript, "The Ballad Singer," became his first published novel. It "wasn't a particularly good book," Harry later admitted, "I look back at it with no special pride." This wasn't precisely true. The main character was given his son Dan's name, and in print it was dedicated to that favored two-year-old boy as well. Besides being his first book, it reflected his approach to teaching and literature, and illustrated how deeply his approach conflicted with the goals and expectations of the college administration.[84]

This manuscript was sent to New York critic and *Editor* editor H. M. Hamilton almost immediately upon completion. It was accompanied by a second, earlier novel manuscript whose title and subject Kroll never recorded, and by an early consolidated draft of the three stories he had written about cotton cropping in the Mississippi delta, under the title "The Peckerwoods." Hamilton, a professional reviewer, returned a lengthy developmental critique of "The Ballad Singer" in September 1927. Of the three manuscripts Kroll had sent him, Hamilton preferred the "Singer" story over the earlier "Peckerwoods" and the other piece; of the manuscript overall, Hamilton liked the story and made several structural suggestions for the narrative. "Considering that I was looking for 'breaks' more than anything else, I think your MS. is practically free of them. As to its virtues, it is full of them." He also chafed about the manuscript title, which he felt communicated something "romantic or Irish," and suggested something more in dialect—"The Mountainy Singer." That title "isn't perfect," Hamilton wrote, "[but] I can't think of a better—can you?"[85] Hamilton also suggested that Kroll first approach half a dozen of the country's larger publishers. If the manuscript was unsuccessful with the major presses, then he suggested trying Dial and other small ones. "Morrow," he wrote of the firm which ultimately accepted the book, "is a good publisher, not as big as some." Against this background of advice and eager for a break to the book market—any break—Kroll immediately submitted the manuscript to William Morrow & Co., which had narrowly rejected "Peckerwoods" only six months earlier. On November 1, Harry Kroll had a tentative manuscript acceptance, but the firm declined his offer to supply illustrations.[86]

It is easy to imagine an ecstatic Harry Kroll grabbing Jesse Stuart and Don West by the collar to tell them the news. Through the winter, Kroll and Frances Phillips of Morrow wrote back and forth frequently, reworking the book's ending, doctoring the continuity of several short sections, and resolving many details to smooth out the story and fit the publisher's preferences. During this time Kroll dangled a newly revised "Peckerwoods" before them as well. It was read but went largely ignored while the "Mountainy Singer" manuscript passed through final story development. Morrow formally accepted the manuscript in the first week of February 1928 and scheduled its publication for the fall list. After the contract was signed, Morrow's Frances Phillips formally discouraged Kroll's hope for contributing illustrations or chapter headings for the book "because the use of them would materially increase the cost of composition and press work on this book" without necessarily contributing to its sales. A few weeks later William Morrow himself wrote Kroll, including in his letter a piece of advice that would be darkly prophetic about his career: "don't, as you value your literary reputation, permit anybody to bring out in book form anything but your best."[87]

"The Peckerwoods" had a Mississippi Delta setting, but for the "Singer" story Kroll adopted the central Appalachian Mountains surrounding Harrogate, inserting autobiographical color from his earlier experience running around the state in a weekend traveling show. At least one of the characters is lifted directly from the latter. The banjo-picking show-stopper Uncle Dave Macon of central Tennessee county fair fame was transformed into the story character Uncle Dave Saxon. *The Mountainy Singer,* published by William Morrow & Co., appeared on the LMU campus a few days before being released to the public on September 22, 1928. Publication of his first book thrilled Kroll to no end. It was a signal personal accomplishment, and the publication was an important event not merely for its author but for the school as well. Kroll's novel was the first book ever published by an LMU faculty member. Having not merely a writer but a novelist on faculty was a major boost for the school and its program. The author inscribed and presented copies to the entire faculty and many of his students.[88]

Vanderbilt professor and book-page editor Donald Davidson, one of the well-known Fugitives and Agrarians, reviewed the book for the *Tennessean* newspaper issue of September 16, probably from an advance copy. Within a few weeks other reviews began appearing in newspapers across the country, and Kroll's first book garnered positive critical acclaim. "It is encouraging to see the welcome that the South is giving your book," Miss Phillips wrote Harry wryly in October, "and I only wish they bought as many times as they praised it." Despite her misgivings, by November sales of *Mountainy Singer* had reached a respectable but unspectacular 1,140 copies. It sold well enough that a second printing was ordered before year-end, and a third was contemplated but is not positively known to have been produced.[89] Caught up in his success, defined chiefly by the fact that he had sold a book manuscript rather than that the book was selling well, Kroll next fired off to William Morrow & Co. a story idea built around a family named Arn, a play on words in dialect for "iron," as one of several "possible next project" ideas. Since he provided the firm with no detailed plot summary, the publisher set aside the proposal, but Harry did not.[90] Two months later Kroll had completed a manuscript with the title "Men of Arn" and sent it off excitedly to Morrow for consideration. The earliest section of this particular story reflected the ambitions he found among students at Lincoln Memorial. Morrow was impressed with large sections and individual characters but felt that the whole was not in a condition even to make concrete developmental suggestions, and eventually returned the manuscript to the author.[91]

Despite the romanticized high point his brief tenure at LMU represented in later decades, Kroll's career there crashed down around his ears within a matter of weeks during the fall of 1928. Publication of *The Mountainy Singer* should have been a step upward. Instead, Kroll naively miscalculated that the book's mere existence would trump its colorful elements for his conservative and religious administrators and colleagues. The book included a few descriptions of rather more physical affection than was seemly, and set teeth on edge. The initial excitement over the major coup for a faculty member soon paled when readers discovered a plot that appeared to hinge on infidelity and incest, and a brief description of petting between two major characters. In the socially conservative, rigidly Christian mountains it was one thing to experience a colorful life yet something quite different to acknowledge it publicly in print. Ignoring the believable character development and lyrical descriptions that so charmed reviewers and publishers in New York, the book landed like a bombshell in the proud and insular school—the students may have been modernizing, but the faculty and community certainly were not. Years later Jesse Stuart credited Lucia Danforth with motivating a negative response among the campus faculty, but the backlash seems to have been general.

> We waited anxiously for the publication of [Mr. Kroll's] novel. Faculty members and students anticipated it. But when the book was published, Harry Kroll was not the popular man with the faculty members that he had been. One professor remarked: "How does he know so much about love? You know what I did with my autographed copy of *The Mountainy Singer?* I tore it in two and threw both parts in the grate! I didn't want my children ever to read that book."[92]

Kroll had made a dramatic miscalculation, and shortly thereafter—shortly, as in within days or weeks—he left his faculty position in mid-term.[93]

There are few and differing accounts of Kroll's dismissal from Lincoln Memorial University and nothing at all in the scattered contemporary primary sources that survive. Precisely what happened is known through rumor and legend but, like most legends, there may be a grain of truth to the stories. One version suggests that tales of the English professor's novel flew to the LMU chancellor's office in New York, and that he descended on the campus from his New York office to excise the godless offender personally. Don West felt the dismissal happened because Kroll had supported student demands for increased autonomy. Another version of the story has Kroll taking the part of Dean Charles D. Lewis in an argument involving the school and losing his position over that disagreement with the administration. Yet another source suggests that Lewis probably took Kroll's side in defending his offending literary production as an academic freedom issue. In any case, Kroll's book was a brickbat against him in an already divided faculty. The administratively unpopular Lewis refused to act on what he perceived to be a minor point of taste and defended Kroll for an issue which the chancellor and others viewed as a moral offense. The book was a pretext to unload the offender.[94] It was a straightforward case. In a matter of weeks the English Department chair was sent packing with great ceremony.

Or was the matter so straightforward? Was Kroll even sent packing?

Since there are no contemporary records of his departure, we are forced to rely on reminiscence. Stuart left his version of events in writing, but little other evidence of a firing can be found in contemporary or reminiscent sources besides his. Stuart's memory about the reception *Mountainy Singer* found among the LMU staff correlates with negative comments made privately years later about his mentor's paperback fiction. Personally, Stuart was always distressed by the steamy scenes that Harry enjoyed writing. Because of a personal antipathy for sexy writing, Jesse Stuart may have projected his opinion onto his memory and missed the professor's real offense at LMU. This book was much more than merely a novel about Appalachian culture and opportunity. *The Mountainy Singer* was also Kroll's indictment of the administrative mission driving Lincoln Memorial University itself.

There was something else going on between Kroll and LMU administrators, of which the book was symptomatic. During the first week of September 1928—two weeks before Davidson's review appeared, and thus at least *three* weeks before the book appeared—Harry Kroll visited Nashville and was featured in an article in the evening edition of the *Nashville Tennessean.* Kroll's new novel had just been published, the article noted (a little prematurely), and the author had "recently severed his connections with an East Tennessee College. . . . Because his ideas of education were not orthodox."[95] Another article was more open about the matter and quoted Kroll directly: "If I had any purpose in the world in writing that book, it was to show how unthinking teachers can spoil the natural talents of the mountain folk, by teaching them how to hold their knives and forks, instead of how to sing their ballads."[96] That was the root of Kroll's offense. What was at stake behind Kroll's market-dominated view of teaching composition as well as in his book, was a direct challenge to the chancellor's entire concept of LMU as an agent of cultural uplift for its Appalachian students. Lincoln Memorial had been founded as essentially a colonial institution. Kroll's entire approach to teaching literature and writing at LMU challenged the assumption that his Appalachian students lacked culture and needed to received it from a well-meaning cultural elite. Harry Kroll would have agreed that his students lacked the traditional sophistication assigned to the European literary canon, but argued strenuously that his students were already cultured individuals. By teaching his students to express their own indigenous Appalachian culture, Kroll effectively denied the superiority of received European tradition. Decades later the Foxfire studies would prove how rich, varied, and skilled "backward" Appalachian mountain culture was.[97]

Unfortunately, this idea of the necessity—the nobility— of cultural uplift was the foundation of the message Chancellor Hill used in his fundraising pitch. Harry Kroll's championing of popular culture was plainly at odds with the paternalistic image of an Appalachian people hungrily anxious for uplift and idealized Euro-American culture that the chancellor was parading before potential donors. John Wesley Hill was a zealously staunch Methodist as well as a fiercely partisan Republican, and was said to have been an ideologue who steered the school from afar and expected its output and image to fit the perception he peddled energetically to potential contributors. At no level did Kroll's colloquial book fit the image of enlightened faculty engaged in cultural evangelism to a noble but benighted hill folk, the country's last "pure" Anglo-Saxons. Hill's point of view from the heights of condesceding elitism was rooted firmly and nourished by the social Darwinism which undergirded American higher education at the time, not merely Lincoln Memorial University. This was no exceptional institutional mission. Harvard University had begun to admit young, poor white men more broadly in an effort to preserve America's perceived native Anglo-Saxon culture and counter the huge influx of uneducated ethnic groups from east, central, and south Europe. Berea College, directly north in Kentucky, was also adopting an educational mission for mountain people, partly to diffuse criticism of its previous goal of interracial education. But Hill was a true believer. Everything about Harry Kroll—his writing, his approach to literature, his teaching methods, his book, his disdain for the fundamental goal of the school—ran counter to the education ideal the chancellor was pitching to potential donors. Lincoln Memorial University was also desperately trying to improve faculty credentials, academic rigor, and administrative functions to a level that it could qualify for academic accreditation, a process that would not happen until John Wesley Hill had departed from the school's management, since he brooked no question or dissent to mar his single-minded purpose to create a financially stable institution. Kroll never admitted in writing that he had left LMU over a disagreement with the chancellor's version of cultural policy, but this explanation seems to best fit the circumstance of the time and personalities involved. Harry Kroll was, in fact, one of many teachers who left LMU under a cloud, symptomatic of Hill's refusal to employ any faculty (especially popular ones) who did not meet his stringent and strident opinions.[98]

The mission of moral and educational uplift which motivated Katheryn Howard and Lucia Danforth, Chancellor Hill, and college founder Oliver O. Howard, had little or no direct relevance to the Appalachian students they taught other than creating modern, well-rounded individuals. Educational uplift had limits in its practical application. Harry Kroll's approach also had its limits, but he was willing to push them. As a result, he contributed significantly to the refinement of a regional American literature—an Appalachian literature—by encouraging the remarkable students among the class of 1929 to be themselves culturally while they refined their abilities to write. Stuart and Still could have developed, like Thomas Wolfe, into generic American literary figures *informed by* their Appalachian experience, but they did not. It would be instructive to study the work of each closely to see just how their experiences shaped not only their themes and messages, but also their expectations about the very function of writing.

Harry Kroll's brief LMU career was a pebble of circumstance whose brief passing left behind widening ripples of influence. By the time he had left in September or October of 1928, Kroll had managed to convince at least some of his students that they had a native culture worth celebrating. Though Appalachian Studies would not become an academic topic for several decades, Kroll laid important footings for a literary cultural appreciation in one corner of the mountain fastness. He also convinced those same students, and alienated others, with the idea that writing was a commodity that could be marketed to interested buyers, like a corn or tobacco crop. Not all of his influence was constructive, but it was still influential even if it provided a reckoning point for rebellion. James Still pursued a more thoughtful and refined expression than his LMU teacher, and Left-leaning Don West rejected Kroll's marketplace sensibilities as literary capitalism (though this might be Stuart's interpretation of the story) but drank deeply from Kroll's use of writing to honor the common man. Roland Carter became a respected English professor in Chattanooga but never a successful writer himself. Louise McCamy became a journalist in Knoxville. Jesse Stuart in particular profited from Kroll's tutelage. Kroll did not make Stuart a writer, Stuart had done that himself through personal drive and perseverance long before the two met. The young writer did, however, seize eagerly on Kroll's model of circulating his work in the literary market. Stuart's career as a fiction writer would eventually slide for precisely the same reasons as his mentor's would after the mid- and late 1950s, but the model worked well enough to establish him as a valid talent with editors across the country.

Precisely when Harry departed the Tennessee hills is not even known with certainty, but before leaving Harrogate in October 1928, he managed to secure a mid-year teaching appointment at Iowa Wesleyan College, where he was hired as Associate Professor of English and as chair of the Journalism Department. Once again Nettie took the boys to her parents' home, three of them this time, while her husband packed their goods for rail shipment westward and then drove down after her. From Mobile the Krolls bundled into the unheated, open-sided family runabout and jounced across Mississippi, crossed the river, crossed Missouri, and followed that river up to Mt. Pleasant, Iowa. Unfamiliar snow eddied past the isinglass windows, sifting around the loose side curtains of the little Dodge and over the laps of its huddled and bundled occupants.

The five Krolls arrived, windblown and road-sore, late in the year and as the fiercely cold winter of 1928–29 was beginning. There they rented a house from a Yankee veteran who, quite by chance, had fought at the Stones River battle in Tennessee during the Civil War. As the family slept on the floor in the cold, empty house the night of their arrival, Nettie sobbed into her pillow but otherwise said nothing.

By this time seven-year-old Harry Jr. was old enough to help with household chores. One of his duties was to stoke the wood-fired stove/furnace that heated the two-story frame structure. In a repeat of the incident his parents had once endured in Alabama eleven years earlier, Son tried to beat back the bitter cold by feeding the fire to the point that creosote in the chimney ignited. Luckily the local fire department was able to punch a hole in the chimney and pour in enough water to extinguish the blaze. A fire in winter could be disastrous, and how close the family had come to tragedy was mocked in the student newspaper with the immature naiveté common to college campuses.[99]

Regrettably, the disaster at home probably represented the climax of the Kroll's short tenure in Iowa. As an instructor, Kroll found Iowa Wesleyan as creatively dry and lifeless as he had found Lincoln Memorial vibrant and lively. While in Iowa, perhaps with an increasing imperative, Harry continued to pursue writing on the side. Not really happy teaching at Wesleyan, his freelance writing became first an outlet, then a goal, then a way out of the oppressiveness of small-scale academia. "Once more the shadow of my mother's fierce indefatigable energy fell upon my life," he wrote ten years later.

> I could write these juveniles in an hour and a half. I have written five-thousand-word short stories at one sitting of three-and-a-half or four hours, mailed them out with no further revision, and had checks back from the pulp [publishers]. I do not mean to say that every such story I wrote was successful. Many—most of them—were not. But a sufficient number of stories did sell to convince me that if I broke from teaching and devoted all my attention to writing, I could make a good income.[100]

Making better income from his writing than his teaching, Harry determined to get out from under administrative control entirely and simply earn a living as a freelance writer.

It seemed like a good time to jump the academic ship to row his own dream boat as a writer. The "good income" that freelance writing represented was a point to ponder—until Kroll's string of employment bad luck held firm and he needed to do more than think. His time in Mt. Pleasant ended sourly when, in February 1929, the board of trustees approved his resignation over an unexplained issue, effective at the end of the term. Just why he was leaving isn't precisely clear. His quasi-autobiographical work *I Was a Share-Cropper* skips the subject entirely. In "Looking Back," a comment on his own career from 1947, he reports only that he began writing fiercely "when I knew for certain I would not be retained in a position I was never very happy in." A story circulated in the family that he had been ungently nudged aside to create a faculty vacancy for someone's recently graduated son. That doesn't seem plausible, since Kroll's replacement, Joseph Morton Harrell, did not seem to have that sort of connection. Most likely, Iowa Wesleyan was simply not LMU and Kroll was not particularly happy there.[101] Ironically, Lucia Danforth lost her position at LMU during the height of Chancellor Hill's purge in 1930 and was hired at Iowa Wesleyan to chair its Languages Department the year after Kroll's departure. She remained happily at IWC, but began teaching summers back at LMU in 1936, and returned there permanently about 1940. Harry did not, and was content merely to vacate Mt. Pleasant after the term ended. He did remain in Iowa long enough to be featured at the fourth annual Journalism Day at nearby Parsons College, where he spoke in the second week of May 1929 on "The Trials and Tribulations of a Scribbler."[102]

"Happily my writing is neither a business nor work," contemporary Tennessee writer T. S. Stribling could remark of his craft, "it is simply doing nothing in a concentrated form; it is doing nothing and making a record of it."[103] Harry Kroll's approach to composition was a complete inversion of Stribling's experience. Writing was work, and hard work, but it was work that paid relatively well. After less than six months in its faculty position, Kroll could shrug off Iowa Wesleyan College and Mt. Pleasant with hardly a backward glance. From his sales record for the year it was evident that he could make a decent living as a writer; he was making substantially more money writing part-time than he was teaching anyway. Looking back archly on 1928 he could report the sale of two novel manuscripts ("Mountainy Singer" to Morrow and "Peckerwoods" to Mims and Co., the latter of which was a premature claim) and 147 pieces of short fiction.[104] The way in which Kroll frames his report of "success" underscores his perspective on writing: writing was a business, a craft or industry like cabinetmaking; so long as he was paid for the story manuscript, whether or not his work was actually published was essentially immaterial. The income and career of a writer seemed much more attractive than the classroom-bound teaching he was doing. After some thought, Kroll decided not to pursue another teaching job at all but to jump with both feet into the market as a freelance writer. "I did and regretted it," he wrote wryly.

Harry's decision to move into freelance fiction turned out to be fatefully and remarkably ill-timed. Four years earlier he had broken into the American pulp market at its height. Like many who had found a good thing, he assumed it would continue and planned accordingly. To characterize Kroll in terms that writers of his generation employed, he was a true hack writer. Walter Benjamin defined a hack as "a man who refused as a matter of principle to improve the production apparatus," or in other words, who writes for the money and has little interest in bettering the quality of his writing for the market. Hacks were hired by the early story papers merely to generate formulaic treatments as rapidly as possible. As the story papers declined and their hack staff retired in the 1890s, to be replaced by the pulp magazines, freelance writers became much more important to publishers. They were under less pressure to write, which raised the literary quality of the material, but it was still a volume-driven industry.[105]

By this point, Kroll's approach to writing as a marketable product had solidified, but so too had the settings he chose to employ. Like many other Southern writers of his generation, he chose to write exclusively about the region he knew best. Yet though he employed the Southern hills and plains as settings, Kroll was not a writer of "place," one identified with a specific geography or culture, such as former students Jesse Stuart, James Still, and later Wendell Barry or Tony Hillerman would become. Regional literature is that "in which action and characters cannot be moved geographically without major loss or distortion."[106] Kroll's personal and thematic ties to the American South were not necessarily cultural as much as they were socioeconomic. Almost all Kroll's work (except the moralistic fiction) drew heavily on the themes of poverty, sexuality, and the South. His work typically incorporates one of two plot-lines: a classic boy-meets-girl romance or a fortune story. As a writer of short fiction, Harry Kroll was fundamentally a romance writer bound by an almost exclusively rural perspective of the last generation of subsistence farmers. These factors together make Harry Harrison Kroll's writing ruralist rather than strictly Southern. His stories fall rather closer to the labor writers of the period, as a writer of condition: the poor or once-poor rural or once-rural boy struggles for opportunity, or returns to the home place to take up the challenge of fitting again into the bucolic origin from which he had risen. Coming up from Southern rural poverty, Kroll was ultimately a literary champion of the one-mule man, which made up the bulk of the rural South he knew. But his focus did not stem from genuine altruism: in the end Harry was in it primarily for the income that stories generated, and was quite willing to strip-mine the landscape and culture for what it offered him. Harry Kroll was thus a participant in what Paul M. Hirsch identified as *cultural industries.*[107]

As it happened, Harry determined to make a go of freelance writing, in the spring of 1929, at the instant that American reading culture was undergoing profound changes, changes to which he was too close to recognize. In 1930 literary commentator Fred Lewis Pattee would say to literate readers, as the world of letters shrank and crumbled silently around him, "So completely did one literary form dominate the forty years after 1890 that one may christen the period with its name: it has been the

Age of the Short Story."[108] But since the mid 1920s new technology had begun chewing greedily into the fat markets for recreational reading, which had previously been Americans' chief form of private entertainment. Though cultural observers could not really yet see it and Harry Kroll never would, the shift would ultimately leave him and thousands of writers like him behind as commercial short fiction writers. The changes in the American publication market were motivated by three major circumstances. The first factor, and chronologically the last of the three, the economic collapse of October 1929 and its attendant spiral into depression, he could not have foreseen; that was purely an accident of timing. Much more influential were two technological innovations, neither of which had anything to do with writing and had actually happened several years earlier. The second factor was the development of radio broadcasting in the mid-1920s and the subsequent creation of arguably the first national popular culture, which was based on national broadcasting. The third, an innovation, was just as influential: the marriage of sound and cinema in 1927 that produced "talking pictures." With recreational reading time now divided between radio broadcasts and movie shows, both magazine publishers and live-entertainment producers saw circulation and attendance figures plummet. The variety of publications themselves fell in real numbers as well, due both to consolidations and cutbacks. Reduced page space increased the competition for remaining space. With an increasingly urban readership, Kroll's rural themes and settings could not compete, and he watched his marketability shrink throughout the Depression.

Nothing in America would be the same.

Freelance Writer

In the late spring or summer of 1929 the Kroll family relocated from southeastern Iowa to Antioch, Tennessee, a few miles southeast of Nashville. Piling into the old Dodge and yet again shipping their few crated household goods by rail, Harry, Nettie, and the three boys drove south across Missouri, crossed the Mississippi River on the Cape Girardeau bridge, and descended across the tip of Kentucky into Tennessee. Decades later both Harry Jr. and Torrey recalled driving through Dyersburg, where Harry pointed out to his young sons the places he had grown up. None of the sites, the two boys realized years later, squared with the descriptions featured in *I Was a Share-Cropper.* As the family settled into Antioch, a few miles south of Nashville, Kroll flung himself into writing with his characteristic energy.

Besides the technological changes involved in the publishing markets, the 1920s were also a time of ferment born of shifts in American demographics and culture. For writers like Harry Kroll and for millions of Americans and immigrants flocking to the burgeoning cities, it was a time to trade the dusty land and old home place for the workplace and street. Warren Susman noted that "As early as the 1920s there were those who were beginning to see that in a sense they were between two eras; they were in a machine age and yet somehow not completely of it; they were caught between an older order and older values and a new social order with its new demands."[109] This drive to Modernity was the change against which the Agrarians set themselves. Time would prove that there was room in the publishing industry for rural themes (much of the best writing of the 1890s and 1900s involved rural settings and characters), but that the available market space would inevitably shrink as readers' attention was drawn away by their distance from rural roots, multiplying complexities, and the varied attractions of urban life.

From his position on the front-lines of national culture, Harry Kroll was too caught up in producing marketable manuscripts quickly and routinely to recognize that the patterns of American popular culture were in the midst of a substantial and probably permanent realignment. By 1929 radio in the United States had made the transition from a craze to an emerging industry. The first primitive two-way radio broadcast/receiver units were commercially available around 1920. Local broadcasting began on 58 isolated private radio stations as early as 1922. By 1924 there were 1,400 stations scattered across the country. Most were in urban locations, ventures underwritten primarily by radio manufacturers to give the public a reason to buy their quickly improving equipment. Initially radio reception picked up a cacophony of disparate signals, as varied and individual as a station owner's interests. By 1927, however, the emergence of network broadcasting by the National Broadcasting Company and its chief competitor, the Columbia Broadcasting System, had imposed a substantial degree of order to the airwaves. By 1929 radio-delivered news and entertainment seemed poised to gobble up newspaper readership. There was even an invention which allowed publishers to distribute printed news sheets by broadcast signal to a receiving device, akin to a modern fax machine. Radio programming flooded into living rooms and carved away huge chunks of the time Americans had previously spent in recreational reading. Evening hours devoted to motionless concentration on comedies, classical music, or radio dramas drove down the percentage of citizens who once wiled away evenings in with a book or periodical. Radio listening weaned huge numbers of readers from their weekly diet of fiction magazines.[110]

The dramatic rise in radio listenership was only the first strike at the reading public. While Harry and Nettie were at LMU, former vaudeville performer Al Jolson sang a blackface version of "Mammy" to theater audiences—*motion picture* audiences. Even in the economically heady months before the 1929 stock market crash, the introduction of sound to movies affected far more than simply the technical production of the pictures themselves. The new equipment that synchronized recorded sound with projected motion pictures produced very scratchy, muted, and hollow voices, but the affect of *The Jazz Singer* and other early "talkies" on audiences and the movie industry was profound. Ticket sales would nearly double in three years, until by 1930, statistically *every* man, woman, and child in the U.S. went to the movies at least once each week. By the early 1930s, audiences were voting with their feet. The popularity of talking pictures halved the number of Broadway shows and traveling theatrical productions produced annually. By 1931 a fifth of Broadway's theatres had closed and been converted to other uses, mostly as movie theatres.[111]

The sounds of movie theatre cash registers was a clanging alarm for literary magazine publishers like Street and Smith, the Ridgeway Company, Popular Publishing, and scores of others. In the eight years between 1927 and 1935, as the time Americans once devoted to recreational reading was reallocated to movie attendance or listening to the radio, fiction publishers watched with alarm as their story-magazine sales declined to the point of freefall. The dramatic rise in talking picture attendance caused a similar decline in recreational reading, of perhaps as much as 80 million hours annually. Sales evaporated, and magazines consolidated or ceased publication entirely. Houses that once published fifty magazine titles were combining and cutting back to maybe twenty. Those that published twenty might slim down the list to six. Those with only a few niche publications simply closed or merged with a larger publisher. While Harry Kroll was beginning his career as a freelancer in 1929, the publishing industry was already reacting to the twin challenges of the new media. Once, monthly story magazines like *Yellow Book* might put thirty stories into an issue of 370 pages and flourish nicely on monthly or weekly sales figures. By the time the stock market crashed in late 1929, publishing companies were already in the midst of reducing magazine page counts, cutting the number of publications, consolidating titles, reducing the number of times an author published in a magazine, and incorporating a new revenue stream—advertising. Collectively these changes sharply reduced the space available for stories, which effectively raised the bar for the quality of the story material publishers were willing to buy. There may have been less space, but the result was that the story magazines could release better quality writing. Competition for manuscript sales increased as sharply as demand for new stories fell. All this change quickly put a substantial dent in the very story-magazine market on which Harry Kroll was staking his new career as a freelance fiction writer. Though he had enjoyed decent placement of his fiction work in nationally circulated pulp story magazines between 1925 and 1929, by 1930 Kroll was unable to place his stories in the pulps at all, probably not because his stories were poorly written but because his rural settings did not attract the interests of an increasingly urban readership. The competition for space had become too stiff.

With the markets in decline he faced the problem of any writer who submitted too much work, even good work, to any one serial publication: name saturation. No matter how good the stories, publishers did not want to print too many stories from any one writer unless they proved both tremendously skilled and tremendously popular. As their page counts shrank, publishers became increasingly wary of putting before their readers too many pieces by an author too frequently. Variety became important. "A successful magazine is like a successful store," publisher Edward Bok observed in his autobiography, "it must keep its wares constantly fresh and varied to attract the eye and hold the patronage of its customers."[112] Printing too many stories by one author could saturate readers' interest and dry up the demand for an author's work. It was a free-market irony—become too successful as a short-fiction writer and demand for your work might dry up. Authors responded by adopting the time-honored ruse of writing under pseudonyms, thereby creating a false impression for readers of how often their work appeared in a magazine. Harry Harrison Kroll was no exception. Proud of his self-driven rise from poverty, he always preferred to publish under his own name, but as he produced and submitted ever more writing, his view that writing was a business ensured he would do what was necessary to achieve sales, even at the expense of notoriety. As early as 1928, attempting to keep his work in at least the comparatively lucrative Street and Smith fortune-story magazines, Kroll adopted half a dozen pseudonyms to increase placement while dodging saturation. Stanley Bright, Wesley Henslaw, Graham Black, and Robert V. Kramer were all *noms de plume* Kroll is known to have used, and there were likely others used in different venues that he never recorded and which remain unknown. The ploy was common among professional writers and it worked, even in Kroll's case. A publisher would not consider including more than one story by an author in an issue, for the sake of variety, but in one semi-monthly issue of *Fame and Fortune Magazine* in 1928, Harry Kroll managed to place three stories under three different names, and on several other occasions managed to place two.[113]

It worked for awhile. Harry was able to sell his work. He was frustrated, and the work was much less remunerative, but he could still land regularly, almost at will, in the juvenile sectarian papers. Unfortunately the payoff per story in this genre was so much smaller than the commercial magazines that he had to produce a dozen or more sectarian stories for each pulp story he could sell. Ironically, it was only after 1929 and then only with maddening infrequency, that he was able to place work of any sort in the slicks—the country's major literary magazines. The popular fallout from Black Monday merely raised the stakes for writers. Like everything else recreational during those difficult days, the popularity of fiction magazines slumped further during the early to mid-1930s as the public's expendable cash evaporated from the economy. Through the Depression decade of the 1930s the sectarian papers became his primary market and provided a distressingly thin grip on financial solvency. Through the Depression, Harry Kroll managed—barely—to support his family as a full-time writer. He produced hundreds of stories and at least three but probably more book manuscripts. Kroll's mailbox was a virtual clearinghouse of incoming and outgoing manuscripts, queries, checks, and rejection slips. For a short time he supported the family well. By late 1931 he could boast of having sold four hundred of the thousand or so stories he estimated he had written up to that point in his life.[114] Though he did not recognize the fact, rural-themed stories (his, among them) were appearing less and less frequently in story publications. He still sold stories and illustrations with regularity, but his writing income slowly and steadily declined. The utter unpredictability of freelancing was fearsomely trying for a family man. Freelance writing was an employment he once described simply as "dark fears mixed with success."[115]

Kroll had evidently maintained contact with Kary Davis at Peabody College, and it may have been to Davis that Kroll turned for help or advice upon returning to Tennessee from Iowa. Fortunately, part of the familial financial pressure was relieved when Harry was offered a term appointment teaching composition at Peabody. The family remained in Antioch. Harry probably rode the train on Mondays and Wednesdays to teach at least one section of Agriculture 413, Agricultural Publicity. He took over the class from Edgar Arthur White, a professor of animal husbandry and editor of the *Dixie Poultry Journal* in Nashville. The course ran for the spring and summer terms. It was, the catalogue noted, "adapted to needs of teachers, county agents, community leaders, and to prospective journalists"—the catalogue number for students needing help with practical professional writing.[116] A face Harry might have been pleasantly surprised to see on the first June day of classes belonged to a former LMU student who had arrived in Nashville to start his graduate education at Peabody College, Jesse Stuart. The twenty-three-year-old Stuart had recently left his school position in Greenup, Kentucky, and was matriculated at Peabody to pursue a degree in education. Besides Kroll's class, Stuart took several other English classes under Bert Roller. He returned to Peabody again for the 1931 summer term, then stayed in Nashville to begin over again at Vanderbilt that fall.[117]

Kroll taught composition at Peabody College twice weekly for the school's big summer sessions over two academic years, 1930–31 and 1931–32. While he was writing the short fiction and teaching the classes that paid the bills, Kroll also flogged his novel manuscripts from publisher to publisher. After working with the "Men of Arn" manuscript over the entire 1929 year while teaching in Iowa, Harry sent the manuscript back to Morrow & Co., hoping for a quick acceptance. It came back, the Morrow story editor still suggesting extensive revisions to the plot, characterizations, and setting.[118] By the late 1920s Morrow was feeling the effects as radio and talkie films cut into the market for their leisure reading material, and the firm was becoming chary of gambling on books of marginal appeal or potentially small sales. The publisher's acquisitions were affected by the general glut in the book trade, a decline fueled by the practice of publishers clearing their shelves by cut-rate remaindering.[119] Morrow desperately needed titles and authors that would sell in its major markets. Despite its social critique, the regional theme of the manuscript worked against Kroll. Ironically, in refusing the manuscript, Frances Phillips of Morrow's editorial department suggested it be condensed to a short story: "fine material, but not a book," she wrote.[120] Six months after that, when Kroll presented yet another revision in July of 1930, the editor praised the revision but turned it down flatly and suggested he try another publisher for the piece.[121] The Morrow staff realized their gaffe immediately and scrambled to rebuild the bridge to Harry Kroll, assuring him that they wanted to see more of his work, but the rejection ended Kroll's association with William Morrow & Co.

Harry wrote furiously, driven now by necessity and hoping daily that the market would realize—soon—the value of his work. While the stream of his writing continued to flow as from a natural spring, story publication continued to dry up. In 1930 he published only a single story in the pulps, in 1931 only two, none at all in 1932 or 1933, and two in 1934. While he still published frequently in the sectarian papers, they paid so poorly that his income from them was a mockery of freelance work (admittedly, their stories were often submitted by housewives and bank clerks with a literary yen, not professional writers.) His success with novels was no better. By 1930, though he had one published book to his credit (*Mountainy Singer,* two years earlier), Kroll's reputation as a writer was hardly soaring. "Peckerwoods" as a novel manuscript was written in 1926 from the early novelettes and the play. It required nearly four years of flogging the manuscript for "Peckerwoods" to find a publisher "Now and then a publisher might think he would want it," Kroll recalled, "but in the end would decide against it. It was a story of share-croppers in the cotton fields. Not a popular theme at best."[122] Harry did not give up. Kroll's commitment to his topic of rural life, his personal certainty in his developing skill, and the story itself drove the cycle of manuscript submissions. By the time Richard R. Smith reviewed and accepted the manuscript in 1931 it had been declined by not only Morrow, but by at least Dial Press, Vanguard Press (a minor social science publisher tentatively adding fiction to its book list).[123] and even Mims and Co., a regional publisher in Texas and Alabama. The latter had liked the book and offered to publish it, but the firm went bankrupt before the book went into publication.[124] Harry later claimed that thirty-five publishers had seen, considered, and rejected the pages before the manuscript was accepted; but he refused to give up on a subject which affected him viscerally. So confident was he in the book's relevance and eventual publication that even before the novel manuscript was accepted for publication Kroll was referring to himself as the "Author of *Peckerwoods*" in short-story bylines. The earliest of these claims appears in "The Opening Wedge," a short story published in the *Young People's Paper* in March 1929, three years before the book was dressed in print.[125] "Peckerwoods" became the best example of Kroll's faith in the market. It circulated with the tireless vigor that characterized his approach to the literary marketplace and writing itself.

Ultimately the "Peckerwoods" manuscript saw publication only by being sold to a start-up venture. Recalling the advice he had been given about new publishers, in the late summer of 1930 Kroll finally sent three manuscripts to Richard R. Smith Inc., an upstart New York publisher that had yet to release a fiction title over its imprint. These included "Peckerwoods," "Seven Daddies" (*Three Brothers and Seven Daddies*), and "Men of Arn" (which became *Rider on the Bronze Horse*). Smith held the sheaves of pages for several weeks, but finally offered Kroll a contract, dependent upon revisions, feeling that "Peckerwoods" would be the most promising piece of the three. Harry was glad enough to get a book manuscript under contract, and was willing to do so at virtually any cost of revision. As Kroll returned the contract, he also offered to illustrate either the book, the jacket, or both. James Van Toor, who handled book production and manufacturing, agreed, as it would both increase the visual appeal and reduce the firm's production costs.[126]

After his first summer term at Peabody closed, in the late fall of 1930 Harry made a return trip to Lula, Mississippi, for some more site research during the cotton-picking season. He returned home to Antioch with the old fire over the economic injustice of sharecropping rekindled. He had the complete revised manuscript in New York by mid-November 1930.[127] The publishers didn't like the revision. It required another six months for Kroll to produce a new "Peckerwoods" revision (by now retitled "The Cabin in the Cotton") based upon the draft he had initially submitted to Morrow, and his own instincts. This time Ray Long, former editor of *Cosmopolitan* and the silent partner in Richard R. Smith Inc., who had just returned from Europe, read it carefully. At his behest, Kroll was invited to New York for a conference about his manuscript and $200 against royalties was wired to him to make the trip.[128] Harry took the train from Nashville in the second or third week of August 1931. He was back home within the week and polished up a final manuscript shortly thereafter. By month-end his jacket, chapter-head, and title page sketches had been accepted and he was beginning to read the initial type in galleys.[129]

Almost coincident with Kroll's final manuscript submission, Ray Long moved into active partnership and the firm became Ray Long and Richard R. Smith Inc.[130] According to a promotional poster issued shortly thereafter by Long & Smith, *Cabin in the Cotton* was not merely a new book, it was the firm's first novel as well. Just as Frank Doubleday and George Doran had done in 1928 at the founding of their firm (producing a special edition of Booth Tarkington's *Claire Ambler*), the publishers determined to bind a special edition of Kroll's book to mark the release of their hopeful venture into the increasingly cutthroat market for literary high culture. Sheets from the first impression were used, but Kroll illustrated a separate limitation page. To get the volume inscribed by both the author and publishers at minimal cost, Long & Smith had the limitation page printed separately and sent the precut sheets for the author's signature. These were countersigned by the partners after they were returned and tipped into the volumes by hand. Kroll's pen-and-ink drawings appeared not only on the book's dust jacket but also on the title page and chapter headings, as well as on the limitation page and the slipcover decoration of the limited edition. The book was released to the public during the last week of October 1931.[131] By December the first printing had sold out and Richard Smith gleefully ordered a second impression.[132]

During these fearsomely uncertain times, the acceptance of "Peckerwoods" in the fall of 1930 brought Harry a needed emotional and financial lift. Through the rest of 1931 he busily knocked out short stories between revisions to the "Peckerwoods" manuscript. Still, the promise of a new book was only a step. Life as a freelance writer was still uncertain enough that Harry was willing to grasp at even slightly more substantial straws. In early summer he submitted a hopeful and very frank fellowship application to the John Simon Guggenheim Memorial Foundation. With the cultural critique in *The Mountainy Singer* still fresh in him, Kroll's Guggenheim fellowship proposal concerned conducting the research for a novel addressing "the wifehood of a typical mountain woman . . . from marriage to death." His plan of work reflected the informal research method by which he had collected material that went into his thesis: the proposed fellowship would support six months tramping through the mountains "while I should talk to folks, women in their cabins especially, hang around, listen, write fragments to use later in the work." He also proposed that the fellowship would underwrite a trip to England and Scotland to explore background, ancestry, and supply a fitting setting for revisions. The application was a not-quite-desperate long shot at best. His confidential references were personally complimentary but two of them returned critiques of either subject or method that undoubtedly doomed the proposal. The imprecision of Harry's proposed study methods certainly counted against him as well. Ironically, Jesse Stuart was awarded a fellowship for travel to Scotland on a similar research proposal a few years later.[133]

Disappointment over the rejection by the Guggenheim Foundation was offset by the publication of *Cabin in the Cotton*, his second book, in October 1931 and the added pleasure of seeing it into a second printing before the year was out. Not only that, but Constable, a British publishing firm, cabled their interest in the British option on the book the very day that *Cabin* was officially published by Long & Smith. Dick Smith happily sent Kroll the first copy of the Constable edition in February 1932.[134] Kroll's novel was obviously off to a good start in an increasingly competitive market. By comparison, Pearl Buck's *The Good Earth* had been released by the John

Day Co. in March 1931, been picked up as a Book of the Month Club selection, and by October had sold nearly two million copies. Buck's book was an exception, however. The Depression was affecting book sales. "I am telling all my budding authors that if they can sell short stories today," Dick Smith wrote Harry, "they had better write them, because one or two stories will give them more income than all the royalties on the average novel."[135] Smith was obviously hoping for a runaway bestseller, but realistic enough to understand the fickleness of the market. But both Long and Smith remained optimistic and planned for a bright future. In February and March of 1932, Ray Long undoubtedly carried copies of Kroll's *Cabin in the Cotton* with him on a European acquisition trip for the firm. On one leg of his travels Long scored what certainly would have been one of the greatest coups in American publishing history—he signed Soviet dictator Josef Stalin to a book contract as a Long & Smith author for a volume of memoirs.[136] Given the subject matter of the firm's first novel, it is conceivable that Long presented Stalin with a copy of Kroll's *Cabin in the Cotton.*

As the Depression deepened and drought continued licking up farmland across the South, *Cabin in the Cotton*'s social criticism gained relevance, especially in light of the unintended consequences of federal crop subsidies. Subsidies were intended to reduce market surpluses without penalizing farmers by depriving them of an income from their land. Conceived far from agricultural reality, federal crop subsidies tried to keep smallholders together by basing subsidies on yields per acre. Subsidies provided starvation-level income for a family on forty acres, but on the large plantations at the heart of cotton agriculture, payments instead subsidized mechanization and allowed planters to divest themselves of responsibility for their traditional human labor force. Even with subsidies, nearly a quarter of the privately owned farms in Alabama were sold out from under their owners for back taxes. In Tallapoosa County, Alabama, the forcible seizure of property broadened into a violent suppression of the black farmers' Share Croppers Union. A market certainly existed for social criticism in these dark days of Southern agriculture.

In July 1932 Long & Smith paid Harry $589.51 in royalty income for sales between November 1931 and the end of the following April, a princely sum. His claim on the book amounted to twenty cents per copy of the $2.00 cover price for the trade edition and an equal amount on the boxed limited edition, which sold for $5.00. Regional book sales are difficult to judge, but it is unlikely that *Cabin* sold particularly well in the South. This is certainly evident in the top-ten lists Kroll pasted into his scrapbook, which show that the book was received well in markets far removed from his region. *Cabin in the Cotton* appeared in the top five fiction sales books tracked in the *San Francisco Chronicle* throughout January 1932, and made the top three in the *Portland Oregonian*'s list during the week of January 3.[137] Reviewers generally praised the work for its realism rather than heroics, which would have pleased the author. On the other hand, closer to home Kroll's book was subjected to biting criticism by Agrarian aesthete Allen Tate, something that Kroll resented forever after.[138] Even that gall, however, Harry could swallow upon receiving word from Dick Smith that the publisher had negotiated the sale of film rights to the book.[139]

The thirst of Hollywood studios for suitable production material was becoming desperate in the 1930s. On average the movie studios were releasing two new pictures every three days, all year long. The stories had to come from somewhere. Payments for story and production rights soared in the competitive market. Broadway playwrights pulled up stakes in New York, and nearly half of the theatres along the Great White Way closed or were converted to motion picture theatres in the decade between 1927 and 1937. A few years later one industry expert suggested three factors which determined the value of film rights: "the author's reputation, the number of copies the book sold, and the success the agent has in working up a competitive interest on the part of the picture people." Huge sums were flung at authors to secure marketable "properties." In that light, the figure negotiated for *Cabin*'s film rights was below modest by industry standards, merely $12,500. Had the publishers had the experience to play the game they could have walked away with two or three times as much, but the figure was exorbitant to both literary parties and the film studio walked away with a steal. Of the sum, 25 percent was claimed by Long & Smith as their share, and an additional 25 percent due the author he waived to publicize the book further. The sale still put more money into Harry's hands than he had ever imagined—much more than he netted from several years writing and at least ten times more than what he might make teaching. Some of the money went immediately toward a new car, suited to the station of a successful writer, a 1932 Hudson Eight club sedan. It was a princely automobile but a practical purchase: the family's old open-seat Dodge was antiquated, and in the Hudson the family could ride through poor weather with the windows up and a heater going. Harry could not help himself to a bit of triumphaism. On one occasion that fall he proudly drove the new car to Nashville, where Jesse Stuart, sculptor Julian Rayford, and Don West together rode with him to introduce Kroll to Sidney Hirsch. Hirsch had been a linguistic lynchpin of the Fugitive group, a well-read gentleman whose taste for etymology had developed in travels in the Orient. His interest in the cultural power of words had once fueled the Fugitives and thrilled and inspired Stuart, whom Rayford had also introduced to Hirsch and had his own love affair with words. Kroll, however, had a more common interest in writing and what it brought. No impression survives of their meeting, but Kroll probably would rather have had the car than Hirsch's sophistication.[140]

The princely sum and the new car also threw a raking light across the never-close relationship between Harry and Nettie, bringing into sharp relief a rift of emotional neglect or ignorance that was slowly and imperceptibly widening between the couple.

Their curiously codependent courtship had not been a firm foundation on which to build a solid marriage, yet like most of their generation, marriage was an issue of economic rather than emotional security, and probably neither spouse ever entertained thoughts of divorce. "I think she thought that success took me from her," Harry recalled to Son after Nettie's death in 1961. "I know once she said, swallowing her tears, 'If it's going to take you from me I hope you'll never amount to anything.'" For his part, flush with the thrill of the moment, Harry was blind to her fears. "I only thought of such writing success as I've had as taking me from no one, only adding me to something I always wanted to be," he protested. "I know she brooded, and I have only the most fragmentary statements as to what went on in her mind and emotions." Driven by his ambition, we have to wonder what effort he made to understand. He also admitted that he remembered "the constant angers she had against me. But when she was not angry she was not happy either, not noticeably." Companionship and economic stability, such as it was, remained in their relationship; what little genuine affection there might have been, however, staled. They talked little. To occupy her sharp and curious mind Nettie ploughed through reading matter constantly while managing the boys and household rather silently. Since family finances were an outgrowth of his writing work, Harry was absorbed with his writing and the constant stream of manuscripts and attendant correspondence. One comes away with the impression that they lived together but inhabited separate and only overlapping, not intersecting, worlds.[141]

As *Cabin in the Cotton* was being released in print in October 1931, Harry eagerly began flinging other book ideas at his publisher. One was for a novel that would relate the history of cotton and labor across three generations of Mississippi families. Harry really wanted to do a big book, and thought this might be a suitably large theme for it. Long liked the general theme but felt Kroll should expand it across more than one volume.[142] Since the novel was merely conceptual at that point, Kroll did not draft anything for several years while the idea lay fallow and other manuscripts took precedence in his attention. The concept remained in mind, however, and would figure into his later writing career.

As large a windfall as the sales of *Cabin* film rights represented, it was a one-time infusion to the family account, which was growing progressively thinner. Now two years into the Depression, his stories were selling to the better-paying pulp venues with less frequency. As his income dwindled, the attractiveness of being a freelance writer was evaporating quickly. Harry moved the family from Antioch about thirty miles farther south to Murfreesboro, Tennessee, in the early spring of 1932, a few months after *Cabin in the Cotton* appeared in print.[143] The reason given publicly was for his boys to attend the city schools, but years later he admitted it was the $13 monthly rent in a house next door to friend and former LMU dean Charles D. Lewis that was the primary attraction. Lewis was a faculty member at the Tennessee Teachers College (now Middle Tennessee State University). Though nothing appears in his surviving letters, it is probable that Kroll was hoping eventually to fill a faculty vacancy at the college. With his two oldest boys now in grade school, Harry was no longer a callow youth who could pursue life merely with unbridled energy, certainty of his own talent, and faith in the future. He began looking about expectantly, recalling the stability and security that a regular paycheck represented.

As Harry fretted over day-to-day financial stability, *Cabin* went into script production almost before the ink dried on the contract. By early spring, film crews were headed to Mississippi to film location shots and provide backgrounds that could be replicated in sound-stage scenery. Production was compartmentalized: writers were typically left out of film production issues once a script was approved, and authors of a story from which a script was adapted were simply ignored. Harry, however, was not going to miss the opportunity to see the work on his film firsthand. During the first week of March 1932 he packed his typewriter into the new Hudson and drove from Antioch back to Lula. Though the route was direct from Nashville to Memphis, Harry detoured directly west for a stop in Dyersburg, probably for the opportunity to boast a bit in the only place he considered a hometown. Returning home from the trip, he found Long & Smith eager for a Kroll manuscript they could put out quickly to capitalize on public attention surrounding the film release of *Cabin in the Cotton*. The publishers finally settled on one of the two other manuscripts they had been holding since accepting *Cabin* in 1930. *Three Brothers and Seven Daddies* was an Appalachian novel blending stereotypical themes of consanguinity, charismatic mountain religion, and bootlegging. It became Kroll's second Long & Smith title in two years, released just as Richard Barthelmess, Bette Davis, and Clarksville native Dorothy Jordan were ready to flicker on silver screens across the nation in the new First National Pictures motion picture *The Cabin in the Cotton*.

Like most minor films of the period, *Cabin in the Cotton* did not have the star-studded debut event we now associate with movie premiers. The film was scheduled for a respectable, two-day opening run in New York at the plush, 2,985-seat Strand Theatre on September 29, 1932.[144] Dyersburg scheduled its own opening night party and was scheduled to hold a screening four days later. However, a week before the premier, in a rare show of sympathy, Warner Brothers broke its precedent of controlling premiers, so that a homecoming could be staged for the book's author in Dyersburg. During the first week of September a telegram from one of the town sponsors summoned Harry to town earlier in the week, allowing Dyersburg to capture the picture's debut credit by moving the party and screening date back to Monday, September 26, scooping the rest of the country. The picture's unusual official release in Kroll's hometown caused a *New York Times* writer to comment that "Dyersburg Tennessee has to be the smallest place in which a Hollywood picture has ever premiered."[145] In the waving heat of September's late summer, and just as *Three Brothers and Seven Daddies* was being bound and jacketed for its release, Harry drove a second time from Murfreesboro to Dyersburg for the "homecoming" activities surrounding the premier of the film. Nettie remained at home with the boys in school. The local folks tried without success to entice one of the film's genuine Hollywood figures, Clarksville native Dorothy Jordan, to attend as well.

Harry arrived in Dyersburg in the early afternoon of Monday, September 26, just in time for the gala dinner and private screening of the film. During the three-day event he was on hand to greet and address the overflow crowds from the stage after each show. Kroll could not have been more pleased. Years later he adapted the experience of the gala event into *Lost Homecoming,* a book that became his final attempt at producing literary rather than popular fiction. In what was probably the truest sentence written in that book, Kroll recalled the emotions he felt walking around the court square before the premier. "You have seen fossil pictures of leaves and fish and backbones in pieces of coal; or weathered eroded names carved in ancient tombstones. Well, my memories of this day would be as enduring on my brain as these."[146] As he walked out the front door of the Frances Theatre, lit by its glowing marquee, Harry could not have missed the cosmic significance that the theater premiering his film faced the Western Union Telegraph office entrance directly across the street. There behind its window he had once sat as a poor kid working as a messenger, envying children who passed on the way to school.

Long & Smith published their second Kroll title, *Three Brothers and Seven Daddies,* just in time to ride the wave of popular interest in the film and its book. After the Morrow firm accepted *Mountainy Singer* in 1927, publisher William Morrow had counseled Kroll about choosing another writing project. He generally encouraged choosing a topic around a "really important theme." Memorable characters were positive, though "habits, superstitions, dialects, and what nots are interesting, but readers will be doubly interested in them if they come in as part of a thoroughly good story."[147] Kroll perhaps kept this in mind as he developed the manuscript that became *Three Brothers and Seven Daddies* while teaching in his second year at Lincoln Memorial University. In this story the Appalachian tradition of primitive charismatic Christianity—liberally blended with folkways, superstition, and dialect—figures more prominently than in any other of his works. The book, in its subject and characters, is virtually an Appalachian caricature. Long & Smith desperately needed another bestseller from Kroll as the firm slid toward insolvency in the deepening

Depression. Setting the publication date near the *Cabin* film debut was a straightforward attempt to capitalize on public interest in the film. Regrettably for all concerned, it did not work. In its critical first two months the book saw only marginally successful sales, partly because it appeared on shelves during some of the darkest months of the Depression. The volume's rather weak reception among the book-buying public did little to enhance Kroll's reputation as a writer and probably handicapped consideration of his other manuscripts as the publishers retreated from using his name as an active marketing point.[148] The publisher negotiated strenuously to sell film rights to the book as the Depression deepened, hoping that another financial windfall like *Cabin in the Cotton* could pull them through.[149] Harry evidently expected the firm to move ahead immediately toward publishing his remaining submission, "Men of Arn." The publisher, looking hard both at Kroll's sales and the market, thought otherwise. Two good books would have cemented their commitment to the writer, but one hit and one fizzle looked suspiciously like the first had been a lucky hit by a marginal author. Dick Smith reconsidered the outstanding "Men of Arn" submission and finally suggested that it be shelved in order for Kroll to concentrate on producing a companion volume to *Cabin in the Cotton.* "If this book [*Three Brothers*] had done well," he wrote Kroll with candor, "then I should have gone ahead with 'Men of Arn' but I think under present circumstances, it would be a mistake to bring this out until some other book of yours has really made a success."[150] In other words, it was not as good a work as the author thought it was.

Kroll was unaware of the straits faced by his far-off publisher, but at Smith's suggestion he leapt into action generating new material. The short fiction which sustained the family was not exactly set aside, but flush with the critical and market success of *Cabin in the Cotton* in 1931 and excited with the pending film version's release, Kroll wrote Richard Smith that he was planning to write a companion volume to *Cabin,* and floated the tentative title of "Cotton Patch Wife." This volume would be a social commentary on the condition of women socially and economically trapped by sharecropping. Smith encouraged him, and Kroll shelved "Men of Arn" to work on the sequel.[151] By the time Harry had a manuscript ready to be put out for a publisher's review the typescript sheets carried the title "Cotton Cabin Woman." By then it was too late: Long & Smith had folded and Harry Kroll needed to find a new publisher.

For another year Harry hung on to solvency by writing, and writing, and writing, pushing out his manuscripts to any venue that would consider them. By 1934 it was clear that Kroll's marketability among the lucrative pulp-magazine markets was declining; and he could never publish enough in the sectarian papers to support a career. Hoping to boost the flagging sale of his manuscripts, in the spring Harry finally accepted that name recognition and energetic output were not enough on which to build a literary career, and he signed with a literary agent, Gertrude Algase, at the New York agency of Hampton and Porter.[152] Having an agent increased his name recognition in the inner offices of America's publishing capitol, but did not result in stronger story sales. Though his work had regularly appeared in the pulp fortune magazines until 1929, after then Kroll managed to sell to the pulps only in dribbles; but two or three stories appeared in the "slicks"—emerging upper-middle-class lifestyle magazines like *Country Gentleman* and *Esquire.*

Harry Kroll was one victim of the consolidations and mergers that constricted the downsizing American magazine industry in the 1930s. By the middle of 1934 Kroll was becoming desperate. He could dump stories into Sunday school papers like *What To Do, Youth's Companion, Girl's Circle,* and *Christian Youth* almost at will, but he seemed unable to place stories in the reduced space available in surviving national story magazines. He was a shoe-in in the Nashville market; he simply could not compete as a writer of short fiction in a national market. This was not really a judgment of his technical ability as a writer. Tied thematically to rural life and the very boy-meets-girl romance of his youth, Harry Kroll was becoming bound by rural, and therefore provincial, themes.

Unable to halt the declining demand for his work, Harry still had to do something to feed, house, and clothe himself and his family. Obviously writing was not doing that nearly as well as it once had. Frustrated, he approached the Guggenheim Foundation a second time about a writing fellowship, this one to produce the broad historical cotton novel which he had conceived while teaching in Lula. Harry was confident enough in the *Cabin* sequel that he listed the title on his second fellowship application to the John Simon Guggenheim Foundation. That entry noted that the manuscript was "Completed, awaiting publication: Probably by Atlantic Monthly Press." It was not, and was offered to at least Harcourt, Brace & Co. as well before the end of 1935.[153] The Guggenheim Foundation likewise turned down his writing fellowship application.[154]

Harry Kroll turned forty-seven in 1935. He continued to write vigorously, spending hours at his typewriter daily, trying to stay afloat in a sea of change, but his fiction sales were declining steadily and he hadn't published a book in four years. As Franklin Roosevelt's "alphabet soup" of economic recovery and work programs began pouring money into the American economy in the mid-1930s, the old saw that "a writer can't eat encouragement" certainly described Kroll's predicament. He wrote and submitted his work at a furious pace. His stories came back with encouragement from virtually every major magazine to which he submitted and many publishing houses as well. It was maddening that the only market in which he could regularly place material was juvenile story papers put out by church publishers like the Methodist Publishing House and David C. Cook Co. His work appeared in these for years, their low pay rates better than nothing. Even the farm magazines were buying less frequently, as paid advertising ate into space once reserved for features. Kroll's frustrating inability to place work consistently with the surviving national short story market—front-rack fiction publications such as *Collier's, Saturday Evening Post,* and *Harper's*—was probably the influence behind his decision to surrender the dream-turned-nightmare of being a full-time writer and attempt to return to teaching. As a freelance writer in a depressed market he had to agree that the school of hard knocks offered a tough curriculum.

CHAPTER 3

College Professor, American Novelist, 1936–1958

"Nobody knew what would happen," remembered Bruce Bliven of the *New Republic*. The Great Depression "was like being on a falling elevator when you don't know how far it is to the bottom—or what you will find there." Worse than the remorseless economics of depression was the sense of directionlessness and instability that afflicted many lives. Was the country on the wrong track? Charles Schwab, the head of Bethlehem Steel Corporation, represented many in America as he confessed his deep-seated cultural fear. "I don't know, we don't know, whether the values we have are going to be real next month or not."[1] There was much more than abstract markets, jobs, and consumer goods at stake. A stable economy stood as a testimonial to the vibrancy of capitalism and the inherent rightness of America itself. Jittery business interests, craving the certainty of cash flow, were openly fearful of the increasing agitation for legislative controls as potential government totalitarianism, but feared economic ruin more. Wanting to be spared any risk of responsibility to lead the way out of the Depression with credit and reinvestment, banking and industry were grudgingly willing to let the federal government regulate. They would endure the sacrifice of trimming off fortune-making peaks in market values if regulation also filled the valleys. Bank and business closures still occurred at an alarming rate in 1935, but at least there were not as many as three years previous.

The Depression shifted the relationship between American citizens and the federal government. Government was expanding because the changed economic situation left no option: some sort of large-scale power was needed. If the business sector abdicated its position as the national economic engine, something else would have to replace it. Historian Michael Barone pointed out that in 1930 federal government as a whole consumed less than 4 percent of the value of the gross national product. Six years later the figure was 9 percent, a 200 percent increase. In addition, federal back-to-work programs accounted 7 percent of the national workforce.[2] It was a desperate economic gamble that did not truly pay off. Only the Second World War provided an engine large enough to smother the dark fears of the previous decade. But in 1935 no one knew that. They were mostly hoping that Roosevelt's measures would work.

The Kroll family was enduring its private niche in the Depression. Harry's sales had not just fallen, they had plummeted. By 1935 Son had turned fifteen. Torrey (who would not commonly be Robert T. till he was an adult) would be thirteen. Dan was nine. Harry's accomplishment as a freelance writer was modest, compared to contemporaries like H. L. Mencken, at the top of his game as editor and contributor to *American Mercury*, or writer-turned-editor-turned-writer Willa Cather, who was approaching the height of her career as a novelist. Harry could boast over a hundred pieces of short fiction and a clutch of essays to his credit, most in small sectarian venues, to show for six years of unremitting creative work. It should have been encouraging. Instead, the slowly declining average return on his investment of time and effort were certain signs that he needed to reconsider pursuing writing as a career.

In fact, Harry had soured on writing as an occupation and began looking for more dependable work. Just when he began inquiring and submitting applications for faculty positions across the South is not clear. Despite two bad experiences with the ivory tower he had no interest in returning to graded or even secondary education. He felt too old to chase kids, and teaching writing fundamentals like grammar while teasing ideas from woolly minds offered him no creative challenge. It would have to be higher education. The challenge of finding work was complicated with colleges and universities still clamped in the jaws of depression, making it a difficult time to find a job, but nationally hope was beginning to glimmer weakly. The late 1920s had seen large numbers of students entering college. Though the numbers of new students dipped markedly during the early 1930s, by mid-decade the trend was increasing again. Growth in student numbers generally foreshadowed a rise in hiring as well. The question was, could he get an application before a hiring authority at the right time? Kroll was doubtless aware that given his background, without a Ph.D. and in his mid-40s, qualifications alone were unlikely to be strong enough to place him in the writing program at a major institution, public or private. Denominational schools like Iowa Wesleyan he may have soured on, but smaller public colleges and junior colleges were numerous enough and stable enough to represent solid employment options. As with his publication record, Kroll left no indication of the number of schools to which he mailed inquiries and applications. It was a drawn-out process, an exercise in stamina that required more dogged patience than energetic vigor. Not that he had given up on writing—he simply needed something to sustain the family more certain than the fiction market was strong enough to offer.

Kroll's surviving correspondence and autobiographical comments provide no clear clue as to when he began his reentry efforts; certainly it was by the spring of 1935 and was likely much earlier. How many schools he approached is likewise an unrecoverable fact, but one of the institutions to which he applied was a small state junior college with a shaky foundation in rural West Tennessee. The University of Tennessee Junior College (after 1951, the University of Tennessee Martin Branch), had been established in 1927 in the facility of a defunct denominational school. The small campus was in the northwest corner of the state, in the small farming community and rail crossroads of Martin. It was fifty miles northeast of Kroll's boyhood home in Dyersburg. The junior college started out solidly enough at its founding, but enrollment during the Depression dropped to the point of fewer than a hundred students, and the University of Tennessee administration threatened the campus with closure in 1933. It decided against that step, however, and simply changed the college's leadership the following year instead. By 1935 the energetic promotional efforts of a new campus executive officer, Paul Meek, began bearing fruit in increasing enrollment. The rise in the number of students merited an expansion in the teaching faculty as well. The previous year (1934) a temporary position had been created in the English Department. Having lost both English faculty members to other employers in the dark year of 1932–33, the outgoing executive Porter Claxton had been remarkably lucky to secure the services of Everett Derryberry, a native Tennessean, University of Tennessee graduate, qualified football coach, and nothing less than an Oxford University-trained Rhodes Scholar in English.[3] For the second vacant position the school relied on a succession of temporary appointments until, at the beginning of the 1935 fall quarter, Paul Meek began looking for a second instructor. The school needed someone qualified not only to teach English composition, but also with at least enough journalistic experience to serve as advisor for the student newspaper, as well as the sensibility to be involved with college publicity and recruitment.

Kroll's application for the UTJC English position was made from Smyrna (where the family had moved from Murfreesboro) in the summer or early autumn of 1935. As it had been for the trustees in Lula a decade before, Harry's record of publication was an impressive credential that probably flattered and excited the administrators of such a small school, and certainly complemented his formal training at Peabody. Even though Kroll's credentials were nowhere near equivalent to UTJC's other English instructor, they were respectable enough. Kroll's general background and writing experience with both journalism and fiction were precisely what the junior college sought. Harry made two trips to Martin during the late fall, the first to discuss the requirements for the position with campus executive Paul Meek, the second to talk over the same matter with Derryberry, the only other English faculty member on campus and therefore the *de facto* department chair.

Meek liked Kroll and, frankly, needed his credentials and writing reputation on campus. During the first week of December, the executive officer visited Nashville on a business trip and took time to interview Kroll's references in person. Satisfied by their responses, on December 10 Meek wrote Dr. Charles Bell Burke of the University of Tennessee English Department, seeking approval to offer the junior college position to Harry Kroll.[4] Kroll accepted the appointment to the UTJC faculty after Christmas, probably with a degree of resignation. For one who craved the kind of creative salon that Lincoln Memorial had been for him, the rank of instructor in a school so small must have been a disappointing relief. The school was less than half the size of LMU and no upperclassmen; his acceptance would double the size of the junior college's English Department staff to two, and increase the school's entire faculty to sixteen.[5] The UTJC job was certainly not a first choice, but finding job offers had been about as difficult as placing his recent writing. In fact, there were no other offers. Nonetheless it was a job. Kroll hastily packed Nettie and the boys and was in Martin in less than a week, quite relieved to retire from freelance writing. He began to teach in the 1936 winter quarter, which opened December 30. Irrespective of how little status the position offered, a steady income represented stability and security that the Kroll family had not enjoyed in several years. "Mr. Kroll" remained a fixture at this small school in northwest Tennessee and taught there until his retirement in 1958. It was while teaching here that Kroll essentially shaped his identity and career as an American novelist.[6]

In making the trip from Smyrna to Martin, Harry and Nettie Kroll completed the seventeenth move of their twenty-five years of married life, again in the dead of winter, a few days after Christmas. They settled into a rented house on Moody Street, squarely in the middle of a tiny community of college professors and administrators that lined the street a block directly south of the small campus. Harry was assigned an office at the rear of an upper floor of the Main Building, a space he would occupy for the next three decades. At the time he arrived in Martin to begin teaching, Harry Kroll was a month shy of forty-six. He had already published hundreds of stories and three books of minor note, two of which had garnered virtually no attention beyond newspaper reviewers. One former student, Roland Carter, opting to follow his teacher, had taken a graduate degree in English at Duke University, and was shortly to begin teaching at the University of Chattanooga.[7] At least two others were quickly making names for themselves as writers. After fruitlessly chasing graduate degrees at Peabody and Vanderbilt, Jesse Stuart was settled back home at W Hollow. He was already garnering national praise for his bestselling poetry collection *Man with a Bull-Tongue Plow* (1934), and shortly to gain still more for the stories in *Head o' W Hollow* (1936) and the autobiography *Beyond Dark Hills* (1938).[8] James Still was selecting poems that became *Hounds on the Mountain* (1937) and placing stories and poetry in magazines that brought him national attention. His work would net him O. Henry Prizes for short fiction in 1937 and 1939. Their teacher, Harry Kroll, meanwhile, was beginning over yet again.

Though he carried a full teaching load of classes, Kroll continued his commercial writing without interruption, though the work was selling far less frequently. Still, it was something beyond the small salary. With the help of the extra income generated by manuscript sales, a year or two later he and Nettie bought an older wood-frame house on Lovelace Street, about two blocks north of their rented home and directly across the street from his office at the college. This move was their last.

At the UT Junior College Kroll's major duty was teaching introductory composition to freshman and sophomore college students, a duty that put him in touch with a good share of the student body. He settled into teaching two of the three composition courses required of freshmen, and a survey of American literature in back-to-back courses every morning of the year's three academic quarters. He often taught through the summer quarter as well. His afternoons would be "free," used for grading, office hours, and writing (if he could squeeze it in). He would maintain that schedule with only slight variations and no major sabbatical breaks for two decades. As a faculty member Kroll was also handed a number of administrative and advisory functions to complement and sometimes compete against his class responsibilities. One was serving as advisor to the Mask and Wig Club, a newly organized student thespian organization. The basketball/volleyball court of the Physical Education Building on

The Kroll home in Martin, Tennessee, ca.1963.

campus had a low stage and proscenium at one end, and the Science Building featured a small lecture hall with stadium seating. The group typically produced one play a quarter, or one larger production over two terms during the school year. One of its earliest productions was Harry Kroll's second foray into theatrical writing, a light comedy entitled "No Kissing, No Romance, No Moonlight." It was a quick, easy local victory for the playwright that cemented him in place within the college community. The production was performed from his typescripts and was never actually a published work, but he claimed it with pride on his trophy list of books that prefaced the later novels.[9] Kroll's second advisory assignment was as faculty advisor to the editorial staff of the student journalistic venture, the *Volette*. Since the school was a junior college division of the University of Tennessee, the paper took its name as a diminutive of the university mascot, the volunteer. The paper was established as a weekly, but during the Depression monthly publication was more common. Drawing on his background as a photographer, a smattering of training at Peabody in agricultural journalism, and his long career as a story writer, Kroll directed and advised the students as they pushed mostly regular issues through editorial discussions, layout and makeup work, and printing. This responsibility he carried each school year until the fall of 1948.

Kroll's advisory roles were generally late afternoon and after-hours responsibilities. Since non-academic administrative duties were shared among the school's small faculty, he also began participating in the developmental activities for attracting new students. But Harry maintained his office for personal reasons as well, and spent much more time there than did most faculty. As soon as the family was settled in Martin, and probably before, Harry resumed his ceaseless routine of re-circulating rejected novel manuscripts to other publishers, between banging out a new short-story manuscript about every other day. Two of these were "My Folks," a fictively autobiographical recounting of his youth, and "The Four-Square Mark," a treasure/mystery story revised from one of his earliest identifiable writing projects from his student years at Peabody College. Neither was receiving any attention. In fact, since the publication of *Three Brothers and Seven Daddies* five years earlier, his novel manuscripts had stirred no interest among publishers. He could not figure out why. The move from central to West Tennessee complicated the ebb and flow of manuscripts from the mailbox. It required some time for the circulation, begun months earlier in Smyrna, to reroute to Martin. One book manuscript known to have been making the rounds when the family moved in late 1935, "Cotton Cabin Woman," finally caught up with the family, arriving in the mail with a rejection slip, and was dropped by one of the boys in the front hall of the new house. According to Harry Jr.'s account years later, Harry gave the package a frustrated kick, breaking it open and scattering the loose pages in the front room, swearing that he would no longer be troubled with revisions. Thus began the long-awaited break in his streak of bad luck. It began, curiously, with Nettie Kroll. She quietly retrieved the discarded sheets from the hall.

Members of the Kroll family still grumble that Harry never adequately acknowledged the significant role his wife Nettie, a quiet and unassuming woman, played as proofreader and critic. She drove the point home this time, however. Since her husband had disowned the story, Nettie revised or rewrote and polished the manuscript on her own. The manuscript does not survive so there is no telling how much she edited, rewrote, or changed. Evidently it was enough that she felt justified in putting her name to it, as well as a new title, "Clementine." How exactly Nettie made contact with the manuscript's eventual publisher Bobbs-Merrill is unclear. Hints survive in Harry's remaining correspondence that some time in 1936 the couple had driven to Indiana, perhaps to visit some of his extended family, who still lived about the north-central part of the state. Passing through Indianapolis they encountered Miss Jerry Laing, an employee of Bobbs-Merrill Inc. Laing introduced the couple to Jessica Mannon, the firm's associate editor.[10] That chance contact might have been the motivation for Nettie's submission. At any rate, the manuscript was hustled off to Bobbs-Merrill that same year.

It is doubtful Harry knew what Nettie had done with "Cotton Cabin Woman," but he certainly noticed when the fat envelope of contract duplicates arrived with her name thereon. Jessica Mannon, who was resigning as Bobbs-Merrill associate editor because of poor health, wrote Mrs. Kroll in November 1936 that she was dramatically impressed by the manuscript and promised to push the firm to get it into print.[11] Prodded by Mrs. Mannon and Miss Laing, and genuinely impressed with the manuscript, publisher D. L. Chambers suggested only minor changes and wanted to meet the author. Since Nettie did not drive, Harry drove them both back to Indianapolis at Chambers's invitation. Harry sat grinding his teeth meekly in the background, watching his wife accept the praise he felt should have been accorded to him, and listening as she discussed revisions to a book he felt he had written. The book went into production almost immediately after they returned to Tennessee. Galleys and page proofs went quickly. It galled Harry that Nettie should have the attention for a book that he felt was rightly his. As long as he published with Bobbs-Merrill the issue of authorship was allowed to lie. Though Harry had published short stories under pseudonyms, including his wife's name, this manuscript resulted in the only book of his printed under a different name. "Cotton Cabin Woman," the intended companion book to *The Cabin in the Cotton,* was published as *Return Not Again.* It had all the power of the prior work and was definitely better written, perhaps thanks to Nettie's revisions.

Harry may never have informed Chambers or the staff who the original author of the manuscript was. Privately, however, he convinced himself that Annette's name on the volume was merely another of his pseudonyms. In a 1963 letter to middle son

Robert, Harry touches on the issue, while discussing the submission of another book manuscript that had gone out under third son Dan's name. If it was accepted for publication, he noted, "I'd have to go on with Dan's name as I did your mommer's on RETURN NOT AGAIN."[12] Beginning with the publication of *Summer Gold* in 1955 Kroll began listing *Return Not Again* "with Annette Heard" among the list of his publications that faced each of his books' title pages.

Encouraged strongly by Bobbs-Merrill president D. L. Chambers, Nettie Kroll supposedly worked until 1939 to follow up her success with other manuscripts, all based upon one or more of her husband's rejected ideas. Harry wrote an ingenuous letter to Bobbs-Merrill in late July, mentioning that "Mrs. Kroll" was at work on "a story of a girl who feared negro blood." Chambers nodded cautiously in writing that such a story "might be admirable for Mrs. Kroll's poetical prose, especially if it maybe saved from an excess of horror and kept romantic—tragic if need be—and not *melo*dramatic." The result, "Winterbound River," was submitted to Bobbs-Merrill under Annette Heard's name in mid-1937. Harry zoomed off excitedly to Vicksburg, Mississippi, in early autumn to capture some local color for the rewrite he was sure would be necessary.[13] The firm returned a rejection tinged with regret in late October. "It is an exciting and stirring story with all the action and thrills one could desire. But it seems lacking in that quality of poetic beauty which we so admired in RETURN NOT AGAIN, and which gave it originality and distinction." After pointing out several flaws, Chambers dropped the hammer. "We have been unable to see how you can revise the story successfully. It would seem that you would have to make a new beginning. And I'm wondering if you would want to attempt it." Perhaps with an inkling of what was happening in the Kroll household and yet hoping that he could coax another genuinely fine manuscript from the author of *Return Not Again,* Chambers encouraged, "You should write something nearer your heart and natural sympathy—that is, if we've guessed right. This plot is too lurid, the characters too unreal."[14] The manuscript's author did get the point, and no revision was forthcoming. It is fairly clear that Nettie had a much larger hand in the final form of *Return Not Again* than her husband would ever admit, but it is also likely that he was responsible for much more of the book than she might admit. Nettie probably never submitted nor perhaps even completed another manuscript, and she certainly never published another book.[15] After two years of encouragement, hoping for another poetic piece, Chambers quit trying.

The publication of Nettie's story, however, provided an opening that allowed Harry to reestablish himself as a novelist when Bobbs-Merrill accepted "The Four-Square Mark" manuscript and published it under the title *The Ghosts of Slave Driver's Bend,* also in 1937. Harry had dabbled with this manuscript periodically since living in Lula and had sent it to Viola Roseboro as early as 1925.[16] It had been rejected repeatedly up and down the East Coast. As other novel manuscripts began to be reviewed more seriously, Harry had put aside this mystery/treasure story to work on more personally rewarding books, including *Cabin in the Cotton.* In November of 1936, with Bobbs-Merrill clamoring for another novel by Nettie Kroll but willing to look at her husband's manuscripts in the meantime, Harry sent "The Four-Square Mark" to Indianapolis together with "My Folks."[17] Following positive reader reviews, Bobbs-Merrill offered the author a publication contract for the former early in January 1937. Having failed to publish a novel since *Three Brothers,* Kroll could hardly sign and return the pages quickly enough. The news made a huge splash at UTJC, just as news of *The Mountainy Singer* had been received nearly a decade earlier while teaching at Lincoln Memorial; the student newspaper excitedly mentioned one of their teachers signing a book contract.[18] In 1937 *The Ghosts of Slave-Driver's Bend* became Harry Kroll's first Bobbs-Merrill book. Harry dedicated the volume to campus Executive Officer Paul Meek, who had hired Kroll as an English instructor almost precisely two years earlier.

Publication of *Ghosts* broke the logjam clogging Harry's writing career, which also allows it to mark a watershed. After 1937 his presently known output of short fiction declined precipitously: nineteen story publications in 1937, ten in 1939, four in 1942, and none at all in 1946 and 1947.[19] With the drastic decline of his short-fiction publication, *Ghosts* allowed him to continue a writing career by becoming a novelist, a role he pursued parallel to that of being a college professor. Discounting his juvenilia produced longhand in the Dixons' orchard two decades earlier, Harry Kroll generated at least eight book manuscripts between 1919 and 1936. Between the 1937 publication of *The Ghosts of Slave Driver's Bend* and his retirement from the University of Tennessee twenty-one years later, Harry Kroll published a total of sixteen adult and young adult novels, and produced manuscripts for at least another ten, all while carrying a full teaching load and reading the tens of thousands of compositions he required of his thousands of students. Harry Kroll's shift from being predominantly a short story writer to being predominantly a novelist was not an easy change, neither smooth nor progressive. It reflected the broader changes within the American publishing market. His late career benefited from and was shortchanged as strongly by shifts in the marketplace as it was by his own abilities as a writer. Not all of Kroll's work, published or unpublished, is significant to understanding either him or his place among American writers. The balance of this book focuses on broad shifts and trends reflected in Kroll's novels and non-fiction books rather than his short work.[20]

Part of the watershed at this point in his career was Bobbs-Merrill's rejection of two other manuscripts at about the same time. One was the "Winterbound River" manuscript described above. The other was a manuscript titled "Rosemont," which had gone from the front-ranked Atlantic Monthly Press in 1937, which expressed little interest, to be shown to second-rank Bobbs-Merrill. It involved a collection of themes on which Kroll held strong opinions—a delta blueblood trying to co-opt a public works project, a favored daughter seduced by a recently returned academic, an unscrupulous lawyer with designs on the daughter, race relations, rape, and accusations all around—a tangled plot. The publisher's reader concluded that Kroll had produced this piece "as a vehicle to propagandize his social theories and air his grievances" and the book went nowhere.[21]

The manuscripts' rejections by Bobbs-Merrill are important because they were the first among many rejections his works would see in the coming three decades. Not that rejection of any individual manuscript particularly mattered; as always Harry continued to send them out until they landed a purchase or till he tired of affixing the postage needed for them to cycle through the mailbox. His market-driven model for the business of writing, born in the late years of American pre-broadcasting print culture, kept him from too firm an allegiance to any one market player but also prevented him from thinking carefully about how his work fit into the world at large. He attention to sales made him myopic as a writer—he simply wrote, rather than wrote *for.* Convinced that most stories and books had a publisher somewhere, Kroll did not focus on what was good, interesting, relevant, or well written, but only on whether it sold. Whether it sold immediately or eventually was immaterial. Having work published was a matter of convenience; he would continue sending work to any one publisher because publication represented a shortcut to his priority: income from manuscript sales. Bobbs-Merrill's quickly offered contracts for *Ghosts* and *Share-Cropper* were a major reason why Kroll tied himself immediately to the second-rank Indianapolis publishing house rather than attempting to climb into other national markets or seeking more prestigious publishers before his work was out of fashion. So long as he focused on advances and royalties rather than sales and reprints, Bobbs-Merrill would be an entirely suitable publisher for Harry Harrison Kroll's major works, but the broader recognition he craved would, consequently, also forever elude him.

The major figure at Bobbs-Merrill was David Laurence Chambers, who had come to the firm in 1903 and had risen through its ranks to the literary directorship in 1926. He would remain at both the business and creative helm for another quarter-century. It was he who took the firm public to finance the acquisition of the Bobbs heirs' interests. "Chambers had excellent editorial ability and executive firmness," observed a publishing historian years later. "He maintained a strict check on the firm's finances; he gladly accepted works of merit if he thought there was an adequate demand for them; he strengthened the text and juvenile lists in his effort to keep the firm on a profitable basis; and he made effective use of the backlist; but during his years of control the firm published few books of either distinction or great popularity."[22] A cynic might observe that Kroll landed in the basket of a publisher on par with his reputation and talents. In truth even Bobbs-Merrill might have afforded his work only cursory notice had he sent them manuscripts cold. Kroll's marketplace view of publishing was grounded on the premise that a good writer would always find a market for his good writing. Harry never seemed to understand that the personal relationship between an author and publisher mattered as much or more in publishing than the quality of writing offered, or the abstract degree of a writer's talent, or a writer's reputation. The importance of the relationship factor increased as markets shrank and publishers shortcut the process of sifting fiction manuscripts for their progressively fewer publication slots. The chance encounter with Miss Laing in Indianapolis, Nettie's introduction to Jessica Mannon, the attention paid to *Return Not Again* during its manuscript review, all likely provided Harry Kroll the entrée with Bobbs-Merrill's editorial department that he needed to have his work reviewed seriously. Once that personal connection had been made they were willing to consider what he sent them. The firm's acceptance and publication of *Ghosts of Slave Driver's Bend* sealed the pact: Bobbs-Merrill remained Kroll's publisher through the major part of his career as a novelist over the next decade. For the most part it was a fortuitous encounter. Certainly it was one of the fateful circumstances which make up life; in this case, Kroll remained tied firmly to a second-tier publisher, rather than working to establish himself with a press that would give his work the cachet and credibility he craved.

The second manuscript Kroll fed into the opening provided by Nettie's book was a work he passed off as autobiographical. "My Folks" was, with "Four-Square Mark," also submitted to Bobbs-Merrill in November 1936.[23] The editors ground the pages through a review and dallied over accepting either; clearly neither work measured up to the standard of *Return Not Again*. With no word from Bobbs-Merrill, Kroll's literary agent, Gertrude Algase, sent a carbon of "My Folks" to the Atlantic Monthly Press in New York. It drew praise from Paul Hoffman, an assistant to the editor, and generated a tentative publication offer from the Atlantic Monthly Press. Hoffman provided a detailed critique and recommendations, specifying that a corrected manuscript be back in their hands by April 15 for consideration in the fall list, whereupon Bobbs-Merrill promptly accepted the manuscript immediately on the strength of its prior submission there.[24] The Atlantic Monthly Press offer was another defining moment, a missed opportunity to be accepted by a major American publisher.

Living again in West Tennessee, fifty miles from where he had spent his childhood but now miles above where the Kroll family had once existed in the social order, "My Folks" (eventually re-titled *I Was a Share-Cropper*) was a treatment of those growing-up years. Building on an ability to construct characters and settings, Harry wrote about what life was like at the bottom. Sadly, the volume fails to compare with former student Jesse Stuart's memoir *Beyond Dark Hills* (Dutton, 1938) which would appear a few years later. Kroll's "autobiography" was more invention than anything else. Stuart's *Beyond Dark Hills* was the autobiography of a twenty-three-year-old, thirsty for social validation as an individual. Conversely, as autobiography, *I Was a Share-Cropper* is problematic, yet it very much fits within Kroll's longstanding practice of using personal stories as a *basis* for fiction. In 1929 the family passed through Dyersburg, Tennessee and Harry took pains to show his young sons the places he had grown up. Years later, both Harry Jr. and Torrey realized that virtually nothing they were shown matched what their father wrote in the book he claimed was autobiographical. As their father later admitted, the autobiography turned out much less autobiographical than the title implies. "What I put in Sharecropper was fictionalized and even so I think I never got deeper than just under the surface of their characters," he confessed to his boys somewhat sadly in later years.[25]

There should be, however, a caveat to his disclaimer. The book falls into various sections that differ in style, composition, flow, and accuracy. The first thirteen chapters, covering a time between moving to "Cottontown" (Dyersburg) and his marriage, are obviously the work of the novelist. The book is set entirely in West Tennessee, for instance, though the Darius and Caroline Kroll family had moved to Alabama when much of its action was supposed to have happened. It is undoubtedly this first section of the book, which talks of his parents' immediate family, which he laments in the admission to his sons. The final fifth of the book—the story of courting and marrying, his education, and his earliest years teaching—is more strictly factual narrative, though he obviously collapses the calendar and skips over some events to avoid clouding the story. For instance, the book skips from teaching at the unnamed Lula-Rich school (which happened in 1925) directly to the also-unnamed school that is Lincoln Memorial University (1927), without accounting for the years back at Peabody completing his master's degree or teaching at either Peabody or Unionville. Despite this, much of the straight narrative seems to be fairly factual material that can be corroborated from contemporary sources. This suggests that elements in at least the latter part of the book are reasonably factual autobiography, but very different writing from the first third. The sections involving dialogue and interaction upon returning to his family are suspect of being turned by an artist's hand and probably constitute the reasons for his lament. He also employed other factual snippets of Dyersburg history in his tale. For instance, the 1913 lynching of John Talley for attempted rape, which Kroll could only have known secondhand, was worked into a personal story.[26] Parts of chapters 3 and 8 were based upon sections of two nearly contemporary stories, his 1937 *Atlantic Monthly* story "My Mother" and "My Father," which appeared in *Esquire* a year earlier.[27] One of the critiques returned by Hoffman was that the second part of the book, the section that really was autobiographical, exhibited a tendency to be overwritten "as soon as your narrative takes you away from the share-cropping scene." Hoffman cited "the fine sensuousness of your earlier 'folk' expression and the wealth of moving implication in that section of your history are sacrificed to what seems too often only prosaic and didactic 'observation' as distinguished from 'participation.'"[28] Sadly, it was Kroll's insistence on a good story that keeps this work from genuine relevance.

Despite the fictionalization, Harry insisted on billing "My Folks" as autobiographical. "A novel does not necessarily take us into the deepest recesses of a character's mind," British critic John Mullan reminds us, "character is one person known by another" in "reputation as well as individuality."[29] So in this sense, Kroll's portrayals of his parents and family may be entirely consistent with their characters. Chambers, however, was concerned about possible repercussions over the use of family members' names given the author's characterizations. Harry's older brother Charles, still known as Soddy in the family and by now living in Anniston, Alabama, granted a plenary permission to use his name in any capacity.[30] Mildred, Harry's oldest younger sister, was either unreachable or less willing to appear as a literary character. Despite Harry's use of her nickname "Murdy" in the manuscript, Chambers instructed the typesetter to substitute "Birdy" uniformly. The same treatment was extended to Dyersburg, which became "Cottontown." Curiously, Kroll's youngest sister Natalie (Nattie) is included only in a completely fabricated experience, the death of a baby sister, Julia. The book retained a few actual names: Harry's older brother Charles's nickname, "Soddy" was one, Harry's father's name was the only other. He uniformly cites his long-dead father as "Darius" rather than father, dad, or some other relational name. His mother, still alive, when called by name in the book, becomes "Sal."[31] In some ways his portrayal of his mother in the book was perhaps a strike back at her for a gauche and domineering personality. She was a sharply critical woman, who fought constantly with Nettie any time she visited. The image Kroll outlines of her in this heavily fictionalized story is unflattering without being directly descriptive. She in turn took his writing personally: Caroline Kroll hated *Share-Cropper* and felt it was untruthful of her character. A letter to her among his papers suggests that the book may have given a more accurate characterization than she wished to admit to herself.[32]

Even *Share-Cropper*'s title was a fiction, but an important one. The negotiated work arrangements Kroll describes in the book are closer to tenancy than genuine sharecropping, but he made a definite choice of terms, one that probably escaped his publishers and most national readers. A. F. Robinson notes that "usually, the courts regarded an arrangement as tenancy where the laborer furnished his or her own stock, farm implements, and other provisions, with the landlord supplying only the land and dwellings; sharecropping was to exist where most everything else was supplied by the landlord, with the cropper providing only the labor."[33] Though the practical distinction between tenancy and sharecropping was exceedingly thin, Kroll's readers from the South in the late 1930s knew exactly what Kroll's book title implied. The term "sharecropper" carried social weight. By invoking it, Kroll was claiming to have occupied and then risen from the lowest possible economic and social status in an agricultural community. The title is used explicitly to demonstrate how high he had ascended through hard work and education. The title itself, then, is part of his fiction. Despite his fictionalization of what he claimed as autobiography, and the fact that little of the family's real character came through, Harry was tremendously proud of the book. Near the height of his reputation, in April 1947, he proudly presented the manuscript for *I Was a Share-Cropper* to the University of Tennessee library, one of its earliest manuscript acquisitions.[34]

Share-Cropper also exemplifies Harry Kroll's writing method. Kroll was not a methodical writer and did not lavish attention on crafting nuance and pondering message. As noted earlier, he typically set down short pieces in a single setting, and he held to this practice even for his longer works. He tended to fix a plot idea in mind and then write around it in a sustained spurt of effort until it was complete. Of *Share-Cropper,* for instance, he recalled with some pride three decades later that its writing had occupied "two weeks and two days." Of *Waters Over the Dam,* his most clearly autobiographical novel, he said that the writing occupied two weeks. Not all the manuscripts were publishable at the point he dashed them off. Many were never published, but revisions constituted a separate writing process. Setting down the form of a work tended to be done in flashes of inspiration. Only late in his career, as he turned to nonfiction, did Kroll retreat into the sort of step-by-step process that builds a work in stages.[35]

During their existence, neither of Kroll's first two books with Bobbs-Merrill was particularly lucrative. By 1947 the firm could report *Ghosts* had sold about 1,100 copies and *Share-Cropper* nearly 2,300.[36] Harry hung on firmly to Bobbs-Merrill because the firm was willing to seriously consider his manuscripts, and even his ideas for manuscripts. One reason Bobbs-Merrill was willing to hang on tightly to Harry Kroll was because it was the late 1930s and he wrote in the genre of historical fiction.

Just before the publication of *The Ghosts of Slave Driver's Bend* in late 1937 or early 1938, on one of Harry Kroll's occasional visits to the Bobbs-Merrill office in Indianapolis, D. L. Chambers asked him offhandedly if he had "a historical novel in [his] system." Chambers's question was substantively more than an idle query. Historical novels were certainly nothing new to publishers, but at the beginning of the Depression they had taken on new life in the taste of the reading public. The American book market had become less of a pursuit of a stable readership through variety than a race for bestsellerdom. In 1931, Pearl Buck's *The Good Earth* had been released by the John Day Co. in March, had been picked up as a Book of the Month Club selection, and by October had sold nearly two million copies. From 1933 through 1936 Hervey Allen's fat novel *Anthony Adverse* became one of the nation's first runaway bestsellers, selling over two million copies in an era when sales of three to five thousand copies was considered reasonable, thirty to fifty thousand excellent, and a hundred thousand exceptional. Publishers noticed. By the time Chambers and Kroll visited in 1938, *Gone with the Wind* was sweeping the country into a lucrative fascination with the U.S. Civil War. The reawakened social memory of that conflict was convenient for the United Daughters of the Confederacy, who were busily reshaping political treason and military defeat into a tragic and noble Lost Cause. To cement its social viability in American culture, the Lost Cause needed a work of wide creative and emotional appeal which could successfully bury the political and economic issues that had set off the war itself. "The historical novel," wrote former Harvard writing professor and *American Mercury* editor Bernard De Voto in 1936, "is a pure form of social myth. It projects into the past reasons why we have become what we are. Our guilt will rest less heavily on us in the dark if we could not become other than we are, if we have done as well with our dust as the components of the dust allowed."[37]

Margaret Mitchell began a career as a journalist, but nurtured a consuming interest in what had become the plantation myth of the bygone South.[38] Mitchell's work accomplished the task admirably. Her single work solidified in the national psyche the Lost Cause myth so carefully manufactured in Nashville through the *Confederate Veteran*, and was unwittingly intellectually reinforced at a critical point by the socially conservative and nostalgic Agrarians.[39] Despite their protests of being nonpolitical and forward-thinking about the socioeconomic issues facing the South in the present, Tate, Davidson, and Ransom had written Stringfellow Barr in 1930 that the South's chief virtues requiring revival were "leisure, kindliness, and the enjoyment of a simple life. These are virtues which thrive in an agrarian climate but do badly in an industrial."[40] This naively patrician ideal of the Southern past utterly ignores the factual realities of either economics or society upon which Southern plantation agriculture was built, and it stands opposite to the unremitting labor required for a genuinely agrarian lifestyle. But such assertive nostalgia for an idealized past presented ideal ground on which to build an historical fiction. Even though its author castigates her main character for adopting the fraudulent business practices that built her fortune, *Gone with the Wind*'s appealing message of survival—even profit—in the face of upheaval, was immensely reassuring to fearful readers in the depth of the Depression. The book's commercial success, and then the fabulous success of the film version, invited mimicry and encouraged work with similar themes.

By 1937 every U.S. publisher was looking for historical novels that would turn over copies even fractionally as well as Margaret Mitchell's spectacular bestseller. Between June and December of 1936 alone, *Gone with the Wind* sold a million copies. Within four years there were seven editions on the market with prices ranging from a photo-illustrated movie edition at an unheard-of price of $7.50, down to 69-cent reprints. A year after Mitchell's work was published, four of the five bestselling books of fiction in the country were historical novels, and dozens of new titles were appearing in a new genre being called Americana.[41] Publishers were actively looking for "ambitious novels with a big theme, a big scope, larger-than-life-size characters, whether written at the 'popular' level . . . or at the literary level." Categorical fiction, like Kroll's rural novels, always had a market (albeit usually a fairly small one), but publishers were constantly hunting for potential bigness: "big in length, big in concept, with a big, central moral conflict, trying hard to be solid, serious, challenging, as well as entertaining."[42] The search for bigness was trumped only by the quest for "great American novel" contenders, of which *Gone with the Wind* was the most recent and *Moby Dick* probably the first. James Hart reminds us that historical fiction of the national past was in demand partly "because many of its most widely read examples dealt with an earlier America, [perceived as] more serene or more triumphant, appealing to the nostalgic urge of people living through a period of distress." Distress came not merely in the form of economic depression but also in the challenge that mechanistic, fast-paced, impersonal Modernism was imposing on the present. Americana portrayed the character of some bygone time and could be nostalgic across any range of senses, from teary-eyed affirmation to bitterly negative indictments. It was "concerned with the exploration of salient national characteristics," qualities that could be lauded even as they oversimplified the messy complexity of real people living in real times. Americana was partly a response to the Depression itself, and rose out of "a people frustrated by the present and hoping to find comfort in the [perceived] happier, younger days of their land."[43] Classics like Stephen Vincent Benét's *John Brown's Body,* Marjorie Kinnan Rawlings's *The Yearling,* and Thomas Wolfe's *Of Time and the River* became important books. Even an urban slum became a bitter but nostalgic setting in Betty Smith's *A Tree Grows in Brooklyn.* Each of these works evoked time and place, and quality and simplicity as well, in ways that had little previous parallel in American literature—or in earlier realities, for that matter.

Chambers wanted such a story. Well, Kroll replied, it just so happened that he did have something like that. Harry mentally pulled out an old idea for a novel that would relate the history of slavery and cotton across three generations of Mississippi families. Ray Long had liked the idea back in 1931 but felt it should be expanded across more than one volume.[44] The project had fizzled as Long & Smith folded; now in Indianapolis the idea was brought up again. On the spot in Chambers's office, working from the knowledge of unpublished manuscripts he had at home, ideas that had been rattling around untouched, and some threads spun simply as he talked through it, Harry laid out a long, winding description of the general plot. "Some of it I had in terms of theme, some in historical background and character, in incident, and in that stuff I call 'nostalgia.'" Kroll rambled out his story until Chambers eventually waved him off and voiced essentially what Ray Long had suggested years earlier, that Kroll's story was really several volumes.[45]

Chambers's interest in Kroll's on-the-spot performance was probably the most significant encouragement the author could be given. Attention earned Kroll's loyalty in a way that virtually nothing else could (and money represented attention). The resulting "Cotton family novels" were never fully completed, but from this discussion came the root ideas for at least the three "Cottontown" works from among Kroll's delta novels: *Keepers of the House* (1939), *The Usurper* (1942), and *Rider on the Bronze Horse* (1943). Harry Kroll returned to Martin from Indianapolis having turned another corner in his writing career—a relationship had solidified with a single publisher. Bobbs-Merrill was clearly interested enough in his work as a whole that they were willing to look at whatever he chose to send them. Harry knew the business well enough to harbor no illusion he could send them just anything, but as a novelist the door was at last open and Harry Kroll finally stood to benefit from a publisher's fairly strong interest in his work.

The conversation in Indianapolis also nudged Kroll's thematic process in a different direction. To this point in his career he had mostly written moralistic stories and social criticism. The first type of writing employed plots that could be inserted interchangeably into virtually any setting; the second type focused on relationships, typically in a specific place and economic setting. Neither type of writing required reference to an actual place or identifiable time. Kroll's writing method tended to first settle on a story line, then he placed it in a setting or time invented along with the characters and action. After his Indianapolis visit, that process inverted. Chambers's desire for a large piece of historical fiction and the growing market for this genre meant that Kroll had to shift the way he chose projects. Settling on a time and place became central to choosing a writing topic. Setting his creative work within identifiable times and real places made most of Kroll's serious mid-career writing into historical fiction. Kroll would follow this historical fiction detour until he returned to his earlier process aiming specifically at the young adult and paperback markets in the mid-1950s.

The discussion between the publisher and author in 1938 was another career watershed. Prior to their discussion Harry Kroll was a short-fiction writer who dabbled in novels. After it he became a novelist who produced short fiction. A few years later, in April 1942, Kroll wrote Jesse Stuart a letter that summarizes in a personal way how the career of one writer reflected the economic shift in the American publishing markets between the late 1920s and late 1930s. "I just don't land on my feet when I write shorts," Harry sighed, personalizing the stylistic and cultural changes occurring far above him. "I sell a few, lately mostly to newspaper syndicates; but I can never depend on it. I guess my best luck is with books. Even there I wish I could call myself bigger than I realize I am. This writing racket is hell." Beyond that, he was through picking his own settings. "I'm turning to historical stuff," he concluded succinctly.[46]

It was not too long after his return from Indianapolis that Kroll's fellow faculty member Everett Derryberry resigned in June 1938 to accept the English Department chair at Murray State Teachers College, forty miles northeast of Martin in Murray, Kentucky. Kroll may have hoped for promotion to the departmental chair, but if he acted toward it the letter was not retained. Later the same summer the University of Tennessee transferred to Martin a thirteen-year veteran of the Knoxville campus's English Department with a nearly completed Ph.D. and the impossible name of Broadus Fleshman Farrar. Though Farrar came highly recommended as a personable character, he and Kroll were at odds almost immediately. Kroll taught writing and composition; Farrar taught literature. Precisely why they clashed isn't known, but it is likely that the perspective on what was important for students to learn differed between the two men—a revival of the disagreement between uplift and expression that resulted in his ouster nearly a decade earlier at Lincoln Memorial University. Kroll wanted students to suck the juices from life and spit it into their stories; Farrar taught students from the lofty canon of the Western literary tradition. Beyond this there was definitely a clash of personalities. In one of his periodic letters Harry confided to Jesse Stuart that he had "a damned moron as a department head, a man who is so small and jealous that he would make life a misery and fire me likely if I did not stand in so well with the administration." But Kroll's own frustrated ambition motivated him as well in the conflict. "I have no complaint to make of the salary," Harry wrote further, "but I have never had a promotion from instructor. I'm easily the biggest man in this peanut organization and as big as they've got in all the university system." He had a point. For all the glowing *alma mater* rhetoric the University of Tennessee generated internally, prior to World War II the school was very much a small state college with ambition but limited appeal beyond eastern Tennessee. Despite providing a sound education on its own merits, the UT Junior College survived chiefly on its connection to the parent school and attracted few students beyond surrounding counties. In that light Harry was not far from correct about his reputation. Even the student newspaper would claim that Mr. Kroll was "the best-known faculty member on campus," and it could probably have been stated as accurately about being one of the university's best-known names beyond campus as well.[47]

Working around Farrar dampened Kroll's enthusiasm for life in a way that repeated rejection of his work never could. Though he remained longer at the University of Tennessee Junior College than in any other position and generally appreciated the stability, within five or six years at the junior college he was "tired of the littleness here. I do small tasks that a high school kid of a good mind could do just as well; we are always overloaded with these fruitless administrative jobs and I hate them."[48] The small town and its junior college were, he said, "a hell of a place to think of dying in."[49] Part of his discontent stemmed from a heavy traveling schedule as a college recruiter. In addition to advising and teaching loads, with his background in journalism and advertising, Kroll had been hired at UTJC to help with the junior college's self-directed promotional and recruiting efforts. For a few years he concentrated merely on teaching classes, but as the New Deal recovery began drawing students from rural areas into schools and cities, encouraging student enrollment became a matter of life and death for the school. Curiously, Kroll seems to have done little brochure or promotional design work on campus as would have been expected, but he was eventually set to work on another front. In 1939, after giving up the advisorship of the campus theatrical group, Kroll began to drive over West Tennessee almost constantly and dipped occasionally into northern Mississippi, speaking to high school students to plug the value of a college education generally and the University of Tennessee Junior College specifically. The assignment continued until fuel rationing cut nonessential travel during World War II.

While it may have been tiring, the travel also allowed him to have a public career as West Tennessee's major literary figure of the day and to accept dozens of far-flung speaking appointments. He spoke before book clubs, civic groups, writers' conferences, and schools. Between September 1940 and the following May he presented talks about writing generally or his works specifically at more than 25 different venues, this in addition to his recruiting stops, sometimes filling engagements at the rate of two a day.[50] Taken together, Kroll's responsibilities were just short of crushing, especially to someone who was also devoting time to creative writing and marketing his work.

Writing, however, provided an escape from academic politics. In the spring of 1939 Harry found or made time to begin setting down one of the large historical novels he and Chambers had discussed the previous year. Once he set out to commit it to paper, the creative fire kindled in him and the story came quickly and easily, filtering through his typewriter in a matter of weeks. The story line drew on the interest in the Civil War that had seized the country so powerfully in *Gone with the Wind.* Perhaps consciously modeling his tale on Mitchell's invocation of Southern placeness, Tara Plantation, Kroll's novel was also shaped around the control of a specific house, Mound Vista, and the family that kept it. *Keepers of the House,* however, was almost a direct inversion of Margaret Mitchell's patrician daydream. Kroll's novel painted a seamy, opportunistic, bitter version of the Old South to answer *Gone with the Wind.* Kroll's story was set in the upper Mississippi Delta just as *Cabin in the Cotton* and *Return Not Again* had been, rather than in genteel Virginia or Georgia.

For his first historical novel, Kroll reached back to his own experience in Mississippi and the seminal season he had taught in Coahoma County during the 1924–25 school year. The native burial mound that is the novel's major physical feature, atop which is built the Dowell home, is probably based on Rozelle Mound, the largest of two pre-Columbian mounds in Coahoma County.[51] Harry crafted the book around the clearing and settlement of the delta, but infused it with his own social perspective about the relationship between the planter gentry and those who worked the land for them. Kroll emphasizes unflattering elements and characters which the public ignored in Margaret Mitchell's novel and David O. Selznick cut from the film version. Kroll's story challenges the idealized fantasy world of Southern plantation life. The gentry are intolerant, adulterous, self-absorbed, and exploitative. The main character is the illegitimate son of the plantation owner and his overseer's wife. Growing up on the same plantation with all the responsibility but none of the privilege as his half-brother the heir, Lett Capers becomes the effective manager that holds together the property, set against the impotent and irrelevant planter aristocracy who inevitably lose it.

The publisher accepted the "Scars Never Sweat" manuscript with reluctant haste. Chambers and his staff had put the typescript through their internal reviewers and were initially lukewarm about its prospects. Kroll was not quite offended, but the lack of zeal by the Bobbs-Merrill staff irked him. "My agent got Macmillan interested in the MS; Macmillan thought they could use the novel if some revisions were made in it," Harry later confessed to Jesse Stuart. "I rewrote and just before sending it to the agent I dropped Mrs. Mannon a letter saying Macmillan wanted the book if it shaped up. They [Bobbs-Merrill] took it immediately."[52] The firm in Indianapolis might not have liked the book immensely, but they were terrified of missing a bestseller if it proved to be one. Mannon, Chambers, and the firm were willing to gamble on a marginal historical novel against the chance that the market proved overwhelmingly less discriminating than they. Bobbs-Merrill was not thrilled with Harry Kroll's work but they did not feel they could afford to pass it by. Their attitude was markedly cooler than had been displayed over *Return Not Again.*

Keepers of the House, the newest of Mr. Kroll's books, was received at the University of Tennessee Junior College with excitement in March 1940.[53] Among his more discriminating former LMU students and associates, the book was not well received. "How perfectly ghastly that story is," Lucia Danforth wrote James Still with a disdainful literary sniff. "How can he get anyone to print such stuff? I hope to see something else of yours soon. I am so thankful that you do not debase your talent." Still's impeccable evocation of the Appalachian ethos, his short novel *River of Earth* (Viking, 1940), was shortly to be published.[54]

A few months later, Kroll decided to change literary agents. He had become disaffected with H. & L. Porter, thinking that the Porter group was ineffective in placing his work with publishers, rather than considering that either the market for fiction might have changed, or that his work generally was not as interesting as he calculated.[55] The change made little difference: though his agents could occasionally place a story in the country's major magazines, Harry Kroll was still unable to publish work there on a regular basis. What he failed to note was that by focusing on producing novels, his ability to generate good short stories with the literary merit to measure up against contemporaries like William Faulkner, Eudora Welty, and even his own former student Jesse Stuart, was becoming increasingly erratic. Later critics might respond that his work of this period was well-written but lacks the stylistic ingenuity and particularly the larger significance that characterizes exceptional literature.

Harry was working hard at being a writer, closing his office door and hammering determinedly at his typewriter, but in contrast to his expectations he was going

Harry, nearing the height of his career as a novelist, standing in a cut of the historic Natchez Trace road, a never-used promotional image for *Perilous Journey* (1942).

relatively nowhere. Physically he was still strong at age fifty. The tremendous stamina that sustained him thirty years earlier as a field and mill worker, and the intellectual drive that won him his schooling and college degrees, and had sustained him in his writing, was still there but becoming less available. He was tiring more after less work—incident, of course, to the natural process of moving into late middle age. Kroll recognized that the virility of youth was vital to writing and lamented the mellowing of his skill and the finesse that was developing. "The gusto of those years when you knew me at LMU is declining. I ain't the man, the boy, I used to be," he wrote mournfully to Jesse Stuart in 1941. "I regret sadly to report that I am an adult. That's bad. Worse than you think, as you'll find when you get there."[56] It did not help, of course, that the simmering conflict with Farrar frustrated and drained him emotionally. Always one to draw upon his own experience in his writing, Harry at least managed to turn that conflict into several stories.[57] Stress was compounded by the fact that he was aging professionally, and he knew it. The likelihood that he could make a jump to a college setting that would allow him to teach students possessing a greater degree of native writing skill and intellectual curiosity was becoming more and more remote. He was willing to try, however. In his favor was the fact that he was already employed in academia and that he had a growing reputation as an author. "It adds up to my going if things turn out as I think they might well do," he confided to Jesse Stuart. "But if they don't—well, I'll eat rue and do the dirty work for the sake of bread and meat, and if I get a little butter on the side it will be from writing."[58] Though his novels were seeing publication, by the 1940s his short-story publication was virtually non-existent.

Part of his writing was as a book reviewer for the major Memphis newspaper, the *Commercial Appeal. Appeal* columnist Jennie B. Gardner edited a full-page collection of reviews, notices, and advertising in the Sunday edition. Though the newspaper's book reviews covered volumes across many genres, the contents and column inches of the Sunday book page varied weekly. Kroll wrote reviews exclusively for works of fiction, but not always Southern fiction or even American fiction. Though he made little or nothing from the reviews, his irregular reviews at least kept his name before West Tennessee's reading public. Toward the end of the war, columnist Paul Flowers took over the *Commercial Appeal*'s book review page. Flowers was a few years younger than Harry Kroll but a writer of Kroll's generation. With a new editor, review policies began changing. The publisher cut back drastically on the number of by-lined book reviews in favor of shorter book notices with merely two or three summary paragraphs. Yet it was clear that Flowers loved Kroll's work and made certain that his novels were glowingly reviewed by the paper. He continued to send Harry books, soliciting reviews by one of the region's major writers, but the number of books Kroll reviewed fell from four or five annually to only occasional reviews, and his role as reviewer effectively ended by 1947.

Book reviews did not offset more substantive areas of dissatisfaction. During the time that Broadus Farrar chaired his department at UTJC, Kroll routinely looked for openings to leave. In 1940 Harry learned that Lincoln Memorial was looking for an English instructor. He could hardly have been more excited and made a bold proposal to return. By this time he might have learned that despite being another casualty of the Hill purge in 1930, Lucia Danforth had also managed to return to LMU.[59] He was disappointed when his application went nowhere, and a year later (1941) was less certain that at his age the jump out of Martin could be made. By then the world was full of other distractions.

High Tide and High Point

As the ceaseless *krump* of Hitler's artillery and nasal whine of Stuka dive bombers reduced Polish cities to heaps of smoking brick, Harry and Nettie's sons were coming of an age to begin striking out on their own. Through 1941, news of European war seeped into more and more column inches of American newspapers until Harry Jr. decided he could not sit idly on the sidelines. America sat determinedly on its hands as the Battle of Britain raged and private pleasure boats evacuated Dunkirk; so Son traveled north to Canada and volunteered for service in the forces of the British Commonwealth. Since a U.S. citizen may not serve in a combat position under a foreign flag, Harry Jr. was put into radio communications and served with distinction in Europe throughout the war.[60] Torrey left next for a radio communications position in the U.S. Army. He, too, wound up in Britain. Finally, toward the end of the war, Dan was old enough to enlist as a Navy communications technician, trained at Duke University and at the University of Wisconsin. He shipped to the South Pacific and Philippines for a long tour of duty in yet another Allied radio post during postwar occupation.

While the Kroll boys and millions like them went abroad for a real-world education, the war had profound effects on American higher education, which lasted until the 1960s. The first effect was an immediate draw-down of student bodies. Both branches of the American military began inducting larger and larger numbers of enlistees as early as 1940, and the draft began culling colleges along with factories and street corners in mid-1941. By the time the U.S. formally entered the worldwide fray in December 1941, the country was already mobilizing its manpower, which sapped classrooms across the country. Most schools lost nearly half of their student bodies—the male half. For West Tennessee, the latter were mostly farm producers. The University of Tennessee Junior College went from approximately seven hundred to three hundred students in less than a year. Eleven of those remaining were male. Nationally, the few male students that were left were either unsuited for military service, were in training programs like the Navy's V-12 accelerated engineering system (which eventually took Dan Kroll), or were deemed essential to the war effort where they were. The spindly junior college out in rural West Tennessee lost so many students that for the second time in a decade the school found it difficult to pay its bills, and faced the possibility of closure.

At the same time, the war represented opportunity for many colleges. They became the research arm of the war effort and important training sites as well. Having mobilized several million men and women, the safest way to insulate military training from attack was to decentralize. The Martin campus found an infusion of desperately needed cash by becoming a Navy V-5 flight training site. The V-5 program trained noncombat pilots. Training was typically divided between three different locations through the course of study. UTJC provided two instructional levels. The first was basic classroom instruction for flight groups, introducing students to the mechanics of flight and basic navigation. A small, private airstrip a few miles south of the campus allowed the institution also to offer intermediate training, which put students into basic aircraft until they qualified for solo flight. Their third stage, always handled at a real airbase, would have carried them through rating for control of specific aircraft. Between 1942 and 1944 UTJC housed, fed, and trained over five hundred V-5 men. By 1944, tuition and fees from the roughly three hundred regular students totaled just over $12,000, while the War Training Service subsidies contributed over $64,000 to campus ledgers, nearly five times the revenue from students.[61] The pilot training program was a financial godsend for the campus, allowing it to remain solvent and open for business during the war. The male trainees and female regular students were strictly segregated for both classes and meals, but the Navy trainees were a social godsend for the UTJC coeds.

For all the horror and suffering it imposed on humanity, the Second World War represented an exceptional opportunity for hundreds of less-than-top-rank writers such as Harry Kroll. Following the dramatic downturn of the late 1920s and early 1930s, the U.S. book industry had to cope with a nearly exponential demand for reading material during the war. The vacuum in the market sucked in publishable work not quite indiscriminately, but its gigantic draft created a bubble of opportunity for marginal writers whose work was good enough to be published in boom times but not good enough or interesting enough to compete well when times were hard. Material demonstrating lesser technical skill, marginal themes, outdated topics, and hack ideas and plots had a much greater chance at publication. During the war, reading once again became popular as other pastimes were curtailed due to travel restrictions and blacked-out electricity. The war-related rise in recreational reading essentially allowed Harry Kroll to establish a minor reputation as an American novelist, and represented the high point for his writing career. When the war was over, Kroll's salability declined, along with the work of many other authors of comparable talent. Between 1942 and 1947 Kroll generated at least fourteen novel manuscripts, at least two of which were probably never completed. Bobbs-Merrill published nine of them. In 1942 came *The Usurper*, a work on the contemporary agricultural South. Three works were released in 1943: *Rider on the Bronze Horse*, *Perilous Journey*, and *Rogue's Company*. Harry's personal idyll *Waters Over the Dam* appeared in 1944. The last year of the war, 1945, witnessed the release of *Fury in the Earth*. The powerful account of the Hatfield and McCoy feud in *Their Ancient Grudge* came in 1946, perhaps Kroll's most notable and praiseworthy work. Finally, as the guns and missiles of the Cold War were towed into place in 1947 came Kroll's last major work as a "serious" fiction writer, *Darker Grows the Valley*. Writing and war production churned on together.

Sadly, death was far too common a companion for American families between 1940 and 1945. With their boys gone to the war, the Krolls, like millions of other households, remained at home praying for their sons. Despite all three of their boys serving somewhere in the world, the red and white service banner in the Krolls' window officially carried only two blue stars; fortunately neither was exchanged for a gold one. Harry's personal contribution to the war effort was twofold: he taught some of the young women left behind—girlfriends, wives, and widows—and wrote "manly books." During the war Harry Kroll entirely quit the still-shrinking short-fiction markets to concentrate on producing books suitable for the popular market, since novels were in high demand for the war effort.[62] Bobbs-Merrill published his work almost as he generated it, expecting revisions, certainly, but accepting it where his earlier work had to be shopped around ceaselessly to find publication. On the whole Bobbs-Merrill did well enough for Kroll throughout the war years, but not exceptionally well. The firm's list, Charles Madison would note decades later with scholarly candor, was populated by work which generally "lacked both unusual merit or wide popularity."[63]

The Second World War disrupted the American publishing industry as much as it did the country's economic and political spheres. There was a genuine yearning for expansive rural simplicity as an antidote to cramped apartment living, the hustle and bustle of public streets and transport, and overly bright lights, yet the pretentious agonies of fictional people that were Kroll's main characters became thin conceits in light of the torrential suffering visible in virtually every newspaper issue, especially during the opening years of the conflict. "Maybe it's my frame of mind because of the war," one reviewer wrote of a Kroll manuscript in 1942, "but the trials, tribulations and nasty little weaknesses of the [Southern] poor white are of little concern to me right now."[64] For the reading public, rural tales should be nostalgic since nostalgia was emotionally encouraging, but Harry Kroll (despite his own idyll, *Waters Over the Dam*) was not a nostalgic writer. His socially conscious romances were, at least, diverting. So long as the war lasted, there was room for books of action-packed diversion and Kroll maintained a place in the reading public.

As it turned out, public interest in the war and the real world at large was neither insignificant nor temporary. Partly as a result of the war, fiction would take a hard knock. Whatever their scope or subject, wrote scholar James D. Hart about this period, books about the war included few novels. "Readers generally preferred knowledge of events and blueprints for a better world. During all the years of American fighting, only two novels dealing with the war made the best-seller lists." During the war, however, book sales and readership skyrocketed. Sales more than doubled in the decade between 1933 and 1943. Neither mobilization-imposed labor or material shortages, shipping difficulties, nor drastic cuts to advertising budgets seemed to slow book sales. Partly this was because with virtually everything else rationed, the American public rediscovered reading. "People discovered books as other goods disappeared from store shelves," wrote one scholar, "and they found time for reading when they were kept home because of gas rationing and dim-outs."[65] Those books had to come from somewhere, expanding opportunities for writers of all sorts, whose work kept minds off the present. The war years marked a short return to the sort of halcyon days literary publishing enjoyed during the 1920s, but it was books and not short work that was marketable. The market for short fiction was irretrievably gone; what was left was just enough space for writers of much greater skill than Kroll's. Harry mourned its passing. "I feel about being a short story writer as you do about being a novelist," he wrote Jesse Stuart. "I'll never make it. I've tried, if not very hard, to make the [*Saturday Evening*] Post, and some of the other slickies, but the truth is I just don't land on my feet when I write shorts. I sell a few, lately mostly to a newspaper syndicate; but I never can depend on it. I guess my best luck is with books."[66] As hard as it was, by the end of the war in 1945, Harry Kroll felt he was at the top of his game as a novelist and expected that his place in the world of American literature had finally solidified. Neither the boom in fiction nor his grip on fame would last, however.

Harry flung himself energetically into his version of war production. The first work through his typewriter became *The Usurper,* the second of three "delta novels" and a contemporary novel of social inversion in the Delta. The protagonist is Stan Butterworth, a name that first appears as a minor background character in his earlier manuscript "Men of Arn," which would appear later as *Rider on the Bronze Horse.* The "Cottontown" setting for the novel is a thin disguise for Clarksdale, Mississippi. Butterworth's store and the small community that surround it were probably lifted from Rich, the satellite community to Lula, though it could have just as factually described scores of similar one-store neighborhoods across the Mississippi Delta. In one respect, this book is an expansion of Kroll's first piece of published writing, "John Jones and His Hired Men," from 1919. This was a moralistic story illustrating how treating one's tenants fairly or generously incites productive initiative. Had he tied that fact to war production in the book Kroll might have had a more relevant and salable work. That point, however, was left as only a minor element of the story. Jesse Stuart felt the book was the strongest Kroll had produced to date and provided a glowing review which Bobbs-Merrill featured prominently in its marketing campaign.[67] Reviewers farther afield were less complimentary, however. In the important *Saturday Review of Literature,* reviewer Bess Jones compared *Usurper*'s themes of social interaction across classes to the work of writer Ellen Glasgow, a Southern writer of forty years earlier. "Ellen Glasgow began to show that a society still had vitality when it could permit a whole submerged class to reassert its vigor and competence and mix its rich red blood with the blue. It wasn't easy, either for her as a novelist in the South (and a woman, at that) or for her characters, but she made her point. She knew where she stood. Mr. Kroll does not seem to know where he stands." Kroll, she felt, held plenty of anger but little sympathy. The book narrated social conquest, not constructive development, although she felt his setting and treatment touched very effectively on a wide variety of social and economic issues. In her eyes, this limited the book's literary substance. "Mr. Kroll's book falls short of true importance, however, because it does not make clear the difference between a genuine social revolution, in which new values replace old, and the turn of a Ferris Wheel, which offers nothing more than a shift in relative positions of the riders."[68] While Ms. Jones may have been looking for an adequate literary venture, the author was attempting to draw an entirely new picture of class and culture. Evidently, the sketch was less well-defined than the author hoped. Despite the praise Jesse Stuart wrote for the publisher's advertising and the budget lavished on marketing this work, *The Usurper* sold only moderately well.[69]

By the time it was in press, however, Harry had already burrowed back into his stack of unsold manuscripts and dredged up one of his earliest story concepts, for his next book. He surfaced with "Men of Arn," which had been first composed as early as 1928, probably before *Mountainy Singer.* It was eventually published by Bobbs-Merrill as *Rider on the Bronze Horse,* but it was not a manuscript to inspire confidence in the publisher. The firm had released enough of his work to see that he might not change or broaden his approach. Harry's career as a novelist was running into rocky ground partly because his themes lacked overall relevance, even as he approached what would prove the high point of his career during the war years. In the first week of March 1942, D. L. Chambers signed a letter to Kroll in which he discussed the publisher's view of the revised manuscript of "Men of Arn" submitted the previous year under the title "The Man on the Bronze Horse."[70] There was much "tangy and eloquent writing in it," but the characters lacked depth. The main character Eli Arn, particularly, seemed "utterly hateful, a man who does not one kindly, friendly, disinterested act." Further, "the conflict within him is not a conflict between good and evil, but simply a conflict between selfish ambition and the gratification of the flesh." Another problem was the date. Chambers, acknowledging the shift in American reading tastes during the war, encouraged Kroll to change the action from a contemporary setting to a point before 1939 and the war in Europe. "Since then the pattern of life all over America has been changing and this change seems not noted in the novel." In other words, Harry Kroll's writing was blind to the present and risked becoming dated; worse, its focus and characterizations were thematically short-sighted, lacking the larger human relevance that makes popular fiction into Literature. The author took the criticism of the manuscript in stride: a near-acceptance only fueled Kroll's ability to rewrite. He quickly produced a revision to the manuscript, generating a new dramatic ending that humanized the main character as Chambers had wished, and yet completely missed the larger fundamental message, which compromised his later career.

Despite the sunny optimism Kroll displayed while discussing his work, the world as a whole looked bleak and lowering in the spring of 1942. The Royal Navy had shipped Son from Canada to Britain; Torrey was deciding whether or not to go himself, and how soon, and into which branch of service. Everyone in town was afraid of how long the mess would last and what might happen to the young men sworn into service at the county courthouse in nearby Dresden. Harry's growing literary success was a miniscule and very personal molehill of verve set against the looming grey mountain of a world at war. His cheer at seeing his work into print—three novels in four years—was reinforced by an invitation that arrived at the Kroll home in Martin that looked like an upward career step. Harry was invited to preside at the Huckleberry Mountain Workshop Camp and Artists Colony, a private retreat outside Hendersonville, North Carolina. Huckleberry had been opened by Evelyn Haynes optimistically in 1940. "New England has had its writers groups at Bread Loaf and McDowell colony," crowed one newspaper column, "and it is the hope of the Huckleberry Mountain Artists Colony to fill this need in the South."[71] An imitation of the prestigious Bread Loaf seminars in Vermont, Huckleberry aspired to become a similar summer intensive retreat for would-be writers and artists. Never exclusive, it accepted anyone who could pay the fee. As a Southern writer with experience in an Appalachian institution and a minor national career, Kroll was invited to contribute his expertise and *gravitas* to the camp. His duty during these summers was to spend six weeks on staff as a resident writer and reviewer. The camp's cabin accommodations afforded him a measure of seclusion to pursue his own work, in exchange for being available to other attendees as a critic and mentor. Eager to get out of town to do some intensive writing, away from the college and possibly from an increasingly dour Nettie, Kroll drafted, rewrote, or polished up most of his novels published between 1943 and 1946 in the North Carolina hills. The arrangement must have also stoked his ego somewhat, for he returned annually between 1943 and 1945 or 1946.

That first summer Harry took fourteen-year-old Dan along to the North Carolina mountains in mid-July. As the sound of his typewriter keys clattered around the bare clapboard cabin walls, between July and August 1942 Harry drafted the land pirate story that he had mentioned to Jesse Stuart in the spring. He went unpaid for his six weeks' tenure on site, but received board and room, space to work essentially uninterrupted during his stay, while Dan ran around the hills.[72] As he returned from Huckleberry to Martin for fall term, *Rider on the Bronze Horse* appeared in August 1942.[73] In mid-October the student newspaper at the University of Tennessee Junior College reported eagerly that the book had reached thirteenth on the national Retail Booksellers' late-summer bestseller list. The following April, Chambers reported that "some 7,600" copies had sold steadily but not particularly well.[74] Kroll repeated the same thing to his former student Jesse Stuart, noting with chagrin that "all at once it stopped selling entirely." "Good or bad seller, the [book's sales] life is generally short," wrote one industry observer. "The most frequent length of active life is between four and five months."[75]

After returning to Martin, the adventurous land pirate story, *Rogue's Company,* was accepted quickly. With several Kroll books on their list, each selling reasonably rather than spectacularly, Bobbs-Merrill was willing to hang on to Harry Kroll, still hoping for a *Gone with the Wind* of their own. The book sold relatively well because reading material was in high demand. By 1947 trade sales for *Rogue's Company,* his most popular work, totaled 12,292 copies, which put the book at the top of his personal list of bestsellers.[76] Even so, the cumulative trade sales figure paled in comparison to the 100,000-copy edition produced for the armed services during World War II.

In terms of numbers and readership, the high point in Harry Kroll's publishing career is clearly the adoption of Kroll's two most popular books by Editions for the Armed Services. Seeking rough-and-tumble books attractive to American GI's, by February, 1944 the Council on Books in War included both *Rogues' Company* and *Perilous Journey* on its 1,322 title list, a date which places the books among of the latest issues published in the series. Editions for the Armed Services books were produced to fit into the breast pocket of a combat uniform.[77] The series clamored for the sort of story that would distract GIs from the hell and ennui of military life, and put copies of his works into hands that otherwise might never have held a Kroll book. Youngest son and naval radioman Dan reported from the postwar Philippines how popular reading material was among U.S. soldiers and noted that the men he knew generally liked his dad's books. In 1945 he had seen a "copy of *Perilous Journey* some Marines had been reading under a palm tree. They were hunting another copy as the last 50 pages were gone. They had rescued the volume from a privy. One of them wanted to know if Jim whats his name found his Pap. I told him to buy a copy after the war." "It strikes me," Dan mused to his father, "that Armed Forced books are building your following more than Bobbs."[78] Harry had noticed. Despite the volume of work the Editions for the Armed Services produced and the series' success, that entire market evaporated in 1945 at the war's end. Its demise portended larger changes in American publishing at every level.

As he was reading *Perilous Journey* galleys in December 1942, Kroll tossed out the idea of another memoir to D. L. Chambers for his thoughts. "This summer . . . I am working on a nostalgic book about when I was twenty or so," Harry wrote to Jesse Stuart in early July 1943. "I wrote it in 15 days, the first draft. Now I plan a summer over in the North Carolina mountains to whip it into shape."[79] The story he had committed to paper was what Bobbs-Merrill publisher D. L. Chambers later pinned down perfectly—an idyll. In fact, it was idyllic in almost every sense of the term: the story was "a picturesque episode or scene of rustic life," and at the same time a rendition of "a carefree episode or experience" and "a romantic interlude." The novel, *Waters Over the Dam,* is also idealistically nostalgic, standing as a romanticized statement of what he wished life would have been, but its setting is also the most genuinely autobiographical and unquestionably the most factual use of real characters among his works. He drew heavily on his early acquaintance with the family of Adlis and Lara Dixon and their eight children.[80] The Rennie of his story, if it is based on a real person, was likely drawn from fifteen-year-old Earma or thirteen-year-old Lula Dixon, using the name of their sister Irene. More likely Kroll used artistic license to dream up the youthful, innocent, vital Rennie by idealizing one of his own UTJC students in the place of the "corn-silk haired" country blossom: Marisue "Kitty" Adams, a vivacious local girl from Martin whose own naturally blonde coif and pliant personality had captured his attention from among his students. The controlling teacher Parnell Dees was based on a Dixons Mills teacher named Ola Carson, but her character was perhaps fortified by knitting in threads of manipulative character that he resented in his own mother.

The most striking feature of the story's telling is that he used actual names for many of the supporting or incidental characters. The author, however, departed from straightforward facts when they interfered with his reverie. Years later, Dixons Mills native Joy Nored noted that "HHK did use so many of the real names, their personality traits, as well as actual places and events, some folks were *very* put out. The ne're-do-well characters in the novel were barely disguised. For years before I saw *the* book, I thought the title was WATERS OVER THE DAMN!"[81]

The final published novel Kroll produced during the war turned on a topic which had interested him since boyhood. The Missouri bootheel and West Tennessee north of Dyersburg, where Harry Kroll spent his childhood, were reshaped by a series of massive earthquakes during the late winter of 1811–12. Collectively known as the New Madrid quake, the shocks shifted a bend of the Mississippi River that marked the western tip of Kentucky, folded and cracked the previously flat landscape, and

The Krolls with the A. J. Dixon family, characters in *Waters Over the Dam* (1944), Dixons Mills, Alabama, ca. 1911. *Back, left to right:* Andrew Joel Dixon, Grady Dixon, Harry Kroll, Inez Dixon, Nora Dixon. *Front, left to right:* Maggie Callehan (Lucretia's sister), Lucretia Dixon holding J. C. Dixon, Nettie Kroll holding Huey Dixon, Irene Dixon. Not shown are Florence and Lillian Dixon. Courtesy of Elizabeth Henderson.

sank a prairie immediately east of the river by a dozen feet or more, which filled with water to become Reelfoot Lake. As a boy in Dyersburg Kroll occasionally wandered through and around the earthen gashes and scarps still tearing through the land a century later, pondering and speculating about what the experience would have been like. Now as an adult and a writer, Kroll decided to produce a fictional version about the effect on the small Missouri town which gave a name to the events. This book, *Fury in the Earth,* was dedicated to Harry's third son Dan, who was touched to receive the dedication copy from his father while overseas. The author was feted by the Stokes and Stockell bookstore in Nashville on the publication date, which held a book signing that afternoon as well. The *New Yorker* noticed the book briefly, damning it with faint praise: in the reviewer's eye Kroll's novel was "a highly moral but not overly interesting tale that is half adventure story and half a feeble try at a study of the psychological effects of disaster on an assorted group of individuals."[82] Ouch.

Biting book reviews were the least of Harry's concerns, however. He and Nettie spent most of the war years in quiet anxiety. Their children's departure for military service left the house on Lovelace Street quiet. Harry and Nettie's relationship was never close, and its silence was rarely broken by conversation. More commonly it was the rustle of Nettie's page-turning or Harry's record albums that provided audible signs of life. Harry did his writing in his office across the street. He poured effort into teaching the young women who remained on campus. Though his output during the war makes it look like most of his effort went toward novels, he maintained the pace of his long-held practice of writing scores of pieces of short fiction for magazines which rarely bought them. Unsurprisingly, this writing reflected the war and the changes it imposed upon society on the Home Front. Most of these short stories were never published and remain the largest amount of material in his surviving papers.[83]

With his sons in service overseas or preparing to go, Harry Kroll tossed his hat in the ring for a journalism appointment at the University of Georgia in 1943, wanting to "get into a spot where I could do some real teaching, as we had it over at LMU." Now into his late fifties and well established at the University of Tennessee Junior College, he had settled stubbornly into an accommodation with Broadus Farrar, and confessed privately that he wasn't trying too hard for the position.[84] By the end of 1943 he had decided that desirable opportunities were dwindling and ultimately settled in emotionally to stay in West Tennessee. Six months later, toward the middle of 1944, the occupational fluidity caused by a wartime economy finally provided Kroll the status he coveted. Farrar was transferred back to Knoxville as a cadet instructor, then left higher education to teach in the Knoxville city schools. Harry was elated. "I've inherited the department head [departmental chair] at last," he crowed to Jesse Stuart, "and it looks as if I am set for life."[85] This promotion to department chair finally quelled Kroll's professional restiveness and he discontinued job hunting. Harry Kroll was finally satisfied to remain on the University of Tennessee Junior College faculty in Martin until his 1958 retirement.

The Postwar Trials and Travails

The almost clockwork regularity to the publication of Kroll's novels during the war years is misleading to some extent, for like his short-story output, not all his work came close to publication. Looking only at his published books masks the dogged zeal with which he pursued his craft. Harry Kroll always produced far more story material than was actually published. Even the market's high demand for reading material during the war did not mean that every book manuscript saw print. The concerns he expressed about what was passed over by publishers, and what publishers said about his work, illuminate his career, abilities, and the times as effectively as does a study of his published works.

One of the early fizzles of Kroll's World War II high-point years was an "untitled teacher story" mentioned in an otherwise unidentified and unsigned Bobbs-Merrill reader's report from December 1941. The reader was not particularly complimentary about Kroll's material. The critic concluded that "the novel seems to me only a long writing about rather petty, trivial, unimportant things." It was a sharp but accurate critique. Jessica Mannon, Kroll's primary contact at Bobbs-Merrill, felt that the manuscript began well enough but then fell off into a rather melodramatic romance/treasure story. The plot was similar to other pieces he had written, including *The Ghosts of Slave Driver's Bend*. Kroll tended to employ conflict, complication, and passion, but his writing lacked genuine narrative drama. The story revolves around a teacher in a rural Alabama school whose budding romantic interest in two of his older female students is being played by a conniving older boy. The theme fell flat with the reader: "The trials, tribulations, and nasty little weaknesses of poor whites are of little concern to me right now," the reviewer wrote, suggesting that book buyers would likely feel the same way. The world had changed in an instant at Pearl Harbor, and Kroll's subjects belonged to another age.[86] Through the war, with the return in reading as a popular pastime, Kroll found his books welcomed; when the war began winding down, that changed, although he never understood why.

Another notable manuscript misfire occurred as a later book, *Their Ancient Grudge*, was going to production. In 1944 Harry latched onto an idea for a fictional treatment built around the story of the Bell Witch, a famous spook of Tennessee folklore. Chambers was willing. The subject came up again a year or so later in a list of three possible new projects, as he finished revisions to *Their Ancient Grudge*. Kroll made a trip to Indianapolis, probably during late 1945, and likely delivered the manuscript to Indianapolis in person.[87] From the summaries found in the surviving readers' reports and correspondence it seems that Kroll wrapped the factual Bell Witch story in one of his standard love-triangle romances. Richard Powell, a schoolmaster boarding with the family, did in fact court Betsy Bell and ultimately married her, but Kroll portrays him pursuing both Betsy and her older sister Esther in turn. This romantic triangle was the heart of Kroll's version of the story, which would have made it historical fiction only in very loose terms.

Since he was on staff at the Huckleberry Writers' Colony during the summer of 1945, Kroll worked at the revision during the summer. While Bobbs-Merrill was in the midst of manufacturing *Their Ancient Grudge* and as Kroll was transmitting to them the first draft for *Darker Grows the Valley*, he sent along a heavily revised draft of "Witch's House." Mrs. York reviewed the revision internally and concluded that there were still major flaws to the structure and narrative. She also identified a key to his popular rather than literary approach to writing. The word "love," she pointed out, inadvertently opening a view into the author's character as well, "has always been used loosely by Kroll when he really means 'desire,'" and she suggested that the story's lusty romance be de-emphasized. Even then the manuscript might not be salvageable. "Personally I hope we can squirm out of this one," she concluded with candor.[88] After more internal discussion did not change the recommendations, Chambers felt that he could neither ignore nor overrule the opinions of his professional staff. "Harry Kroll is going to be awfully disappointed if we turn down this script," Rosemary York warned Chambers in an internal memo, "when he was here it was evident that he thinks he has 'arrived' as a novelist. (He is even touchy about our editing.) And he likes this story."[89] On the strength of those reports Chambers wrote Kroll saying that the firm still didn't feel the manuscript was in publishable condition. Mrs. York had been correct. Though he had seen his work rejected before, this rejection was an important stress crack between Harry Kroll and publisher Bobbs-Merrill.

Even ideas that had produced books generated missed hits. Though the concept for an expansive novel about Mississippi Delta plantation culture had sparked as early as 1931, Kroll chose not to work on the eponymous Cotton family historical novel for nearly a decade and a half while he knocked out other projects. Eventually, with the war both depressing and fostering specific action genres and on the heels of Stuart's praise for *The Usurper,* he decided to pick up the project again. By the middle of 1943 Kroll had brought the old idea back into his sights and set about converting it to manuscript form. The novel was described summarily to Jesse Stuart, who was also mourning the downturn in his own publication:

> I am plugging at a three-decker on cotton in three wars, the Civil War, [first] world War, and the current mess. But all around the life of King Cotton, who was a small boy in the beginning, and dies in the present. A long span, with cotton woven through a dramatic plot, around one family, the Cotton family; but with the idea of showing cotton in relation to war. Now that's a hell of a dull idea, of itself. But I'm going to heave in flood and feud, hell and high water, slavery, hard times, *people,* and after about 500 pages emerge with what I hope will be pretty good.[90]

His comment leaves open a question about precisely what Kroll intended to do with his "Cotton novel." "Three-decker" could refer to either a three-volume series of novels, or instead to a three-part single volume. Given the 500-page count he names, presumably the latter is more likely. He had employed Cotton as a family name once before, for the discredited governor Solomon Cotton in *Rider on the Bronze Horse.* It is tempting to speculate whether he would have tried to tie together King Cotton of this book and Solomon Cotton in a family relationship across volumes, as he did with Stan Butterworth in *Usurper* and *Rider on the Bronze Horse.* Unfortunately all we can do presently is speculate. The manuscript or manuscripts, if the author produced fully developed drafts, represented Kroll's last attempt to write about the South's culture of rural agriculture. As has been noted elsewhere, the market for socially critical fiction was essentially dead by the 1940s.

Harry Kroll's last three major novels, all published after the war between 1946 and 1950, include his best work, his most inventive work, and his deepest failure. As a writer, Rosemary York had correctly read the situation: by the end of the Second World War the sequential publication of several novels had given Harry Kroll confidence that his technical ability as a writer should and would carry him into literary prominence—if he could find the right manuscript as a vehicle. In 1945 he came very close.

Nearly twenty years after his first attempts at a Hatfield-McCoy novel, an illustrated article in *Life* magazine in 1944 reawakened Harry's interest in the tragedy's possibilities as a literary topic.[91] The idea simmered for months and he finally roughed in a new outline to his son Dan by letter in the summer of the same year. After further thought about structure and narrative, the idea dawned on him that it was the families' women who had suffered most through the fights, whose stories possessed both pathos and strength. Present interest in emerging minority perspectives and voices makes it tempting to consider *Their Ancient Grudge,* told essentially from the points of view of the female Hatfield and McCoy family members, as a forward step in modern literature. Regrettably, Harry Kroll was not so motivated or enlightened; telling the story from the women's perspective simply seemed like a clever device. It was, however, precisely the angle he needed to add human dimension to the conflict. With a major stylistic block cleared, work on the manuscript progressed quickly. D. L. Chambers jumped on the proposal when it was made several months later. It was thematically the largest subject with which Kroll had ever approached the firm.

During the Christmas holidays in 1945, Kroll enjoyed the postwar relaxation of fuel rationing to drive from his home in Martin across the length of the state to the Tug Fork River region between Kentucky and West Virginia. As ever, Nettie was left at home. He devoted the three-week excursion to drinking in the ethos of the landscape and interviewing Hatfield and McCoy family relatives on both sides. "I came away from the feud country," he wrote in his note on sources, "with a sense of having been in the most somber region I had ever seen; of coal mines, mist, rain, snow and ice, and a feeling of futility that suddenly made the feud wholly plausible." After that, the story flowed quickly through his fingers and the typewriter.

The rough manuscript dispatched to Indianapolis from Kroll's home in Martin was titled "Their Ancient Grudge" rather than "An Eye for an Eye," as tentatively stipulated in the book contract. The author had chosen to adopt a line from act 1, scene 3 of Shakespeare's *Merchant of Venice* as a caption for the work. In the playwright's setting,

Shylock, the money lender, determines to take a pound of flesh rather than accept cash payment on a loan, a senseless measure of opportunistic revenge that stood emblematic of the tit-for-tat exchange between the two Appalachian families of this story. When the book went to press, the publisher put the new title into context for Kroll's readers by setting the line from the play on the title page in an epigram: "I will feed fat," Shylock whines in an aside to the audience, "the ancient grudge I bear him."

Even with this wholly real, larger-than-life event as a canvas, readers will quickly see how much extrapolation and literary license Kroll employs in the finished work. He refused to allow history to determine either the precise scope or details of his work. This was part of his fundamental problem in working within the genre of historical fiction. In working the historical facts of the real Hatfield-McCoy feud into a narrative, he tells the story rather loosely, collapsing time between elements of the feud, dropping dates entirely from the story (both to underscore the isolation of a backwoods setting, and to imply the timelessness and senselessness of hate and reprisal), and using dialogue—pure invention on his part—for both exposition and emotional effect. In a major oversight that shows how far out of touch he was with contemporary literature, Kroll also decided to present dialogue in dialect. Dialect, popular through the 1930s for the color and authenticity it contributed to works, was rapidly falling out of favor with the reading public. When compared to the complexity and international flavors injected by the Second World War, dialect seemed backward, and distracted from ease of reading.[92]

What Kroll does not employ in his account is as telling as what he chooses to feature. He glosses over the long period of legal trials. He includes only an offhanded sentence or two about the feud's treatment in popular literature of the time. Emphasizing "bad blood"—malice between just the two families—he skirts how long they had interacted without conflict, as well as the fact that some members sided with the other side against their own kin in legal disputes. He also fails to acknowledge or even recognize the pop-culture fictional approach to the feud's factual history: that the turn-of-the century motif of wild-eyed violence was employed by non-local writers to help culturally define Appalachia for the rest of the country. Being written when it was, in the 1940s, Kroll's novel (and earlier his short fiction) turns that cultural definition on its head and uses Appalachia to explain the cultural reason for the violence there.[93] While he was creating sympathetic characters, he was doing so by basing them on stereotypes as much as on the research he had done. In fact, Kroll couches his tale more like the sensational contemporary accounts appearing in the newspapers, which painted the feud in strictly familial terms. The Hatfield-McCoy feud wasn't simple, but when it was boiling it made for a great story. The author's purpose for this venture into historical fiction was not historicity for its own sake, but rather to let the pathos of the situation bleed as freely and as inevitably as the characters. Part of the book's power can be glimpsed here between its lines: that one's character and meaning—even one's mortal fate—results from how firmly we hold to the sides we take. That point, however, is perhaps a glimpse into Harry Kroll's personal experience and not that of either the Hatfields or McCoys. Put back into its proper context, Appalachia's classic feud thus becomes complex and not very literary. Focusing the novel straightforwardly on the action and the characters was the easiest way to avoid the messy contradictions and contextual details of reality. Regrettably, the tendency to prefer conflict to understanding was part of Harry Kroll's weakness as a writer.

On the advice of at least one reader, Kroll's publisher suggested cutting the revised manuscript's length to tighten the story, while excising some of the horrific descriptions of violence escalating beyond control. "There seems to be evidence that a tendency to overdo grimness and terror has restricted the sales of your earlier books," wrote Chambers carefully. "This is what our salesmen report in their talks with booksellers." In one of the few letters about his own writing, Kroll agreed to make cuts, but brandished his literary license. "I am willing to make such changes in the name of art and good taste, though I think I have less interest in doing so to meet the taste of book readers." His books, he continued to affirm, dealt with "life," which to Harry Kroll was always earthy, usually petty, frequently coarse or venal, and sometimes downright brutal and ugly. This book was brimming with the latter. His reliance on "vivid, often crude technique" characterizes Kroll's work and is the stylistic foundation of *Their Ancient Grudge*. Chambers's suggestion to moderate the manuscript put him in a funk. "Frankly I decline to rewrite from the suggestions of some one [*sic*] so utterly out of sympathy with the whole performance as this reader. I'd rather return the check and take the book elsewhere," he grumped.[94] Kroll chaffed at the criticism; these new cracks in the relationship between he and Bobbs-Merrill would widen and end their association three years later. In a day or two Kroll's attitude turned around and he began working on revisions. It was well that he did so. The completed manuscript was tighter, more evenly paced, and possessed a balance and realism lacking in some of his other work.

Kroll struck a chord with his novel, and *Their Ancient Grudge* sold well. "Fighting like the Hatfields and McCoys" remained a common phase in American speech and perhaps provided a basis for readers' interests. Chambers was thrilled to report that the book had sold ten thousand copies between its publication in August and October 19, 1946, a very respectable showing; a second printing had already been executed. The figures pulled the book into thirteenth position on the national bestseller lists for a week, and sales remained strong. Then disaster struck. A two-week labor strike by New York truckers cut off deliveries to retailers, and the entire industry shortly thereafter descended into a period of severe material shortages. No further reprints were possible, or even needed, as demand for the book evaporated. A few more copies trickled out as the title remained in print, but readership is fickle. Once gone, public interest simply could not be reclaimed. Circumstance robbed Harry Kroll of his best chance at a genuine best-seller.[95]

Though *Their Ancient Grudge* is a fictional treatment of the Hatfield-McCoy feud, Kroll's book is itself a cultural document. On one hand, Kroll's violent novel, published in 1946, was virtually the last major stylized treatment of the feud, and effectively closes a chapter in its literary history. Thereafter, writers would be more interested in prying up the wild tales to examine what was behind the action. On the other hand, Kroll's rendition is an excellent example of the mid-century Appalachian stereotype, and one of the last books published in the country to rely heavily on stylized vernacular speech. Towards the end of Kroll's life, student and friend Jesse Stuart continued to push *Their Ancient Grudge* toward paperback publishers, hoping to keep it before the public. "It's I believe your finest book," Stuart commented to his former teacher. "It should be, if it isn't, in print."[96] Harry perhaps agreed, but never did see his crowning Appalachian story go back to press. He continued writing, but by almost every measure, failed to regain the high mark of story, style, or sales that *Their Ancient Grudge* represented. It does, however, retain its standing as Harry Harrison Kroll's finest book.

After publication of *Their Ancient Grudge* Harry sat back and had to regain his bearings. For the first time in awhile he did not have another project nagging him to be written. He found one in a uniquely relevant subject: the Tennessee Valley Authority. Kroll's rural-born populism led him into being a liberal Democrat during most of his life. By the beginning of the war, like many others, he became disenchanted with Franklin Roosevelt's policies, growing increasingly conservative about the wisdom of federal development programs for the rural poor he had once celebrated. As Harry aged and settled into the personal comfort of central heating and paved streets, he became more and more comfortable in his middle-class existence and increasingly distant from the daily strain of his rural experience. Eventually he put his disdain into a new manuscript. It was inventively well written, telling the interwoven story of families in an East Tennessee valley across generations. But, the book offered little of the large themes or exceptional craft that publishers now required literary fiction to carry. *Darker Grows the Valley,* released in 1947 to virtually no notice or sales, became Kroll's last title for Bobbs-Merrill. Despite the truncated success *Their Ancient Grudge* had enjoyed, it seems that Chambers finally realized Harry Kroll would not be the author to supply his publishing company with a major historical novel. The firm continued to review Kroll manuscripts periodically when Harry grew desperate, but their increased discretion effectively cut him loose.

Even as Harry, Nettie, and the rest of the nation welcomed their sons back from their far-flung service, the war's conclusion seemed to cut loose Harry Kroll from the moorings he had established a decade earlier. Bobbs-Merrill's editorial control seemed to be creeping more deeply into his work. It was shaking his confidence in the ability he had long had to generate marketable work requiring little change prior to publication. Editorial revisions were not simply bothersome and tiring, they gnawed at his faith in the writing market, which was a keystone to the writing practices he had established decades earlier. If a manuscript was not good the first or second time it was seen by a publisher, then he may not have been convinced it would be any good after four or five rounds of tiresome revision. That challenged his fundamental approach to writing. Discontent over the intrusiveness of Bobbs-Merrill's editing was not the only nagging issue. By the spring of 1948, Harry had become thoroughly disgusted over Evelyn Haynes's management of her establishment at Huckleberry and her expectations of him. Feeling his market-fed oats as an author with a public presence, he refused to participate in egalitarian chore assignments about the camp, which were expected of attendees. Ultimately Harry decided that he could establish and run an arrangement on his own terms that was at least as productive, one that could compete with Huckleberry directly, or at least undercut it.[97]

Still brimming with confidence borne by the run of his war books, with a portion of his *Ancient Grudge* royalty advances, he had bought a small, run-down hill farm from Mattie Drake outside Ashville, North Carolina, in 1947. The following year, having quit Huckleberry, Kroll set about establishing his own summer writers' retreat with his reputation as a writer/educator as the main attraction. The farm then required additional investment to construct suitable cabins and other amenities. Through the spring, back in Martin, he generated his own advertising, and handled all the correspondence, booking, and billing arrangements. He managed to hold the camp open for one year, but finally admitted that there was more to operating a public establishment than merely showing up, reviewing manuscripts, and encouraging authors who paid for the privilege. He was pushing sixty now, and establishing the camp proved to be too much of a reach. The camp's primitive accommodations proved impossible to advertise successfully and the effort involved in running the camp's details was too much for him. He enjoyed the event enough, however, that he was willing to cheerfully admit he was in over his head and carry forward.

Harry's participation at Huckleberry Camp and later purchase of the North Carolina property was symptomatic of two larger forces in his life. First, by the middle of the war he had essentially abandoned a stagnating career in short fiction to concentrate on enhancing his career and reputation as a novelist. Buying the Ashville farm, four hundred miles from the Kroll household in Martin, was intended to provide time and space specifically for the intense writing and continuity that a novel required. Regrettably the farm also symbolized the fraying ties binding his and Nettie's marriage. "I'm somewhat of a novice at giving voice to my emotions," Harry's son Dan wrote candidly to one young woman he had met during his service, "for my family was never a demonstrative one. We even stopped observing Christmas. I don't know the birthdays of any of my folks; we never bothered to observe those, either." "The only time I saw my mother cry was when I left on my last leave. Dad didn't say anything."[98] As time passed, Harry and Nettie's relationship, perhaps never very close, grew increasingly distant. Perhaps to compensate, perhaps an excuse, perhaps simply because he could, Harry's eye began to wander.

Sadly, it was not a new issue. Harry had kept a mistress in Nashville at least as early as 1934. Huckleberry merely provided the opportunity to indulge the latest of a long string of casual extramarital relationships. Hints about similar recreations can be seen throughout his writing. A few years later while his youngest son was in the Philippines, Harry wrote a long, private missive to Dan on the subject, explaining and thereby justifying his behavior to an extent. Despite the lofty themes of love and respect in some of his writing, on a personal level, "love" to Harry Kroll seems to have been primarily a hormonal force. If hormones changed, then "love" simply found another object of desire; marriage under those terms, it seems, became mostly a social convention. Dan wrote back just as frankly, "As for your amours, in truth I look at them with an eye that is at least tolerant if not downright sympathetic. I suppose you are old and wise enough to know what you're doing, and young enough to enjoy doing it. As for Mom, I don't know how to make a stand. I can see her side, too, but I am no Dorothy Dix, and see no solution. You aren't keeping anything from her, for her intuition is absolutely uncanny. I don't think you're doing quite right by her, but I know that when a man needs a woman he needs her with every fiber of his being. It's a yearning in the guts."[99]

Harry may have been very discrete about his affairs, but Nettie was neither blind nor a fool. She knew that her husband was "riding out" on occasion and despised him for it. Their relationship was evidently not close enough that they could resolve or even discuss the subject. Most dalliances seem to have been assignations of convenience, short-lived things conducted at professional conferences or while visiting distant cities. "I was always able to get my dirty doings far enough away not to smell up the domestic arena," he wrote Dan. "Huckleberry was remote; Beersheba was far enough. When I'd meet a woman in Nashville or Memphis I always was lucky in having schoolmarms on the string and meet them at teachers' meetings." He did manage two or three local relationships through the years, and it is little short of miraculous that in a town as small and morally straight-laced as Martin, Tennessee that word of his liaisons did not circulate. But Harry did not fool Annette. Nettie knew of her husband's philandering, swallowed bile over it, and said nothing. Their relationship probably survived on her stable refusal to push the issue. "She could see there was nothing better in the crystal ball for her than me," Harry told his youngest son with an air of condescension, but the couple's relationship strained increasingly as time passed.[100] Just how strained it was is reflected in a story told by one former UTJC student, who happened to meet the couple together just after the war. Of an afternoon he was hitch-hiking the thirteen miles between school in Martin and home in Union City, and recalled being picked up by the Krolls. Even though Harry and Nettie were sitting together up front and he was in one of Kroll's classes, there was not a word spoken between the pair or to their rider during the entire forty-five minute trip.[101]

As autobiographically motivated a writer as ever, Harry eventually began weaving extramarital *affaires d'amour* into his novels as plot devices. The earliest appeared between the first-person main character Eli Arn and a school acquaintance in *Rider on the Bronze Horse.* In 1950 Kroll worked a similar liaison into *Lost Homecoming,* the fictionalized account of his reception in Dyersburg at the premier of the *Cabin in the Cotton* film, and a sequel to *I Was a Share-Cropper.* In this latter novel the female love interest Clara Bell is probably an invention, but the sentiment expressed in the closing pages as Kroll's first-person Darie confided in himself and his reader as he left his wife at home for the festivities, seems to be written as autobiography:

> When I left for this other homecoming I had sensed it. She hadn't wanted me to go from her. She had guessed I would see Clara Bell again. A woman's intuition in such matters is unerring. I hadn't pressed her to go with me, and she had remarked the omission. I'd return restless, frustrated, moody. Olivia [Harry's frequently used pseudonym for Nettie] would guess the cause. But that would be only the beginning of a long season of unhappiness. After a while she would be just another discontented wife of the breed whose husbands have traveled away from them in growth and achievement and culture.[102]

Harry Kroll never seemed to understand that Annette had talent, interests, and hopes of her own. He failed to recognize or appreciate her stability in his life and ignored her personal sacrifices; he was too focused on chasing his writing career. It seems that it was not until after her passing that he began realizing the lot he had handed her.

At the same time, his wandering eye was manifest in a more subtle and public fashion. Kroll was an enormously popular professor on campus. The comments of former students almost uniformly agree that as an instructor he played to the girls, most of whom were aware of his guarded attention and, in the interest of their grades, conspicuously occupied the front rows. An avid photographer, Harry shot thousands of slides and prints of dozens of different subjects. On the UTJC campus, Harry Kroll and his cameras were as inseparable as he and his black notebook had been among LMU students twenty years earlier. At school he often photographed students informally with a still camera or his early 8mm film camera. His largish office became an informal portrait studio. Occasionally he would invite a particularly pretty coed to dress up in her finery and pose for a studio portrait in his large college office after hours. He always presented them with prints of the best image for their trouble. To be the subject of a Kroll portrait was considered an honor among UTJC's female students.[103] This, however, was merely the public face on his hobby; privately, one of his favorite weekend pastimes was photographing willing models more naturally in outdoor settings. An irregular succession of more discrete and less inhibited young participants were flattered to share an afternoon of conversation, a picnic lunch, and the novelty of being the exclusive focus of a photographer's attention. There is no clear indication that Kroll was intimately involved with any his UTJC students, but a few hints in letters to other correspondents suggest that he shared at least one and perhaps two dalliances in the mid-1940s, though not necessarily with students. These would have been conducted with extreme discretion.[104]

As Europe staggered out of bombed-out hiding places and refugees began rebuilding from heaps of rubble, French translation rights to *Keepers of the House* were sold in 1946 by a Dutch literary agency acting on behalf of Bobbs-Merrill. The buyer was Librarie Lardanchet, a firm in Lyon, France. The book appeared in the firm's foreign-author collection in 1947.[105] Kroll's work was only one of hundreds of American titles which flooded into the hands of European readers, perhaps one manifestation of the pro-American feeling following the Allied victory in the Second World War. Harry hoped more foreign editions of his work would follow. Other than a Spanish edition of *Their Ancient Grudge,* none ever did. As the world's political climate cooled into the Cold War, Harry Kroll began to feel personally the decline that the publishing industry leaders were already seeing and planning toward. Kroll recognized that his reputation and salability as a novelist were chilling as well, and it bothered him greatly. During the war his son Dan had once observed that "Armed Forced books are building your following more than Bobbs."[106] That was truer than Harry liked to admit.

It was not until 1948 that the Bobbs-Merrill staff finally admitted to themselves that in Harry Kroll they had a writer who was not likely to produce work anywhere near Margaret Mitchell's masterwork. There did not seem to be enough history in his historical fiction to carry readership, and his themes, like the Bell Witch, seemed too small or provincial for a national readership. Looking back from our vantage point in the present it is clear that the war years mark the high point of Harry Harrison Kroll's career as a novelist, but *why* they were the high point had as much to do with circumstance as it did with either the opportunity to land in the lists of a reputable publisher, or his popularity, or ability, or even thematic choices as a writer. The fact is, that during the war public morale was a booming business opportunity, and diversionary books were morale builders. Magazines never recovered from the post-Depression market contraction, and most began to rely heavily on photography to carry readers' interest. When the war ended, so did the demand for the work of hundreds of writers of Kroll's level of talent. In this way, Harry Kroll's cut-short career, as well as the careers of others like him, might be considered collateral damage of the conflict. Throughout the war he remained busily at work between his classes and office hours at the University of Tennessee Junior College, then for a few years he continued a career as a serious novelist, but in retrospect it is clear that his marketability was in decline.

American publishers, despite the boom in reading material occasioned by the war, despite the heady weeks after VE and VJ days, were well aware that American reading habits were changing. As the war was winding down, the book industries (publishers and sellers) became seriously concerned about their future. Everyone in the publishing industry seemed to recognize that something had indefinably changed; the problem was that despite the decades of experience among publishers, there was nothing at all concrete to quantify or define precisely *how* publishing had changed or to hint at the direction or speed it might move. What was understood with crystal-like clarity was that no longer could publishers afford to pick up manuscripts and push them through the expensive publication process on a general feeling about what the public would likely buy, hoping for decent sales. Because of rising costs of paper and especially machinery, margins were much slimmer even as the volume of printed material available increased. Publishers needed to target specific buyers to be sure their literary wares sold. Everyone could tell the industry was experiencing a boom through the war, but publishers, executives, bookstore owners, and librarians were equally unsure whether they were at the leading edge of a growth curve or near the precipice of a post-war bust. Since book production involved months of investment in editing, production, and manufacturing *before* a title was on shelves for sale, studying readership before the end of the war seemed like a good idea. "The ever-recurring phrase is that we will increase our business by ten-percent over what it was before the war. Sure the soldiers have acquired a taste for reading books, but does that necessarily mean that they will want to own them too?" wrote one recently demobilized New York bookman, A. van Duym. That question was entirely open, and no one had a good answer. What van Duym did realize presciently was that competition for book sales would not be between publishers, but between the book trade and the rest of the manufacturing economy for a share of the goods flooding the post-war market: appliances, automobiles, furniture, audio equipment, and even housing. "Apparently," observed the introduction to one industry study, "no one in the book business had any authentic information as to what was actually happening, particularly in relation to 'People and Books.'" War-time price controls would be lifted, ensuring that costs were certain to rise, whether from additional investment in plant capacity or post-war inflation, so "profitable future operation becomes increasingly dependent upon the accuracy with which market trends can be gauged." The American publishing industry had just abandoned its traditional basis in instinct to adopt a modern business model.[107]

Another significant shift in the publishing industry involved the function of literary agents. Into the 1930s Viola Roseboro continued the Gilded Age practice of reading everything that came in the mailbags. Even then the practice was antiquated. The in-house reader was replaced by freelance critics that publishers did not have to pay. By the 1940s this change was complete. Literary agents no longer exclusively represented authors. The publishing industry adopted them as the frontline of talent scouting and manuscript development, weeding poor writers from good ones and passing along only the likely prospects for direct consideration by publishers.

Some of what the industry learned from its studies was not surprising—that the level of education was a better predictor of readership than income or economic status, and that reading of all sorts declined among older Americans. In the 1940s, however, the older generation was generally not well educated and tended not to be readers, so the demographic decline in reading could be more related to schooling and culture than to age. As public education reforms of the 1920s reached a second generation and the general level of education increased in the population, reading should have increased as well. Half of one statistical study's subjects had read a book or magazine as recently as the preceding day and within the preceding month. They were classed as active readers. Inactive readers, those who had read something only sometime within the past year, represented 21 percent (the same percentage which had read something only the day before). The remaining 29 percent of the population were those who had not read in a year and were considered non-readers. Of the latter figure, nearly half could not recall having read something within even five years. Thus, seventy percent of the books sold in the country could be attributed to the activity of merely 21 percent of the national population, and 94 percent of reading material of any type was handled by merely half of the country's potential readership. Kroll's favored historical novel genre did not rank high on readers' priority lists, landing only 6 percent of respondents' first preferences in the book survey.

The study clanged alarm bells for the industry. It suggested that half the American population, more literate than ever before, read effectively nothing at all. Most significantly, despite the boom in book sales and the increase in reading during the war, of the people who had read a book the previous day (21 percent of all respondents), the average time spent reading was merely thirteen minutes, less than the average time devoted to movie-going the previous day. By far the most significant recreational activity reported by respondents was listening to the radio, which occupied eight times the number of minutes devoted to reading. The fundamental question the industry wanted to know was this: "was the buying of books in recent years a war-time luxury which will abate now that the war has ended?" What publishers learned, in short, was that more Americans were reading, and that reading still occupied 40 percent of daily time available for recreation and improvement. They also learned that the relative importance of fiction to the book market was declining over the halcyon days of two decades earlier. Publishing generally seemed to be on good ground and was probably poised to grow after the war, but in 1945 books were not nearly as significant in daily life as were radio, film, newspapers, and magazines.[108]

How did the trend affect Harry Kroll? First off, he likely never saw the study or its report and may not have been interested in something so broad, but even he was aware that it was getting more difficult to sell his work. At the beginning of the war, Jessica Mannon at Bobbs-Merrill, who today would be considered the firm's developmental editor, noted that "historical novels, adventure, detective and war stories will continue to sell. 'Social' novels had already started dropping off before December 7."[109] Her comment pegged what the industry study would later confirm, that the era of muckraking journalism and social literature was substantially over. Readers were more interested in characters than exotic "color" stories, and what remaining reader interest existed for colorful settings was being drawn toward non-fiction. Isolated in still-rural West Tennessee, connected to the rapidly changing writing markets only by mail, Harry did not see what was happening. Part of the challenge he faced was the growth of interest in new genres and themes for popular fiction. Harry wrote for people like himself, those who had left the farm but recalled what it was like to live a rural existence. The problem was his demographic did not buy many books nationally, and he was not a good enough writer to appeal to those with sophisticated, eclectic reading tastes. Harry continued to write about the mundanities of rural life, while the urban "hard-boiled" detective stories by Raymond Chandler carried mystery and adventure stories into the realm of negative character studies, and new writers like Robert Heinlein were pointing readers toward the stars.[110] First the national pulp markets had shrunk to a fraction of what they had been two decades earlier, and now after the war, the fiction sector of the market seemed to be moving the same direction.

These shifting realities stranded a class-conscious regional writer Harry Kroll far above the market tide for two reasons. First, Kroll and others like him came into the trade-book market as the swell in book buying and reading during the war induced publishers to accept material they may not have published in more competitive markets. Kroll's career as a novelist is evidence of that. It had been difficult to get his writing accepted in the 1930s and would become that way again in the 1950s and 1960s—but not during the early 1940s, the war years.

Second, hundreds of novels were still being released, but fiction's importance as a fractional part of the whole trade-book market was lessening. The drop in market share during and after the war increased competition between the writers whose work was vying for acceptance and presentation to the reading public. Though the proportional balance between fiction and nonfiction book publications changed by only a few percentage points, it represented a sea change in American book sales and readership, showing how deeply war had affected the country's reading habits. Anecdotally, interest in fiction plummeted as public attention shifted from the unrealities of fiction stories to the unrealities of the theatres of war. Harry recognized at least that aspect himself. "Novels don't seem to do as well as these 'I-was-the-last-man off Something-or-other' books," he complained to Jesse Stuart as early as 1943. "Fiction of the soil in this country has never been popular. It has to muckrake, or be socially critical before it will be taken at all."[111] His "fiction of the soil" reflected another problem also represented in the demographic statistics of readership. While Harry's work focused on rural themes, the majority of American book buyers were urban, living in the Midwest and in the increasingly urban Northeast. Rural book buyers were relatively scarce.

Riding the wave of war-borne popularity, which he was sure stemmed from a preternatural trust of market forces as the effective measuring stick for good writing, by the mid 1940s Harry Kroll was feeling that he had finally built himself a literary career. From its height he kept looking further up expectantly, certain he had now become an American author and not merely a regional one. From his position as a front-line participant in the book industry, an author, Kroll could see none of what the book industry was studying so carefully at the close of World War II, nor could he understand why his work stopped selling. All he knew was that his long-time publisher was suddenly less enthusiastic about his work. About his own ability he remained supremely confident, so the public's lack of interest could only indicate that its taste—not his ability—had shifted. In fact, his career's impending decline curved downward out of view. The postwar years would witness Harry Kroll's deterioration from being perceived as a serious literary figure into a paperback and juvenile writer.

In fact, by 1950 Harry was tired of working with Bobbs-Merrill. Though they published his books with moderate success, he was irritated by their requirements to tone down his language and heavily edit the physical and romantic action that he craved to put in print. While he did not argue with their marketing or promotion, Kroll came to feel that their editing was holding him back from greater sales. "Southerners write with brilliant intensity," observed one contemporary book reviewer, "but their subject matter runs to horror—social, psychological or economic." Like fellow realists William Faulkner, Erskine Caldwell, and John Steinbeck, Kroll always preferred laying out conflict and action without resorting to literary devices like understatement or implication to soften the violence. As early as January, 1946, as he worked on the second round of revisions to *Their Ancient Grudge,* he wrote Henry Holt & Co. asking if they would be interested in his work. "What I find myself needing is not reports from elderly lady readers, but he-man readers who won't emasculate a man's goods. I am a realist and often a brutal one. But I am also a damned good writer, and I am short of stature because of trying to meet the wishes of readers who are not writers and never . . . will be."[112] Holt may have answered him but the firm never did publish a Kroll book and may not even have reviewed a manuscript.

Sales for Kroll's last Bobbs-Merrill title, *Darker Grows the Valley* (1948), were so small that Kroll quit working on another novel and returned to writing short stories, which he could still produce in one sitting and therefore tended to pay better for the effort. "To work six months on a long novel and have it go into a market where sales are not as much as school teaching is a little more than I like to think about," he grumbled to D. L. Chambers.[113] It was frustrating—bitterly frustrating, but just as Holt had given his work a cold shoulder, Harry's work got similar responses from dozens of other publishers.

Kroll's writing career demonstrates two of the three challenges facing would-be writers as outlined by publishing executive Ann Watkins in 1941. First, she noted, few writers could depend on their work alone for an income; he had tried that and had gotten out as early as 1935. By the late 1940s writing mostly provided a critical outlet for his energy and his quest for reputation, though he enjoyed the money. Second, his long record of writing and publication exemplified her point about cultivating the industry and patience to be a writer. His ceaseless cycle of submitting work until it was hopeless or accepted was proof of that. But, "most important," Watkins noted, was her third challenge:

> Have you the perception, the power of interpretation, the capacity for reflection that are the basic requisites of authorship? Anyone can master technique, and style will develop with time, but few are sufficiently endowed with the fundamentals [of insight] to qualify as professional writers. At best writing is a long, heartbreaking, uphill game.[114]

At the height of his moderate success as a novelist, Harry Kroll seems to have lacked this basic quality that would have given his work relevance and perhaps an assured place in the constricting fiction market of the 1940s. His faith in the strength of the marketplace allowed him to assume that because he could write well technically, because he could craft a story, his work would be marketable. Both the European and American book markets were losing broad interest in the themes he preferred. The market, in which he had such faith, had changed dramatically without his noticing. Kroll wanted to be a best-selling author of work he liked to write—he wanted his work to be relevant, but not to be required to figure out what readers felt was substantive. He neglected to develop depth, a search for first principles, a cosmic relevance that cut across time, class, and the rural-urban divide.

In his separate comments to Henry Holt & Co. and to Chambers, Harry revealed something about himself and his craft that he should have studied very carefully. It boiled down to the difference between the widening popular market and the elite market for fiction. During the Depression publishers debated and worried over serving a very traditional, well-educated, literate, book readership, or joining film and radio as another mass-entertainment industry. "The soul of the industry was at stake," writes David Welky, "as firms sought a balance between artistic and commercial considerations." Book publishing was shifting from an art-driven craft to a profit-driven industry. "In order to expand their readerships, bookmen needed to think more like hard-nosed businessmen than litterateurs. They had to focus on books that appealed to broad audiences, not those making profound statements."

By the time Kroll grumbled about his craft and realism to Henry Holt & Co. in 1946, the industry was settling into its choice. In short, the industry was being taken over by corporate America. Texas oil millionaire Clint W. Murchison quietly took over Holt's stock in the late 1940s, and other large publishers followed shortly in the 1950s, especially the textbook publishers catering to returning veterans being schooled on the GI Bill. The takeovers contributed to a feeling of unease in the editorial trenches, and the decline in fiction sales portended stiffer competition for the available investment slots on the publishers' annual lists—a book had to be newer, or wilder, or just plain better than what had been acceptable in the past. Wall Street, which dines hungrily on markets with rapid growth potential, strode into board rooms as the elderly owners of firms across the country were quite willing to protect their heirs from rapacious inheritance taxes by divesting their interests for cash. Publishers to which Harry Kroll was sending his work had largely given up the popular fiction market and gambled that they could provide literate America with relatively sophisticated literature. Kroll's approach to writing was closer to popular literature than to fiction of the sort most publishers would take a risk on for high-culture audiences. Harry Kroll wrote for people like himself, those who had left the farm but recalled what it was like to live a rural existence. Unfortunately, he was not a good enough writer to appeal to those with sophisticated, eclectic reading tastes. Handicapping him further, his demographic was shrinking, and it did not buy many books nationally. For instance, Tennessee had less than two percent of the nation's literate public—in real numbers and percentage, greater than Virginia; considered together, the rest of the South could only muster 12.63%, while just New York and Illinois counted 17.26% of the nation's literate individuals. It complicated matters in that those two states held over a quarter of the nation's urban population, but the worst figure was in the market distribution for books: five states accounted for 62% of the books sold in the country, of that figure New York alone bought more than 30% of the nation's books; California (even before it became a megalopolis), Illinois, Massachusetts and Pennsylvania rounded out the figure. Demographically, in terms of literacy, in terms of the urban-rural market share, and given the sea of other material in the market, Harry's rural stories drowned in the struggle for readership. The fact that his books appeared on weekly book lists only in places like San Francisco and Seattle suggested that his work could not swim effectively against the tide of other writers' work—but then, neither could anyone else. Of course, there were exceptions. Alfred A. Knopf, one of the highest of the high-culture publishers, produced the mystery fiction of Dashiell Hammett, George Harmon Coxe, and John Ross Macdonald, but the old popular fiction was no longer really popular. By the end of the war Harry Kroll was essentially a popular writer trying to attract the interest of a high-culture market. Even Zane Gray and Max Brand could not do that. Kroll had the wrong sort of approach and material for that sector of the industry. He would eventually try to place his work in the paperback market, which succeeded the popular-literature markets of the 1930s and earlier, and which exploded after the Second World War. The American publishing industry was enduring a second fundamental shift.[115]

Through the 1930s fiction remained the most popular genre for readers nationally. Around 1,900 novels appeared in print annually, and fiction books accounted for about 85 percent of books circulating through public libraries.[116] The Depression and the Second World War swelled readers' interest in nonfiction, and American fiction markets began slumping. Postwar economic expansion pulled the U.S. population into suburban areas from both the urban cores and the countryside. Faced with a declining fiction market, Rosemary York eventually warned Harry that "The public at this time is very selective, and the fiction market very skittish," but Harry was so confident in his writing and storytelling ability that he seems to have missed the implications behind this warning.[117] Mrs. York was not the only publisher to notice the trend. After one of his many scouting trips, New York publisher Alfred A. Knopf's scout Herbert Weinstock reported back that "Among the booksellers I saw (they are often the best central intelligence posts in a city) there was a unanimous depression about fiction, but also a general feeling that the book business is a healthy and going concern."[118]

It is a truism that the national list of bestselling fiction of the postwar years displayed a thirst for quality, or at least the illusion of serious importance, but for those who cared to look the nonfiction bestseller lists revealed the dramatically changed nature of postwar America. *Betty Crocker's Picture Cook Book; The Baby; Look Younger, Live Longer; How I Raised Myself from Failure to Success in Selling;* and *Your Dream Home* were the top-selling books for 1950. "The war had restored American productivity," observed Michael Korda, "brought a final end to the Great Depression, and made Americans yearn for a quiet life at home in the new suburbs that were already redefining the American Way of Life. Succeeding at your job, buying your dream house, looking younger and living longer, and cooking food that looked pretty was what Americans wanted after the deprivations of the Depression and the excitement of war, though even as people settled into 'the good life,' the first tremors of [social] changes were taking place around them. . . ."[119] Harry Kroll's writing bore no relation to this brave, new world. He was still anchored firmly in a rural past, his rural past, both personally by living in rural West Tennessee, and thematically by personal interest. There was, however, another limiting theme in his writing that had grown larger and larger in his evolving career as a novelist.

Romantic relationships had characterized Kroll's writing since his first juvenile attempts at writing, forty years earlier. He found it difficult *not* to employ, not merely romantic, but increasingly sexualized historical fiction. It just did not have a market, at least not as he wrote it. He professed no interest in bodice-rippers or sappy adventure books, but had he looked critically over his own correspondence, he would see that his work displayed more and more frequently a sexual edge, which his editors at Bobbs-Merrill commented on more than once. His inability to transcend carnal desire eventually compromised his publisher's view of his work; worse, it threatened to offend potential book-buyers.

Around the turn of 1947 Kroll picked up and read with approval *The Wilderness Road* by former Middlesboro, Kentucky, newspaper publisher Robert L. Kincaid, who was now Lincoln Memorial University president. The book was one volume of the American Trails Series, an historical treatment of the passage across the Appalachian Mountains into Kentucky, through which the country began expanding westward. A few weeks after Kroll completed his reading, Jesse Stuart told Kincaid how impressed Kroll had been. "He thinks one part of it has material for a fine historical novel."[120] The part Kroll had in mind was the 1770s settlement expedition made down the Tennessee River and up the Cumberland River by a group under the command of John Donelson that resulted in the founding of Nashville.

In June or July 1947, Kroll was invited to speak before a "Southern Life Class" at Peabody College in Nashville. His remarks involved discussion of a story on which he was working. Kroll's presentation at Peabody was probably an outline of the story and some suggestions of how he would bring in particular characters, coupled to a reading of a few draft pages. Like most class presentations it would have gone unnoticed, except that Mrs. John Lawrence Merritt, a descendant of John Donelson, was in the audience. Mrs. Merritt took offense at the characterization Kroll proposed to make of her ancestor. In mid-August she wrote Kroll, challenging his interpretations. "We have a worthy heritage which we expect to pass unstained into the hearts of our children," she wrote, warning him that anything negative that might be said of the "founder of the clan" would have to be "accurately, and very definitely proved, to be true."[121] Merritt challenged Kroll's use of unquestionably historical characters in nonhistorical events. Her major complaint was Kroll's creation of a passionate and entirely fictional *affaire d'amour* between John Donelson and the much younger Rachel Henderson, an event which never happened but certainly could have (or should have) to Kroll's mind. Harry ignored her and did not respond.

In Nashville, Mrs. Merritt's ire simmered unassuaged for several weeks as she awaited an appropriately abject answer. After a month she wrote directly to Bobbs-Merrill, enclosing a copy of her letter to Kroll and stating that since he had not responded, her charges—that he was intentionally besmirching her progenitor's character—must have struck home and should thus be interpreted as true. Her assumption was a logical fallacy (lack of contrary evidence does not constitute proof of a point), but the threat of libel spooked the conservative Chambers to the point that the publisher wrote Kroll hastily. Bobbs-Merrill's president pointed out that Tennessee had a libel law that included the dead—even the distantly departed. He suggested that family names should be changed.[122] Harry refused categorically, and for good reason. Doing so would have shredded the importance of the book as a historical novel. After letting the issues simmer through the weekend he hammered out a closely written, three-page reply to his assailant, waving his own "great artistic integrity" like a banner in a line of battle, rebutting her veiled threat of libel and picking apart her interpretations and arguments point by point.[123] Her threat induced Kroll to avoid a direct challenge to the book's historicity—or at least his fictional treatment of historicity—by recasting the story entirely. He put Donelson's efforts within the larger context as merely one activity of the Transylvania Company, a private group of eighteenth-century adventurers penetrating the territory that became Kentucky and Tennessee. "Probably the novel I finally write will be the tragedy of the Indian in dealing with the ruthless if godly white men and their passion for land and riches," he wrote Mrs. Merritt.

> I know of nothing more inexorable than this slow but steady and bloody defeat of Dragging Canoe and all that he stood for against Henderson, Robertson, Donelson, Caffrey, Peyton, and the others who made up the Transylvania Company. Declared three times illegal these men nevertheless contrived to establish themselves on lands and enrich themselves. Henderson took advantage of the preoccupation of the Revolution to sieze [*sic*] Kentucky and Tennessee lands, and after the manner of mighty men in God all of them justified their methods and results.[124]

From this perspective, history was not on her side. Richard Henderson, John Donelson, Daniel Boone, and others secured land grants, brought groups of settlers across the Appalachian range, and attempted to treat with native groups, hoping to capitalize on Euro-American claims and expansion into the region, a frontier version of eminent domain. A book of this broader scope, it was evident, would have made a libel charge involving one character impossible to argue. It was her turn to have nothing to say, and though nothing more came of Mrs. Merritt's challenge to his approach, the exchange of letters committed Kroll emotionally to the writing project more firmly than any advance royalty check could have. It also sensitized him to challenges of his literary interpretations of characters or situations, editorial or otherwise.

The exchange helped reshape Harry Kroll's approach to historical literature and represented a minor turning-point in his career. This manuscript became a transition piece between his earlier, historically informed fiction and his late-life nonfiction. Though the shift required twenty years, Kroll finally seems to have learned the lesson that actual individuals cannot be played too fast and loosely if a work is to be billed as historical fiction. He could get away with the trope of overblown romance and trail right along the edge of credibility for a failed story on a Confederate officer and his slave concubine, given the sparse correspondence between the real people. For "Men of Empire," the limited and well-known number of people descending the Cumberland River in the Donelson party complicated his work. Rather than add an invented character to the group to provide a romantic foil, Kroll tried to employ but rearrange the biohistorical material at hand. It didn't work, as Mrs. Merritt's challenge demonstrated. That was only his first problem. A second, more personal shortcoming to be conquered before he could write effective nonfiction was his adamant devotion to romantic entanglements for his characters. The Donelson story, as he first explained it to Chambers, had the makings of the important book he noted it could be; however in the 1940s Kroll seems to have lacked the sort of descriptive and narrative literary skill to recognize and build a story around issues more substantive than hormones and opportunism. Despite his earlier work with historical fiction, it seems that Kroll's perspective on the past was taken from the standpoint of imagination, not fact. His work on this expansive idea throughout 1947 and 1948 converted the project into a fictional history rather than the standard rollicking romance of a couple in the wilderness. The research he began drew him away from fiction and closer to nonfiction generally. For perhaps the first time Kroll could genuinely claim to be writing *historical* fiction and not merely historically inspired fiction.

Six months after the exchange with Mrs. Merritt, Chambers had still heard nothing at all from Kroll and prompted him in April 1948 with an inquiry about the book. Kroll responded that he had set the project aside to concentrate on the magazine fiction market.[125] Chambers's note, however, proved that the publisher still trusted Harry to turn out a respectable piece of work. He decided to pick up the manuscript again, worked at it furiously for several weeks, then forwarded the stack of typescript to Indianapolis. Rosemary York was tentatively impressed. Kroll had set a huge task for himself. Dozens of characters were involved, historical fact had to be followed, and he was limited to a page count small enough to result in book of salable size. There were problems, York wrote, with historical fact discussed without being introduced, too many plot lines involving too many individuals to be adequately or easily followed. "It really needs a careful scaffolding—a controlling plan leading to unity of impression," she concluded. York suggested that the manuscript be set aside for a time to give him a chance to come back for a second revision with fresh perspective.[126] What she did not say was that for the third time in as many manuscripts (*Their Ancient Grudge, Darker Grows the Valley,* and now "Men of Empire") Kroll had employed the structural device of dividing the manuscript into sections based on the points of view and actions of different women in the story, and the firm felt that the device was becoming hackneyed.

Not exactly pleased with the review, Kroll replied in two letters, the first asking straight out for some clarification and explaining the broad sweep he was seeking to portray, and the second (a day later) with a more measured consideration of the manuscript's historical and narrative sweep. In this, above all his work to date, Kroll felt that he might at last have the makings of a genuine bestseller, and he wanted it to be fully ripe.[127] Rosemary York replied with sympathetic encouragement, explaining that the firm felt the book suffered chiefly from being *too* historical, that Kroll was pulling facts into the story needlessly, which complicated it. "If a fact . . . cannot be made an intimate or relevant part of the story, why mention it at all?," she asked rhetorically as a broad hint. She also encouraged him to plan carefully in his revision so that parts that remained were rationally related.[128] Kroll worked the revision through the summer of 1948 and turned in a second revised manuscript in September that proved to be a disaster. The Bobbs-Merrill staff was shocked. The reader report forwarded internally to David Chambers was blunt. "What is the matter with Harry Kroll? Usually he's very good at revising a first draft that we've criticized severely, been able to bounce back with a highly creditable job. . . . Kroll is now completely off base. The present manuscript is far worse than the first draft."[129] A second reviewer shared that opinion. "History has left a mighty larder from which to draw; the trouble is, Mr. Kroll has not made his material into a good novel."[130]

Though Bobbs-Merrill's rejection letter to Kroll does not now survive, it landed on him very heavily, and he fired back a claim that he had been treated unfairly, coupled with a threat to take the manuscript to another publisher. Having tried to put the matter as fairly and carefully as she could, Rosemary York replied a little defensively but certainly with encouragement. "We know how much work there is to writing a book, and it's certainly no fun to have to tell an old friend when we believe the results of his hard work don't measure up commercially, in our judgment. I wish more than I can say that we felt such confidence in *Men of Empire.* The fact remains that we still do not. . . ."[131] Her confidence did not mollify him at all. By this point he had invested a tremendous amount of time and personal energy in revising the manuscript, particularly after Mrs. Merritt's jab two years earlier. He was convinced that the result was a literary masterwork. In November, Kroll quietly made good on the threat and shipped the manuscript to Harcourt, Brace in New York. They unwittingly confirmed Bobbs-Merrill's perception when the manuscript was rejected virtually without comment.[132] Kroll self-confidently waved aside the implication and returned to his old practice of cold-calling his manuscripts to potential publishers. He sent the manuscript in turn to Lippincott, Doubleday, and A. A. Wyn, in the first half of 1949.[133] They each turned it down; Wyn rejected it twice. By the middle of 1949, with the school year closing and distracted by the need to respond to queries and registrations for his summer writers' camp, Kroll parked the "Men of Empire" manuscript with Franz Horch, a literary agent in New York, for his critique. Horch responded in mid-September, agreeing that the manuscript needed work and "tightening" but evaded giving a straight answer as to what to do with it.[134] Absolutely convinced of the story's historical significance, literary value, and his marketability, Kroll would return again and again to tweak, cut, rearrange, but never publish the manuscript.

"Men of Empire" was not the only drain on Harry's time and attention. The rigors of conducting his summer writing on his isolated North Carolina property were simply too much. Harry gave up the idea of converting his hill farm into a summer writers' colony or even workshop. The conditions were too primitive to attract the late-middle-aged clientele he hosted, and he could not afford to upgrade the accommodations. Instead, Harry changed venues and arranged for his "school" to spend its two-week 1949 summer session at the more amenable Beersheba Springs Hotel. The antebellum resort in Grundy County, Tennessee north of Chattanooga, provided a much better facility than the primitive cabins his hill farm offered. This year proved to be his most successful event. Kroll's advertising was a three-page, mimeographed, undated letter to which he attached photos of his own making.[135] How widely it was distributed isn't known, but a surviving group photo of the attendees shows that the camp attracted at least forty-four people of late middle age, or who today would qualify as senior citizens, thirty-eight of whom were women.[136] One of these was Corinne Hodges, a staff writer for the *Commercial Appeal* in Memphis, who wrote a personal account of the gathering.[137] At the fading elegance of the hotel Kroll was in his element as an appreciated don, and he discovered that he rather liked playing the part of the literary tutor. For his part, "I had a hell of a good time teaching those folks," Harry later wrote of the experience, "and the project was a ripsnorting success."[138] It was not so successful, however, that he would repeat it. Harry decided that the writing school operation was a hugely time-consuming proposition that did not attract the sort or quality of writers he had hoped for, paid back very little on the investment, and netted him nothing professionally. Two years' effort as an independent camp operator taught him chiefly that the work involved in a camp was inadequately repaid by the "fun" and income. Getting too old for chasing wild hares, Harry quit the pursuit and closed his writing school after 1949. Thereafter, with one exception made after his retirement a decade later, he was content to stick out his time in the faculty position at the University of Tennessee Junior College. He held onto the North Carolina hill farm for another decade.

By 1949 Kroll was determined to demonstrate that his career as a salable serious novelist was not over.[139] It was, however. He would still produce several juvenile novels, a couple of steamy paperbacks, and a raft of new short fiction, but none of it would rekindle the critical acclaim in which he basked with his earlier books. But he didn't know that in 1949, and he plunged ahead on a new tack. Two years earlier, while "Men of Empire" was being shaken together and Mrs. Merritt stormed threateningly, Harry Kroll produced what would prove to be his last major piece of substantive fiction, conceived as a sequel to *I Was a Share-Cropper.* The 1936 *Share-Cropper* story had ended as the first-person narrator returned to Cottontown for the premier of the film based on an unnamed novel. Now a decade later, Harry picked up the story and in *Lost Homecoming* continued the fictional treatment of the week-long event, again told in the first person, opening with his arrival and built around the interaction with people from his past and concluding with his departure from town. Despite Harry's confidence about the book, it was rejected by most American publishers and finally ended up in print by Coward-McCann, a minor publisher. A comment D. L. Chambers had made about the manuscript when rejecting it two years earlier turned out to be prophetic: the story simply did not carry the emotional cocktail he had once stirred up and poured into *Share-Cropper.* The royalty sheet from the critical first few months notes that *Lost Homecoming* experienced positively dismal sales: fewer than 3,200 copies worldwide, approximately a fifth of which would eventually be returned to the publisher, if normal industry projections held accurate here.[140] This book was the final publication of a serious novel for Harry Kroll. To national publishers already deeply worried about their fiction lists staying viable, a marginal book or appealing to a niche market was not a good investment. Throughout the rest of his life, though he would continue to write and publish, the works would be young adult fiction, mass-market paperbacks, and nonfiction—neither the historical novels nor serious literature for which he wanted to be known.

The competitive, edgy opening years of the 1950s for the fiction industry and book publishers saw Harry Kroll's career and reputation as a novelist evaporating. Between 1950 and 1967 Kroll would produce at least twenty-six book manuscripts. A dozen and a half of those would be worked on and worked over between 1950 and his retirement from teaching in 1958. While there were enough successes to encourage him, they were few. Six novels and three nonfiction works would see publication, but all of the former would be either paperbacks or young adult fiction. Harry Kroll occupied his campus office in the Main Building after hours and between classes—writing, rewriting, and shipping his work almost constantly, unaware that his days as a competitive figure in American twentieth century literature, albeit a minor one, were essentially over.

The motivation he needed for a style change finally came in the middle of 1951 when Kroll was approached by the Western Printing Company of Racine, Wisconsin, which was interested in producing a paperback reprint of *Cabin in the Cotton* and asked about copyright. Copyright registration had been made by the original publisher, Long & Smith, but that firm had been bankrupt for two decades. It was unclear if Harry could legally approve the venture on his own, or whether he needed the permission of one or both of the partners or their heirs (Long had since died a suicide). Since his career as a novelist was flagging Kroll jumped at the chance to get his most successful creation back into print. Kroll immediately wrote back that of course he owned the copyright, then sent an immediate query to the Copyright Office at the Library of Congress to be sure. Harry's youngest son Dan, who was living and working in Washington, D.C., did some investigating and initially reported that the copyright was still within its original protection period and had not been reregistered. Kroll heaved a sigh of relief and gladly signed the re-publication contract.[141]

Dan's initial confidence was incorrect, and so while Harry carried on a casual business correspondence with Western, he was also pursuing the steps necessary to reregister the book's copyright extension in a process that was only slightly less than frantic.[142] Harry wanted to claim copyright based on the fact that he was the book's author and keep what had been a profitable property out of the hands of potential creditors of the Long & Smith bankruptcy. In February 1952 Dan wrote to tell his father that the copyright to the book was unresolved but that he most assuredly did not have copyright. His rights had been sold to Long & Smith in the original publication contract and he had no legal recourse. A copyright lawyer approached the New York clerk of court, who resolved the rights issue, which revolved around the bankruptcy proceedings twenty years earlier. Long & Smith had been put into receivership, but the rights to *Cabin in the Cotton* had not been sold and thus were unresolved when copyright protection expired. Western ultimately decided to hedge on the issue of who owned what, included the original copyright date of 1931 in its new paperback version, and went forward with production.[143]

Harry wanted to expand the novel's text slightly, and Western agreed. Busy with two other book manuscripts and with the question of copyright registration, he put off the revisions until late in December 1951 or the first week of January, when a high-pitched telegram from Western pleading for the text set him busily to work on the revisions. Twenty years earlier, Long & Smith had given him a free hand with the sexual overtones of the action. "Bring Danny and Nordie as close to sex experience as you want," James Van Toor had written, and with a handwritten postscript to the typed letter added "The limit, if you wish, says our reader, but I thot my secretary might blush at that."[144] As he completed the manuscript in 1931 Kroll took what he felt was Van Toor's unspoken advice about offending potential readership, and thus limited the details of the tryst to innuendo. Twenty years later, however, with a paperback printing in the works, Harry asked Smith if he might add rather graphic detail to the bedroom scene of Danny's seduction by Nordie Lord.[145] Smith was amenable, since the type would have to be entirely re-set for the paperback. Harry thus made explicit one sexual encounter between Danny and Nordie Lord, painting her specifically as the sort of nubile seductress he personally found so motivating.[146] Smith sent Kroll five copies of the Dell paperback edition in the first week of May 1952. The firm pumped out a quarter-million copies of the book in its first run and paid the author royalties of a cent per copy. Six months later it was supplemented by another run of 50,000 copies, which netted him another $500. It was not a dramatic return but was certainly the best real income he had enjoyed from writing in years.[147] Sadly, time proved that it was as much a one-time event as the sale of the film rights had been two decades earlier. He could not see that, of course. Harry was pleased enough with himself that he bought a new car with the proceeds, a pale blue Buick sedan with a massive chrome grille that leered like a lecherous grin.

Little motivated Harry Kroll's writing as effectively as income. As he aged he was more and more willing to chase down what limited success he had found with the hope of repeating it. The relative success of the paperback reissue of *Cabin in the Cotton* in 1952 drew his attention toward the popular paperback market, the one fiction format thriving in postwar America. The industry could hardly claim to be literary but it was lucrative. In some ways the appetites of the 1950s American paperback market paralleled those of the pulp and fiction markets of earlier decades. Book quality was abysmal, but it was sales that mattered, not quality, and there were so many genres and subgenres to fill that the paperback market seemed a business that a writer like Kroll should be able to stir around in easily.

After the new printing of *Cabin in the Cotton,* Harry finally squirmed uncomfortably in the new realities facing the American writing industry, gathering himself to jump genres and land in what he described as "a hard-boiled mystery story." During his heyday in the pulp-magazine market of the late 1920s he had produced scores of mystery stories and felt he knew the formulas well enough to stretch them out into short novels. Three decades later his trial book-to-be carried the title "The Guilty Flee" and appeared under a pseudonym drawn from his three boys' names, Dan Torrey Jr. The use of a pseudonym was perhaps a ploy at preserving the remaining shreds of dignity of a "serious" novelist. The sheaf was sent to and returned from everywhere.

Other work was similarly ignored. Harry had mentioned an idea for a fictionalized treatment of Chattanooga patent medicine millionaire E. W. Grove in a letter to Jesse Stuart as early as 1943, along with other book concepts. These included a celebratory book on "the two horse farmer of the deep South," and a less-than-celebratory send up of "Alan [*sic*] Tate and his ilk" over the "damn snooty ways that make realists in the South."[148] Among these three, Kroll is known to have committed only the Grove book to physical form, probably because it represented the most marketable topic. By this time Harry realized he was struggling to find a market for his work, but was patently unwilling to shift his topics or writing style by much. Confident in his own

Harry and Nettie at home in Martin, Tennessee, 1955.

technical ability to carry a story, he kept generating manuscripts and sending them to publishers.

Perhaps it was the act of returning to *Cabin in the Cotton* in 1951 which occasioned for him a new flash of nostalgia. At about the time he sent the emendation pages to Western Printing, Harry sat down and, over a week and a half, drafted an account of his experiences teaching at Lincoln Memorial University. It was a piece of literary work as serious as any he produced, but he felt that the personal or family timing of the story was not particularly right and did not send out the manuscript immediately, as was his custom. The ream was shelved in favor of other projects, hopefully ones that paid more. In 1956 Harry was invited to present a keynote address before the Tennessee Philological Association meeting, held that year at Lincoln Memorial University. It was a perfect venue to revisit his past. At the conference his presentation consisted of reading the opening paragraphs from "The Golden Years" and discussing its genesis.[149] Like most of Kroll's work, the manuscript was strongly autobiographical. "I had started the novel 28 years ago while I was still here at LMU," Kroll told his hearers (the beginning he cites was probably a rhetorical device), "but abandoned it. I wanted to write a novel about a mountain college where a great many things happened to me, and all of them important." The novel revolves around the two years he spent teaching English at LMU, including his mother's disruptive visit near the end of his career there. One major character is Iris Granberry, a woman that wielded the effective power on campus. The character was a thin disguise for Iris Grannis, librarian and editor of LMU's magazine, the *Mountain Herald*. Former student Jesse Stuart read the full manuscript in the spring of 1956 and was favorably impressed with it. Stuart's opinion, however, was that the manuscript would be much more effective as a straightforward reminiscence than a novel.[150] Despite this advice, still hoping eagerly to reestablish himself as a novelist and probably also spooked by the reminiscent ghosts of threats for libel over *I Was a Share-Cropper, Darker Grows the Valley,* and "Men of Empire," Kroll avoided the morass of autobiography and insisted on casting the whole work as fiction. He then put away the pages. LMU represented too much to discard.

On the other hand, he kept after the paperback publishers. Kroll submitted a manuscript under the working title "The Dance of Death" to Lion Books and to Western Printing in the first few months of 1953, and then through the Writers' Service to Gold Medal Books and Popular Library.[151] No one wanted the book's steamy and stereotypical images of Appalachian family feuds, corruption, and bloodshed. Eventually the sheaf of pages landed at Ace Books, a mass market paperback firm, toward the end of 1954. They were willing to consider it with some revisions. In January 1955 Kroll submitted a revised manuscript and was delighted to receive a contract in the first week of February. Pushing his opportunity, he also tried to interest Ace's Donald Wollheim in another manuscript, "Murder in the Mist," which went nowhere.[152] "Dance of Death" appeared later the same year under the title *The Smoldering Fire.* Having just read his mentor's vibrant account of LMU, Jesse Stuart was troubled by Kroll's publication of such a decidedly low-brow effort. Stuart respected his former professor and had praised his fiction highly a decade earlier. Kroll personified the solid grass-roots tradition of hard work and bootstrap effort that Stuart respected. Stuart regarded this popular market title as a sell-out. "Why should he write a lousy, sexy, pot-bolier [*sic*] at his age when he should be getting a little reputation," he grumbled to Lincoln Memorial president Robert Kincaid. "He lost ground on this lousy piece of filth for a few degenerate dollars."[153] Stuart had no use for stock characters or blood-and-thunder writing, yet entirely missed the fact that Kroll's reputation had been in steep decline for nearly a decade. His serious writing had been rejected by every major publisher in the country and most minor ones as well. Paperback publishers across the country—whose standards were not nearly so high as trade publishers—had rejected half a dozen Kroll manuscripts in the previous three years, one right after another. Harry Kroll had slid from his previous position as a minor but serious novelist toward the point of wanting something—anything—in the hands of paperback publishers. Kroll's "reputation" in American literature during the early and mid-1950s was virtually nonexistent. The lingering taint from Stuart's opinion of this book ensured that Kinkaid tabled any consideration of awarding Kroll an honorary doctorate from Lincoln Memorial a few years later.

While Harry probed the paperback markets with limited success, he decided to return to writing moralistic stories for the Baptist, Methodist, Presbyterian, and other sectarian newspapers, most of which continued publication from Nashville. He could still knock out stories quickly, and though the papers published far fewer stories than twenty years earlier, at least the pay was better. One important acceptance came in 1949 for a twelve-part serial life of John Wesley, the founder of Methodism. By the time the story ran in 1951, Harry was ready to propose it as a separate publication. The publication of *The Long Quest* by Westminster Press introduced Harry to the niche young adult market. Through the 1950s he mined other serials similarly. From the Southern Baptist Convention's Sunday School Board youth magazine *Upward* came "Barbara's Farm," a story adapted out of his own 1948 attempt at converting his hilly smallholding outside Asheville into a viable writers' retreat. In the serial and book version, Barbara Estwicke is a college girl who inherits a mountain farm and determines to convert it into a summer girls' camp. Harry was even able to coax Westminster into a sequel for this book while he considered producing young adult biographical novels on Puritan dissenter Roger Williams or on Methodist missionary Bishop Asbury. Since he had already drafted "a farmlife novel" and wondered about

Westminster's potential interest, he let the other ideas lie. "I don't mean a manure-on-the-boots farm story, but the tale of a young man of education and culture who got fed up on the hectic life of our times and went back to the land." The inspiration for this was his son Dan, successful as a technical writer for the Navy Department but eager to get out of Washington, D.C. A girl was involved in the story's plot, of course. Westminster, of course, was *not* interested in such a topic—they had edited out the word "kiss" from the *Long Quest* manuscript.[154]

Despite this moderate success with young adult fiction in the mid-1950s, Harry was puzzled why he was no longer able to get his serious novels to press. From what little he said on the subject it must not have troubled him too deeply, for by this time Kroll felt instinctively that he had found a new niche with young adult novels. His shift in attitude was not so much that he had abandoned the novel form but rather that he was always ready to follow opportunity. Despite his relative success with juvenile books, Kroll had not entirely surrendered his hopes at renewed recognition as a serious writer. By 1955, having not sold a novel manuscript in half a decade and unable to land on two feet in the paperback market, Kroll again picked up his historically informed subjects and tried the major publishers again with two pieces of autobiographically informed fiction. The revived "Golden Years" manuscript was one; the other was "Soddy and I."

Harry's son Dan came home to Martin for a visit in the summer of 1955, a visit during which the father and son discussed Harry's early life in Alabama. After Dan left to return to Washington, their discussion became a story idea. Kroll sat down and spilled the story into his typewriter in a little over a week toward the middle of July. The Soddy of the title is the author's older brother and former itinerant-photography partner, Charles Kroll. The manuscript was a treatment of lessons learned on his and his brother's time drumming up business among the southern Alabama pinewoods towns half a century earlier. It was written as an adult story, but Kroll told Westminster Press, which had just released *Summer Gold* and was working over *My Heart's in the Hills,* that he would consider rewriting it as a young adult novel and offering it to them first.[155] So far as is known, he never did. The story may have been too personal or he may have lost interest. Harry even tried a return to idyll. "Old Chat's Girl" was yet another Kroll boy/girl Southern romance, known solely from a rejection by Western Printing and Lithographing (Dell) in late 1957. About it the managing editor could soften the rejection with the compliment that "This has the feel and mood of back-country South about as authentically as one could ask. I'm afraid, though," he continued, "that Harry and Fairy just don't generate the sort of warmth and interest that they should—and the story really depends on how much we can be drawn into their intimate little affair."[156]

Late in 1957 Kroll was secretly invited to California for a guest appearance on live national television in a *This Is Your Life* episode featuring former student Jesse Stuart. The weekly NBC series was wildly popular. Started as a morale-boosting radio program for returning veterans, it proved so popular that churches were said to change their prayer meeting schedules when the show leapt to television in 1952. The thirty-minute show featured a different honoree each week, whose life and accomplishments were profiled in a narrative done by the host, and through personal reminiscences by several guests. Honorees on *This Is Your Life* might include a major sports figure one week and a small town teacher the next—an important draw for the audience of a live show grounded in the premise of reconnecting long-lost friends and significant influences. The real-time broadcast arrangement and lack of editing provided a genuine and often emotion-filled experience which affirmed the Everyman nature of postwar America. It also left viewers just as surprised as the person being profiled. The show always began with a classic audience hook: springing the surprise on an unwitting honoree, whether in the studio audience or nearby. "The honesty of that moment was so important that [a planned episode] was scrapped if the secret leaked out."[157] Part of the show's appeal was involving virtually anyone, from well-known stars to common heroes. Stuart was a heart attack survivor and serving an appointment as the American Heart Association spokesman. Expecting to come to the studio to record a Heart Association interview, Stuart was instead surprised by host Ralph Edwards

Kroll in retirement, beside his career trophies at home in Martin, Tennessee, 1957.

MARTIN, TENNESSEE—TUESDAY, MAY 20, 1958

Named
ha Oe

; twenty years was
st annual Aloha Oe
mores. This candle-
letic Field prior to
ssive of all activities
way" or "farewell,"
from the university
. Due to inclement
college gymnasium.

Townsend
rd Annual
Contest

e Dallas And
ra Brooks
In Event

'ownsend, Paris sopho-
the third annual David
emorial Speech Contest
. Jimmie Dallas, a
from Memphis, placed
l Barbara Brooks, a
Memphis, won third

l's winning speech was
old—the Turtle." In
he urged the student
take a stand on cam-
He emphasized his
comment, "the turtle
sses when he sticks his
and added that this

Presentation to the college of a portrait of Harry H. Kroll was a highlight of Friday night's Aloha Oe services. Pictured with Mr. Kroll are Jere Freeman, ASC president, and Dean Paul Meek.

Kroll To Retire At End Of Quarter

Bishop Recital Is Well Received

Hal Bishop, talented UTMB pianist, presented a highly successful recital the evening of May 13. The program featured a number

Thirty
Receiv
At Con

Culmination of fo
30 UTMB seniors.
Commencement exer
Principal speaker
P. Craine and Dr. Ke
Craine, pastor of the
deliver the Baccalau
dress by Dr. Knicker

Commencemen
Dance Ends Th
Social Season

The annual Comr
Dance Saturday night
fitting climax to the so
on the campus. Under
sorship of the Freshma
large and happy group c
made the dance one c
events of the year.
At intermission, the g
welcomed by Adam S
president. Scott asked
iors to lead the way t
freshment tables whe
cakes, orange punch, a

Kroll, student body president Jere Freeman, and Dean Paul Meek unveiling Kroll's portrait, 1958. University Archives, University of Tennessee at Martin.

and whisked into the television studio before a live audience during a commercial break. Kroll was one of several fellow guests. Aired on network television as a live broadcast, Kroll was afforded half a minute or so to visit directly with Stuart in an unrehearsed exchange about their time at Lincoln Memorial University.[158] He strode onto the set right on cue, grinning, but his voice was that of an old man, a reedy husk of its once rolling timbre.

Other aspects of life were not as pleasant. The strains of silence and personal differences on Harry and Nettie's marriage were beginning to ravel their relationship. Sadly, the tension was not new. Nettie had always been taciturn, and had became sullen over the years as her husband quietly stepped out on her. One of his means of adjusting to her silence was through writing. Someone reading his work with a critical eye might look carefully at the vibrant, "corn-silk"-haired young women of his stories to see what qualities and features he idolized in women. Nettie seems to have had none of them. As early as his nostalgic *roman à clef* story, "Honeymoon Summer," published in 1940, he draws word pictures of Nettie's quiet character in at least veiled terms, but the distance between them remains visible. She is Olivia in *Share-Cropper* and *Lost Homecoming,* his last literary novel to appear in print (1950). Nettie is portrayed there with something less than affection, a passive wife who appears only as a timid background character, while the action revolves around the narrator's brief affair with a childhood flame during a visit to his hometown. In "Soddy and I," Harry retreated further into their past to introduce her character, still passive and almost emotionlessly stoic. In that story Nettie is the schoolmistress to whom the main character is initially indifferent but eventually courts and resolves to marry. She is brought only slightly closer to the foreground in "The Golden Years," the story written about his brief career at Lincoln Memorial University. In this treatment the marriage itself is described as flawed. Harry's seemingly unfulfilled craving for passion and vivacity—evident in his paperback books and a long string of discrete peccadilloes—began cropping up visibly in the treatment he afforded his wife. His longtime publisher Bobbs-Merrill finally realized how closely the problems in his marriage were spilling out onto the page. In turning down both "Golden Years" and "Soddy and I" in the same letter, Harry Platt laid out the issue with candor. "No matter how well superficial characteristics and physical descriptions may have been altered, Miss Olivia is a very real person indeed. If she is alive, . . . she is almost certain to recognize herself and, because of the great honesty with which you report your feelings about her, almost equally certainly to feel her privacy has been invaded." Harry's self-vaunted "integrity" as a writer in some respects merely reflected a fundamentally selfish, emotional callousness which plagued him throughout life. His publishers knew this too. "It would seem to be best all around if you concentrate on fictional treatments of subjects of which you are not an immediate, active part," Platt admonished. "You do your best writing when you are not too close to your situations and characters."[159]

After Nettie's passing, Harry would write their sons that "I have thought many a night about her, trying to decide what manner of person she really was at heart" since "I have only the most fragmentary statements as to what went on in her mind and emotions." Though he could name the clues throughout her life, he never seemed to understand that Nettie craved stable relationships that she never had as either a child, a young woman, or married wife. "I think her real unhappiness dated from about the time of the sale of the Cabin to the movies," Harry finally admitted to his sons and himself, "I think she thought that success took me from her. I know once she said, swallowing her tears, 'If it's going to take you from me I hope you'll never amount to anything.' I only thought of such writing success as I've had as taking me from no one, only adding me to something I always wanted to be." He may never have understood, nor tried to understand, either her or himself.[160] By the time Harry retired as a University of Tennessee faculty member, he and Nettie had been married nearly forty-five years. His retirement would put them back at home and close together at a point in their relationship where they were perhaps furthest apart.

Harry Kroll retired from teaching at the conclusion of the 1958 spring term. He was sixty-eight years old. "Mr. Kroll" was easily the most well known and one of the best-liked faculty members at the small school. The campus student body organization, the All Students Club, afforded him an unprecedented honor when it commissioned an oil portrait of Professor Kroll for the new library under construction. The artist was Paul Penczner, a young Hungarian émigré who had settled in Memphis in 1951 and quickly became the city's leading portraitist. The Harry Kroll portrait was unveiled at its formal presentation to the college during the traditional Aloha Oe, the campus pre-graduation awards ceremony.[161] The portrait was no small honor. In a hundred years of its history, the only other portrait ever commissioned by the student body (and a decade after Kroll's) was of college dean Paul Meek, also done by Penczner. Meek's portrait still hangs in the campus library that bears his name. Though the Kroll family has several photographs of Harry posing with his own portrait, the painting itself has disappeared.

Retirement also meant that Kroll could at last clear his office of the stacks of themes and other student compositions. For years they had seemed to sift in and eddy untidily onto shelves like snow blown between an ill-fitted door and sill. He had been a common sight trudging up or down the creaking wooden stairs of the aging Main Building carrying a deep stack of student compositions to or from classes. He was famous, or perhaps infamous, for the pages and pages of writing assignments he required weekly. Keeping straight the incoming and outgoing currents was a chore often delegated to part-time assistants. Students grumbled that he rarely looked at their work himself, and they were probably correct. What concerned him was that those who registered for his classes keep writing. An overworked or underappreciated writer in class reportedly once asked why he required so much writing from his students when other professors did not. Kroll summed up thirty years of teaching experience and his own literary career with his answer: "I want to see my students as far down the road as they can go when they leave my class," he reportedly replied. "You can't become a writer in ten thousand words, it takes a million."

CHAPTER 4

Professor Emeritus, 1958–1967

Though Harry Kroll had always dedicated himself to writing during his summer breaks from teaching, the change in status from being a full-time teacher to an emeritus professor left Harry without a defined responsibility or employment for the first time that he could remember. He was sixty-seven and retirement looked like a good time to restart his career in literature—an exciting and rewarding prospect without the pressure of regular teaching. The campus had been elevated from a two-year junior college to a degree-granting unit of the University of Tennessee in 1951. New construction that had followed programmatic expansion eased the cramped office and classroom accommodations. Both the new English departmental and campus administrators agreed that Harry was welcome to maintain his office in the old Hall-Moody building, which sat as it always had, directly across Lovelace Street from his house. Maintaining and working in his office of twenty-three years provided Harry with familiar surroundings. It also maintained his distance from Nettie's circle of daily life.

During his first retirement summer, Harry taught a private writing class in Martin for nineteen motivated students. Most were newspaper staff members from the surrounding towns, and a few college-bound students. He was delighted with the quality of work they produced and for a time he began thinking that it was possible to reawaken the spirit of literary excitement which had characterized his classes three decades earlier at Lincoln Memorial University.[1] The experience was rewarding enough that he seriously considered reestablishing his writing workshop. Unfortunately the class proved to be a flash in the pan, the only group of interested writers he was able to gather in the small town of Martin. That few weeks of concentrated effort and direction represented the effective end of his long career as a writing teacher and college professor.

On the other hand, being retired but having an office left Harry plenty of time for what he liked best to do. Between his classes and some new personal writing, during the first calendar year of retirement Kroll concentrated on placing the manuscripts he had on hand. "The Mystery of Mabrey's Mill," "The Golden Years," and "For Cloi with Love," all went out repeatedly. He even pulled out the manuscript of "Men of Empire," gave it a new name, and sent it out again. All of them came back with rejections. Though he had no way of knowing, ultimately only two of the dozen book-length fiction manuscripts he would complete after retirement would ever be published: one was his last juvenile novel and the other a decidedly steamy trade paperback. He and thousands of other writers, including contemporary Tennessean and Pulitzer Prize winner T. S. Stribling, were creatures of an earlier generation. The American popular fiction market by the late 1950s was half of what it had been a decade earlier, and a thin shell of what it had been when Harry was an energetic young writer in the 1920s. "We're positive that, contrary to many critics, the novel is *not* dead, but only dormant," a contact at Bobbs-Merrill wrote encouragingly in what was their last rejection of a Kroll manuscript, the same year that he retired from teaching. "Nevertheless our business office instructs us to pare down our fiction lists to the barest minimum for the next few seasons."[2] In August 1958 the latest in a long round of rejections included a suggestion that he submit the piece to another press that had both a commercial arm and a subsidy business.[3] The entire concept of committing his work to a vanity press was anathema to Kroll. He trusted deeply in the marketplace's ability to winnow poor writing and reward good stuff with purchases. But the simple fact remained that his work *wasn't* selling. If he were to exist any longer in the writers' marketplace, his style, his topic, or his approach, or something, would have to change. Perhaps being retired would provide him the time to figure out what.

A postscript inked at the bottom of a letter to son Robert shortly after his retirement in 1958 provides a clue about his post-retirement plans. "Haven't sold a book yet but I'm trying. Going to start on the Reelfoot night riders for a paperback."[4] Harry had plunged into Tennessee local history for his first post-retirement writing project. During the 1910s a disagreement had arisen between locals living in the northwest corner of Tennessee—who made a spare living as market hunters and fishermen on Reelfoot Lake—and two lawyers who registered ownership to land around the lake, attempting to cut off the squatters' historical access to "their" property. Banding together extra-legally to meet the challenge, the locals formed a group of vigilante "night riders" to answer the legal manipulations. They caught the lawyers and lynched one.[5] Harry's account was a popular version of the story. It went nowhere. He also picked up and reworked a number of manuscripts from his crate of rejects. At the top of the list was "Men of Empire," which got the new title "Empire Dreamers" but still did not garner attention from the half-dozen publishers to which he sent it. Within a couple years of retirement Harry had so tired of frequent rejection that he became concerned

Kroll at the Peabody College alumni breakfast, May 1959. Courtesy of George Peabody Photograph Collection, Vanderbilt University Special Collections and University Archives.

that his reputation itself might be the problem preventing his sales. For a couple of submissions he fell back to using a pseudonym. One of these was the resurrected Reelfoot Lake book. To his second son he confessed that "My Reelfoot night riding book I sent out under Dan's name, and it's been at a New York house 3 months now, and it just might be the thing will go through."[6] It didn't. Otherwise, his retirement year, which he had approached with eager optimism, concluded as perhaps the low point in his career as a novelist. Fortunately, the turn of the 1959 New Year brought with it a pair of honors in the form of invitations. One would allow him to form an important new friendship.

Toward the end of May, Harry took the car, leaving Nettie in Martin, and drove himself to Nashville. There he was one of a trio of writers honored at the traditional Peabody College commencement breakfast. Two other writers with historic ties to the college—former student Jesse Stuart and longtime faculty member Alfred Leland Crabb—were Harry's companions for the day.[7] In 1958 Stuart was near the height of his success as an American fiction writer, with his career as an essayist and writer of memoir still largely before of him. Crabb's fiction, grounded in Nashville, remained popular, though some of his great work remained to be written. Kroll, four years younger than Crabb, and Stuart's former instructor, had the largest oeuvre. The event featured a display of the three authors' published works. For Harry, it represented the first time he was honored as an American literary figure and not chiefly as someone with a recent book. He considered the event portentous, especially because on the heels of this invitation another had arrived. Early in the year Harry had been flattered by an invitation to lecture, opine, hold forth, and otherwise participate at the eighth annual summer writing workshop at Morehead State University in Kentucky's eastern hills. As one who reveled in being in front of a rapt audience of appreciative budding writers, he was delighted to accept. When the Peabody breakfast concluded, he continued by road from the Cumberland Plateau up into the central Appalachian hills to Morehead.

The Morehead Writers' Workshop was already well established. Its driving force and major figure was James Still, who would donate his papers to the school and have a room named for him the following year. Jesse Stuart was on hand as a lecturer as well. Since leaving LMU and Vanderbilt, Still had traveled in Europe and published *River of Earth* to critical acclaim in 1940, then settled into a cabin without electricity at Wolfpen Creek in Knott County, Kentucky. Still was librarian at the Hindman Settlement School, a private institution modeling progressive education and community service, but also an institution dedicated to conserving Appalachian culture. From the mountain quiet outside his cabin door flowed a stream of evocative fiction and poetry that would earn Still the sobriquet "the dean of Appalachian writers."[8] He was a thoughtful writer, whose crystalline prose and poetry welled up like a rock-walled spring, presenting a smooth but not-quite-still surface roiled by the subtle agitation of current in its depths, brimming over the rockwork into a rill. His work could not have been more different than Harry Kroll's.

The 1959 writing conference in Morehead became a reunion for the former Lincoln Memorial writers and they quickly found an ideal venue for after-hours conversation. Still was a close friend of Benjamin and Calia Hicks, both local schoolteachers. She was the aspiring writer; he was the consummate host. After the first invitation the Hickses' home, just out of town on a low rise with a view of the Appalachian hills, became the gathering place for the workshop's literary figures and old acquaintances. Harry joined them there. One of Kroll's longest, most intense, and complicated relationships blossomed between he and Calia Hicks in the summer of 1959.

Ben Hicks's ticket out of the Depression-era Kentucky backwoods had been the U.S. Navy, but the umbilical attraction of the Appalachian hills proved impossible to resist permanently. Ben was from Floyd County, deep in Kentucky's southern mountains. After a stint at Caney Junior College, where he met and courted Calia, he enlisted in 1939. They married and moved to California, where the first two of their five children were born, and in time for him to be drawn immediately into the post-Pearl Harbor mobilization. Ben served as engineer's mate on a succession of ships across the Pacific. Natively garrulous, he earned a reputation as a consensus-building non-commissioned officer who could whip the most troubled engine room into shape. After the war he decided to remain in the service as a Navy recruiter and was assigned the Southeast coast. He met the challenge and a war-borne wanderlust by towing the growing family—three strapping boys and two girls—up and down the East coast in a travel trailer. By 1958 that mobile accommodation had been the family home for over a decade. The tenuous living arrangements were a tremendous strain on Calia, who was never sure when they would move or to where. Her husband's last posting as a Navy recruiter had been at Grayson, Kentucky, within driving distance of Morehead. When his twenty-year hitch with the Navy was up, he compromised with his wife, who desperately wanted a settled existence after two decades of constant motion, and they settled down in Morehead for a formal education.

Benjamin Franklin Hicks was a real man in the days before the term was derisive. He was a gregarious and engaging host, a born storyteller, a glad-hand, hail-fellow-well-met, and sociable to a fault with the school's other male students half his age. He was not studious but got through classes on charm and with the tutorial help of his wife. Older than his classmates, world-wise, tall, and athletically strong, Ben flourished as an informal leader in the virile, sports-dominated college scene; his wife gravitated toward and became deeply involved with the campus writing club.[9] Calia Hicks, short and dark, had lived a mountain woman's life even when beyond the reach of Appalachia's hill shadows. "Kentucky," she would tell her girls with a vein of ruefulness chilling her warm laugh, "is heaven for men and hound dogs and hell on mules and women." Her Kentucky, she implied, was as much a set of gender relations as it was a place. Growing up as the oldest girl in her family, tradition delegated to her the responsibility of raising her younger siblings and carrying on most of the work around the house, while her mother kept the babies and looked after the menfolk. Determined not to be kept down by cultural expectation, Calia had won an education by inches and earned her normal degree before she and Ben married. She held the family together in his shadow as they trailed rootlessly up and down throughout the eastern seaboard during his years as a recruiter.

The pair had settled into Morehead and into jobs as secondary teachers in 1958, just the year before Harry Kroll arrived. The family lived south of Morehead in a rambling old mountain house with a deep porch running the width of its front. In the days before air conditioning and insulation made houses livable in the summer, the front porch served as the living room, and hosting visitors on the porch was perfectly acceptable company manners. In 1959, while the Hickses' sons devoted their evenings to energetic personal pursuits, their oldest daughter Claudia, a shy and observant girl just into her teens, comfortably settled into a corner behind the circle of creaking chairs to listen to these writing men, who were so unlike the men she knew.

Kroll happened upon the Hicks family at a crucial time. The cultural fastness of the central Appalachians was breaking down. The Tennessee Valley Authority had threaded wires and electricity into most Appalachian towns and hollows before the war. Paved roads, telephones, and television accelerated a generational change. Ben and Calia Hicks, beneath their veneer of education and sophistication, retained a solid core of the traditional mountain attitudes regarding social place, gender roles, and propriety, in which they were raised. That culture favored their sons, all of whom were strong, virile athletes. In the postwar mountains, athletic prowess was quickly replacing the cultural position held by the woodcraft valued by earlier generations. Their fourth child and oldest daughter Claudia, however, was among a new breed of postwar Kentucky mountain women who were educated from a young age; influenced strongly by broadcast media like radio, movies and television; and much less bound by the anxieties about the still-rigid gender roles possessed by adults around her. As an adult she recalled that Calia excused her children from household work if she found they were reading—a trait they soon learned to exploit, keeping a book close at hand should they hear her footfall, irrespective of what they might really be doing.

Years later Claudia Hicks recalled that summer of afternoons and evenings on the family porch as Jesse Stuart, James Still, Harry Kroll, her parents, and a few others would come for supper and talk until darkness drove them indoors. The succession of feedings and discussion linked Kroll to his hosts as he struck up a friendship with Calia Hicks. She appreciated the older man's notice of the effort that went into cooking for the group. He had always wanted a daughter to indulge. She craved a sympathetic male figure. Soon he was spending time with her and a circle of female friends between writing sessions. By the time he departed for home, they were deepening their fast friendship.

Perhaps knowing beforehand that he would again meet several of his former students, Harry brought with him to Morehead the "Golden Years" manuscript and allowed at least Still to read it. After doing so Still quietly pulled Stuart aside to discuss the thing, perhaps unaware that that his old classmate had seen it already, but before they could begin a discussion the author walked in and Still broke off the subject.[10] Their reaction suggests that the novel had drifted further from its roots in fact and, like *I Was a Share-Cropper* twenty years earlier, was now far less autobiographical than Kroll considered it to be, but still true enough that the major characters could find themselves easily. Since Harry tended more to paint his characterizations with rouge than to sketch them with pencil, the highly colored narrative did not sit well with those who knew the subject personally.

Harry was also busily flogging work to the young adult market at the same time. Near the first of April of 1959, Harry had sent an edgy story about basketball and a romance between a high school coach and one of his players to juvenile/young adult publisher Lothrop, Lee and Shepard. Beatrice Creighton, the press's juvenile editor, accepted the manuscript subject to some technical editing, insisting that some of the heavy detail about basketball that infected the last pages of the manuscript be cut back.[11] After a name change, the *For Chloe With Love* manuscript was accepted by Lothrop, Lee and Shepard the next week. Thus it was squarely in his mind when he encountered the Hicks family in Morehead. The next summer (1960) Kroll returned to Morehead for an extended visit. He brought with him a copy of this book, his third juvenile novel, for Calia Hicks's oldest daughter. He had commissioned a copy of the basketball story bound in full green leather with a gold-tooled spine. Still in the hands of its original owner, this presentation volume is unique among his works.

Harry Kroll did not teach again at the Morehead Writers' Workshop. It didn't matter. His 1959 summer workshop residency and after-hours socializing with other presenters on the Hicks' porch was sufficient for Kroll to strike up a lasting friendship with the family and with Calia particularly. For several years Harry returned each summer, alone, to stay for several weeks with the family. After the sale of Harry's North Carolina hill property, the Hicks household in Morehead became his summer writing retreat. The tension between he and Nettie at home, and probably his private chafing over his writing career being essentially ignored by both the college administration in Martin and the university administration in Knoxville, left him thirsting for appreciation. In the Kentucky college town his status as a published writer provided Harry the reputational *gravitas* to play the Grand Old Man among the small group of literary acolytes. Kroll loved the attention lavished upon him in Morehead. He soon took to wearing linen suits with crisply pressed shirts, affecting the dress and deportment of the planter class he had hated with passion as a young man. He pandered to the small crowd, petted and praised by a group of Calia's friends who vied for approval and attention as he tutored and encouraged their literary efforts.

With Calia and the two Hicks girls, Harry was more familiar. Soon he persuaded them to drop "Mr. Kroll" in favor of "Daddy Harry." In Calia he found someone else with the sort of literary ambition that had once fired him, someone who had also struggled up from rural poverty, and the daughter he had longed for himself. Despite the difference in their ages—he was seventy, she was in her thirties—she opened up to his attention, which she found completely opposite to the sort of compartmentalized relationship she had built with her husband. The visits to Morehead represented a new idyll for Kroll. "It was the last carefree summer of my life. I felt young and I was happy . . . ," he wrote one former attendee.[12] There in Morehead and among a coterie of Calia's friends and family Harry was once again respected as a writer of importance.

Calia Hicks and Kroll at Morehead State College, Morehead, Kentucky, probably 1960. Calia Hicks papers, University of Tennessee at Martin.

More importantly, he was welcomed into a family that had the strong, active, assured, literate girls he had long ago craved as daughters and which he had written into his fiction for decades.

Calia, in particular, began turning to this new friend for the emotional and personal support lacking in her marriage. Privately, behind a veneer of community propriety and stability, the family was in flux. Ben and Calia's marriage was raveling. He was the social *bon vivant:* popular, eager, and well liked by his high school students and their parents. She and her household were frequently ignored. Her lot in life had made Calia introspective and thoughtful. Though she was an excellent schoolteacher and very well respected in the community, the strongly conservative world of the hills expected that her needs and interests be secondary to her husband's. She was ground between that hard place and the firm rock of her own ambition in the modern world, in which she was a respected professional teacher and emerging writer. The situation reflected something of the lopsided and unlovely domestic relationships Kroll had employed in the six sections of *Their Ancient Grudge* more than ten years earlier. Calia felt trapped, unappreciated, and alienated in her own home. Harry Kroll represented a heady world of literary self-expression and individual creativity, as well as being a confidant that was not part of her local society: a private safety valve for the pressure in her life. Kroll, easily old enough to be her father, contributed to her emotional fulfillment. Little is known about their relationship, but from the scattered letters, a few photographs, some poetry manuscripts, and family memories, it is evident that they shared confidences and emotional intimacies that neither could nor would confide to their respective spouses.

During his summer visits, Calia and Harry spent hours alone together. Claudia later recalled that when Mr. Kroll visited, Calia would call one of the children to accompany she and Daddy Harry on a country drive or picnic several times a week. The boys often were not interested or committed to another activity, so Claudia would frequently be invited along. The trio would depart together, but as often as not, before leaving town Claudia might be dropped off at a friend's house to spend an afternoon after a suggestion that she might find that more fun than remaining with the adults, leaving her mother and Daddy Harry to drive on alone. Harry and Calia walked together for hours in the warren of hollows leading back between the ridges and hills around Morehead, anywhere beyond the paved streets—along the roads shaded by overhanging limbs and sun-warmed leaves, past abandoned homesteads, alongside brooks and fields. They often climbed to a pond on the property at some distance from the house. A lifelong shutterbug, Kroll typically brought along his cameras and photographed Calia occasionally. While they were apart through the rest of the year, letters delivered to his departmental post office box at UTMB or to the Morehead literary club, of which she was secretary, kept them connected.

Wrapped up in his own interests and activities, Ben Hicks was seemingly oblivious as Calia and Mr. Kroll's relationship deepened. Nettie was not. To cover the deepening connection between them and justify the summer weeks he spent away from home in Morehead, Harry offhandedly once joked about Calia being his "bastard daughter." The comment was completely groundless and mentioned infrequently, but it burned like banked coals in Nettie long enough that she began believing the story, widening further the emotional gap between them. Nettie knew of her husband's earlier philandering just enough to not ask questions to which she did not want answers. The Hickses were not welcome in Martin. Following a round of surgery early in the spring of 1961, Calia once telephoned good wishes after Harry returned from the hospital stay. Harry confessed confidentially to his son Dan, "there your maw sat, grim as hell, making something out of it. I think she is convinced this woman is my bastard daughter. I can't change that now, for a mistress would be worse."[13]

There seems to be more than abiding friendship at work between Harry Kroll and Calia Hicks, but no clear indication of precisely what degree of intimacy they shared. After Calia's death, the family discovered a manuscript poem, "The Iron Weed," between the leaves of her Bible, written out in her hand.

I give you this little bouquet of iron weed
In remembrance of an hour with you
At a little white school house with a broken window
Under oak and walnut and hickory trees.
We are saying farewell[,] tho the heart never forgets
I will dream of you in the long winter nights
And the memory of you will walk with me in the sunrise of many days
Tho I pray but poorly, I shall pray for you,
So the love I give you God may share also.
I am old and you are young,
But love knows no years or seasons or ages.
So I touch your lips with reverence,
And give you this bit of ironweed,
Because it is so rude and forsaken and lovely.[14]

Years later her daughter realized that Calia's garden always contained a clump or two of ironweed. But the question remains an open one. There is no direct evidence that either Harry or Calia was the author of the poem, and the relationship implied in it is circumstantial evidence attested by nothing concrete. Even if the poem was his work and accurately reflected a liaison, Kroll was often given to overstatement when he wished to impress someone, and his favorite son Dan was one he always hoped to impress. It is possible that his use of "mistress" was an indication of what *could* have happened given the chance. The reality of their relationship may have been different. For a public school teacher to conduct an affair in a town as small, as closely bound, and as staunchly conservative as Morehead would have been a significant risk which it is doubtful either rational adult would have taken. If their relationship was adulterous, it was both of limited duration and exceedingly discrete. We could assume that theirs was an emotional rather than a physical adultery, and as evidence offer perhaps the only bit of concrete proof to survive. Sometime in the early 1960s Harry sent Calia a poem, "Honeymoon Cabin."

We had stopped beside the mountain road
    to look down at the old deserted cabin.
It was a forsaken spot in the golden winter sunlight.
I remember I looked down at the glow
    on your dark hair,
And the mute thoughts that I could read in your face.
I said, "Can you see yourself spending the rest of your
    life with me in that cabin?"
I remember you were a long moment answering. You nodded guardedly.

"Yes," you said. "If things were otherwise—yes."
"Would you," I asked, "give me a child?"
Once again you were a long time nodding.
"If things were otherwise I would seriously
consider giving you a child."
So the old forlorn cabin by a lost and lonely road
became the symbol of a moment that is still
bedded deeply in my heart.
We drove away in the golden winter sunlight.[15]

The poem and its implied sentiment is certainly not proof of moral innocence, but suggestive nonetheless.

On the other hand, Harry was tremendously proud of the Hicks family's accomplishments and drew them all under his emotional wing. The boys were old enough and active enough on their own that they looked on Mr. Kroll only as a friend of their parents as they blew through the house to one activity or game after another. While Nettie brooded about this younger woman's possible claim on her husband, Harry wrote in a letter to his youngest sister, Natalie, concerning Kroll family history, Harry included a line that "Calia is married and has four children, and she and her husband are both in college. I'll write you more about this branch of the tribe some other time."[16] He referred to his host as "my 'daughter'" in a published account of visiting the Hickses' summer family reunion.[17] In his private letters he employed "Daddy" to close, the same signature which closed letters to his sons, or "Papa" or "Daddy Harry" when signing letters to Calia or the girls. Her letters to him were sent to "Papa" and signed "Baby." Jesse Stuart once wrote Kroll that he would certainly be happy to forward an inscribed copy of a new book to "your daughter," indicating that Kroll had written to him about Calia Hicks in that vein.[18]

Complex personal relationships at home in Tennessee and deep in the Kentucky hills were not the only complications in Harry's life. Just before Christmas of 1959 a letter arrived from a neighbor of his North Carolina property, Gladys Hagglund. Her letter was the first round in a series of events that could have been dictated straight out of one of Kroll's mountain stories. In it she mentioned that their common neighbor Will Glaspy was eager to cut out some beetle-killed trees from Kroll's fallow hill farm above Hendersonville. A few weeks later as Kroll was in the midst of a creative fever, old Glaspy himself showed up unannounced at the Kroll's front door in Martin. Stunned, Kroll invited him in. Over breakfast a reluctant verbal plan unfolded between the two of them for Glaspy to clear dead pines on the property for pulp wood. Harry had planned to visit Son and his wife Nelle in Knoxville in the coming month, and promised Glaspy that he would drive a couple more hours to Hendersonville to see the situation himself. He gave Glaspy a verbal go-ahead. The old man departed for home, having gotten what he wanted. Shortly thereafter Harry's better judgment prevailed and he fired off through several channels clear instructions not to proceed. A visit in April confirmed that the less-than-straight account from the old man had already resulted in two loads of good timber logs cut from the property and some of the land cleared and fenced for the benefit of Glaspy's cattle. Harry's boys collectively felt that Will Glaspy was playing a game, first to get the timber and then the land itself. Harry declined to play and turned the matter over to a lawyer.[19]

Half a decade of summer excursions to see the Hicks's in Morehead left Harry annually invigorated, but he always returned to Martin to face less rosy domestic and literary realities. Since his novel manuscripts seemed to be caught in a ceaseless eddy of editorial disinterest, Harry shifted his output and began again producing stories and articles. By the 1960s there were virtually no important commercial fiction venues left for work of the type he produced. Even the venerable *Southern Agriculturist* had given up being a farm-life magazine to become a farm-operations magazine. Once the magazine had been a chief source of farm-family entertainment, with one story for the farmer, perhaps another for his wife, and short vignettes for children. By 1960 it published a story of any sort only very occasionally as filler, and often not at all. It became effectively a trade journal for the business of farming, much more focused on production than enriching rural life. The editor of one magazine in which short stories once appeared regularly, wrote Kroll plainly about the shift in his business. His publication represented most publications of the same type. "We, as you may have noticed, have abandoned 'culture,' pass-the-time-away, and so-what type of material. In other words, we don't want any stories . . . [with] which the reader can pass the time away but can do nothing about. If there are enough facts to challenge other communities and tell them how they can do the same thing, then we would like it."[27] Harry was also not a science fiction writer, another of the few surviving fiction genres. He was unable to break into westerns, despite repeated efforts. About the only remaining markets for the "boy-meets-girl" stories he knew best existed in the "slicks," the generic, middle-class national lifestyle magazines that were more interested in other themes. The one short-fiction market in which did he manage to place stories tended to be the sort of magazines sold from behind counters or that were mailed in plain brown printed wrappers. But because they bought his stories, that was the market for which he chose to write.

By the time he had retired, Harry had discovered the men's magazines that cropped up like weeds in the otherwise straight-laced 1950s. Hardly a literary genre, these new magazines nevertheless blended Harry's longtime interests in photography and fiction with nubile young women and sexual conquest. Presumably he kept this sort of reading material out of the house and out from under Nettie's certainly disapproving eyes, but he shared them with two of his sons. Because titles like *Gent, Modern Man, Mr.,* and *Swank* represented a potential new market for his work, such publications turned his attention and writing interest in a new direction. After the war Harry had reestablished a modest publication presence in the old Sunday School fiction venues, but these high-paying magazines would forever pull at his attention, and their preference for subjects would color further his penchant for romantic subthemes in novels.

In May 1960 Harry had written *Male* magazine with a story idea for a fictionalized piece of West Tennessee folklore. With the Civil War centennial the next year, war stories were good. Harry's tale involved the relationship between Confederate cavalry commander Nathan Bedford Forrest and one of his female slaves at the Civil War battle at Johnsonville, Tennessee. By mid-July it was in draft form and sent to New York. The magazine wanted an extensive rewrite, which the author was only too glad to do. Regrettably the new version did not impress the editor at all and the magazine chose not to encourage the author further. Another story idea went to *True* and then *Saga,* both men's adventure magazines, with a rehash of the 1887 Tolliver-Martin feud idea he had proposed elsewhere the previous year.[20] Harry even attempted to interest magazines in a story about college cheating.[21] Finally, after several revisions and late in December, the story involving Nathan Bedford Forrest was accepted by *Male.* The payment of $225 was dramatically more than he had received for similar work decades ago.[22] Prices were substantially higher because magazine publishers had become much more selective about what they bought to populate the pages of progressively fewer magazines. The corollary, however, was that they also paid much better for the work that was accepted. This broad, deep shift in the industry could be seen even in markets as staid and seemingly unchanged as the juvenile sectarian papers. Kroll received $600 on a serial story for which, twenty years earlier, he would have once gladly accepted a tenth the amount.[23]

Even as he wrote poetry for Calia, banged out occasional fiction for men's magazines, and worried over his hill farm, Harry made time to write, but good story ideas were becoming scarce. With only occasional success selling his work to prime his creative pump, ideas came less frequently. With no cosmic issues before him, no social axes to grind, he gave up writing serious novels. By the time Harry retired in 1958, his attention was focused on the American paperback markets. The cheap productions had far more niche publishers. Their wares included plenty of stories with rollicking passion, comparable to what he loved in his works. Even so, his effort went nowhere. "Corpse in the Hearse Ahead," a mystery known solely from two rejections in 1960, was probably the one Kroll was hard at work upon during the imbroglio with Will Glaspy over the timber on his North Carolina hill property, but it was not the only failure.[24] Harry even reached across the ocean with a hope to restart his career as a novelist. He submitted "Wind in the South," to the Hutchinson Publishing Group in Great Britain just after the start of 1960. Harry was more confident in this than his other recent work and asked that this manuscript to be considered ahead of an earlier submission, "A Debt of Honor," which was a western. Hutchinson had a strong hold in academic titles but also had several imprints producing trade publications as well. One of these was John Long Ltd., which had produced the British editions of several earlier Kroll titles. "Wind in the South," Harry described to Gerald Austin, was a story growing out of legends around Nashville and Murfreesboro after the Civil War. "The issue" in the book evidently addressed the social problems of what to do with freed slaves during Reconstruction. The British editor turned down both submissions a month and a half later. Kroll had woefully miscalculated his submission. A story about the U.S. Civil War "will be a difficult one to put over in this country," Austin wrote, and "there is a certain lack of drama for the English reader." Hoping for a different response, Kroll responded by commissioning Curtis Brown Ltd. to represent him and shop his work to other publishers in England.[25] His own round of U.S. publishers was no more successful. About the only constructive comment on any manuscript came from Vanguard Press, which was emblematic of Kroll's late-career appeal. Vanguard called Kroll's story "a vivid and difficult-to-forget picture of reconstruction days in the South," but noted "it certainly won't be easy to find a public for it."[26] The editor was correct.

Kroll labored at "a manuscript for Dell," a paperback publisher, through 1960. Initially the manuscript was cumbersomely titled "Watchman, What of the Night," which featured the relationship between the main character (a night watchman) and a host of brutish supporting characters, including the sexually eager mill-owner's daughter, in the southern Alabama pine woods. Whether or not Dell looked at the pages, it was accepted for publication by Ace Books in mid-December 1960.[28] It appeared on shelves as *The Brazen Dream* in April 1961, and represented Harry Kroll's last book-length work of fiction ever to see print. According to data on a single surviving royalty statement, Ace Books printed 104,037 copies of the paperback. Calculating sales from the figures given on the sheet, only 14 percent of the books—14,563 copies—had sold through that date. Of the thousand dollar advance made by the publisher, $796.11 was still outstanding fourteen months after publication.[29] Meanwhile, hoping to follow *The Brazen Dream* with another paperback, Kroll quickly knocked together a second story with a similar setting and submitted it to Ace. "I have just written the last page, 173. It's a good story. The same setting down around Mobile as the last one. Back in the timberlands," Harry wrote his son Robert in January. Probably spooked by the lackluster sales of *Brazen Dream,* Ace was unwilling to risk anything more on Kroll titles and never published another of his books. The editorial department generated a printed-form rejection for the second manuscript, which arrived in Harry's mailbox around mid-March without a note of explanation. He was crushed.[30]

Oblivious, still convinced of his salability, and with manuscripts once again flying all over the country, Harry needed some constructive personal distraction. Before Christmas 1960 he wrote to his older brother Charles (Soddy) in Birmingham, renewing contact that had been infrequent or nonexistent. Charles wrote back, with pencil, as he always did, in the cramped but legible hand of one who had lettered architectural drawings for years. Soddy had retired, his wife had passed away, and there were no children. With the line reestablished between them, the brothers began writing occasionally back and forth, but never met again. Their only contact remained their infrequent letters and Nattie (Natalie), their youngest sister.

Soddy's letters were not the only sign of age. Sometime in January 1961, Harry noticed that an itchy spot on his upper back was also discolored and slightly raised. Since it would not go away he made an appointment to see Joe Priestly, a local family friend turned dermatologist. During the last week of the month Dr. Priestly identified the growth as a melanoma and urged Harry to have it removed soon. On February 1, Kroll drove from Martin to Union City, where the mole on his back was removed.[31] More melanoma sites were discovered, requiring additional work. Harry spent a good part of February and March in and out of the hospital, either preparing for surgery,

Robert Torrey and Dan with their father, 1958.

in surgery, or recovering from it. Though no one knew at the time, the cancer had already spread more deeply and widely than was recognized. The melanoma was serious, though how serious he would not realize for several more years, since there were more significant, immediate problems facing him at home.

With their boys gone and only the two of them in the house, there was no need to hide the strain between Harry and Nettie. Nettie began feeling an odd pain in her innards around the time her husband had begun planning his retirement in 1956 or 1957. By 1960 the pain was a persistent force. To make matters worse, as the pain became sharper and more constant, she began to medicate her pain with alcohol, a coping mechanism growing from being terribly afraid of doctors and hospitals. Almost as if the will of her denial and the alcohol would push the symptom away, she refused to investigate the cause. Instead, the pain worsened; therefore first her desire and then the need for relief increased. She drank more, and drank more frequently. Like her father, she declined steadily into alcoholism. Though he had once been a teetotaler, Harry himself had settled into genteel imbibing, a habit which was dragged downward by his wife's own slide. Harry later confessed to his sons that their evening drinking strained to breaking the remaining affection the couple may have felt for each other. If intoxication at least dulled the pain of the malady that ultimately claimed her, it also loosened the mutual inhibitions that had kept their marriage on an even keel for decades. The alcohol provided the opportunity to dredge up old hurts. Through the years her even temperament had been ballast to the household. Harry, however, had been blind to the importance of that stability for his career.

Passionate himself, his preference for character development often involved the vicarious creation of similarly passionate female characters. "Your maw has never been a wife," Harry wrote Dan with a chilly clatter of typewriter keys in April 1961. "She's lived with me and born children, but being a wife is a different thing. I won't try to define it, but you'll know it when you have it." Harry once described his wife in a story setting as "secretive and with no more humor than a fence post."[32] Such an unflattering characterization, which appeared more frequently in his novels in later life, could only have driven the cold tooth of a wedge more deeply between them. Now, as she writhed with the pain that had become a more faithful companion than her husband, those hurts were brought to the surface. Slights, thoughtlessness, and all the small inconsiderate acts of a long marriage were dragged out anew and flung down like gauntlets between them. "Not too long before she laid down and died," Harry finally confessed to Son, Robert, and Dan a few months later, "we both were in our cups . . . and I said 'Somehow I guess you just got the wrong husband.' And she said bitterly, 'Maybe you married the wrong wife.' You would think that after fifty years of marriage, in what is known as serene old age," he wrote with a wistful pang, "two people would have another set of remarks to make about each other. It filled me with sadness."[33]

Nettie held herself together until the first week of May. By then even Harry could tell something was wrong. He sent her to bed and took on household chores himself. "I'm going to keep her there two or three days and then if she doesn't get better from bed rest I'm going to put her in the hospital and find out what ails her. Part of it I am sure is psychological," he wrote their youngest son. Nettie's condition was not psychological and there was no improvement. Finally, her physical constitution wrecked, Harry drove Nettie twelve miles to the Obion County Hospital in Union City, where Nettie was admitted on May 12. Perhaps he was shocked and remorseful when a physician came to tell him that her pain was not at all psychosomatic. Two days later she lay unconscious, a consequence of acute hepatitis as first her liver and then other organs shut down. At 9 a.m. on May 15, 1961, Hattie Annette Heard Kroll passed away, eight days short of their fiftieth wedding anniversary.[34] Harry left no record of his feelings upon learning only after her passing that the pain, which he dismissed so easily yet had been her most faithful companion, was due to metastatic cancer that had slowly and painfully eaten into her internal organs.

Despite the recent bitterness between them, Nettie's passing left Harry empty and very alone for the first time in his seventy-three years. She had not wished to be buried in Martin, so Harry Jr. drove to Martin from Knoxville to ride with his mother's body back to his home. She was buried in the Edgewood Cemetery, close to the high school where Harry Jr. taught physics, on the brow of one of the Tennessee hills overlooking the river that make up the city. Back in Martin, despite the lively student scene across the street at the college, the Kroll house was empty, uninviting, and falling slowly into disrepair. Craving the company of youth and vitality, Kroll spent as much time as was practical reading or writing in his retirement office across Lovelace Street in the Administration Building. He developed a habit of sitting back in a chair at a stairwell window outside his office, silently gazing out over campus, watching students walk between classes and perhaps looking for a new story idea in a loner or a couple or a group.

Concerned about his well-being, Ben and Calia Hicks brought their family to Martin from eastern Kentucky for a visit in the summer of 1961. Harry put them up in the house and for a week reveled again in the welcome imposition and routine noises a family made. The Hickses returned leisurely to Morehead, arriving to find that a letter from their recent host had beaten them home. Dan, Harry reported with some worry, had been in a serious automobile accident just as they had left. Though thrown through the windscreen by the impact (these being the days before seatbelts and automobile safety glass), his injuries were miraculously limited to a badly gashed face.[35] Concerned about his son's own downward spiral into what he feared was becoming alcoholism, complicated further by the latest in a string of Dan's unsubtle adulteries, Harry could only hope for a miracle and expect the worst. He piled into the Buick and drove to Maryland in October to visit Dan and his wife Evangeline. Their household was a tense emotional wreck and Harry could not even stand to stay. "I'm at my wits end about him," he wrote Robert upon returning home. "I still feel I have done wrong by him, running out on him. But that stuff there was killing me."[36]

Both Dan's marriage and his life were raveling quickly. "There is nothing sacred about a marriage that has gone sour," Harry wrote his son with conviction the following spring, offering a somewhat hypocritical list of advance suggestions for his next marriage. Harry drove himself to Washington, D.C., again in January, 1962 and tried to help Dan collect himself and his belongings prior to the pending divorce. A week after returning to Tennessee he received notice that Daniel Wesley Kroll had died February 10, 1962. It was not automobile-induced; a decline into depression complicated by alcoholism had been the cause. He had simply shut down. Dan had appointed his father as executor. His favored son's passing was perhaps a deeper blow to Harry than Nettie's had been the year before. He was not in a personal position to do much about Dan's unsettled affairs from nearly a thousand miles away. As the family member closest to Dan's home in Maryland, middle son Robert Torrey Kroll handled most of the immediate, practical arrangements in discovering outstanding debts and settling the estate.[37]

His wife was gone, his sons were grown and gone, one now dead, and his career was only slightly more than in shambles. Harry had busily but unsuccessfully hawked book manuscripts for two years, not only to publishers across the country but also to publishers across the Atlantic. By 1962 he admitted to Son that he had given up "commercial writing, unless it's a paperback of the kind I enjoy writing."[38] But even his tales of lust and carnal passion did not sell very well, leaving him hollow and despairing about his abilities. There was more. Still pondering deeply about the quality and sum of Nettie's character in the second year after her death, he wrote to Robert, "I wonder why I have never been able to see the side of her she showed to a great many other people—her church friends, you children."[39] There was no comfortable answer for him.

It was perhaps as a way to look for an answer to the riddle that was his wife that Harry again dug out and began again to revise his "Golden Years" manuscript, which concerned teaching at Lincoln Memorial in the mid-1920s together with Dan's birth and infancy. In April 1962 Harry spoke at a writing conference at the University of Chattanooga where he stayed as a guest with former LMU student and now English faculty member Roland Carter. For part of his conference talk he again fetched out the opening pages from the "Golden Years" manuscript. After hearing it read, Carter extracted a promise from Kroll to give him an opportunity of reading the full manuscript. After reading through half of it, he wrote Kroll with praise. Spurred by his former student's professorially positive criticism, Harry began seriously revising the manuscript yet again in May. Part of his immediate loneliness was eaten up as this story spilled out from his memory. Dan had been born during his Lincoln Memorial idyll, and his passing spurred Harry to re-approach the fictional account of the time to make it emotionally truer. But so close to his wife's passing, one of his major character-development challenges became integrating Nettie's inscrutable emotionlessness in what, to him, had literally been his golden years. In the interest of literary value, and probably revealing more than he cared to, Kroll eventually succumbed to portraying Olivia in the manuscript as more lively, emotional, and involved than she had been in life. Neither the memories nor the writing came easily. "I'm moving toward the end now, the most difficult part of a book to keep sustained and interesting," Harry mused to Robert. "I'm all messed up with Maw's visit, and your Mommer's and Maw's feudin, and my anguish. Doesn't sound very golden, when you think of it."[40] While the liberal use of dialogue was entirely contrived for the benefit of the storyline, details remembered independently by other family members suggest that the general unfolding of events and other factual data seems to have been accurate. Except for the altered characterizations, the resulting story was essentially rewritten as a *roman à clef*, a story related factually with only the names changed.

Kroll and University of Tennessee, Martin Branch English departmental faculty in his final year of teaching, 1957. Mildred Payne sits at right. University Archives, University of Tennessee at Martin.

But nothing changed, really.

Since he had not published a substantial novel in years, Kroll was skittish about submitting new work to the major New York presses, but initial publishing inquiries for the newly revised "Golden Years" manuscript were promising. After a few new rejections, Kroll reached far afield and sent a query to Alan Swallow of Swallow Press in Denver. Swallow said he would accept the manuscript if he liked it personally, but on no other condition. Kroll sent a carbon westward and waited. Harry dismissed vanity presses on principle, but probably banking on Swallow's acceptance Kroll decided to put aside $1,750 from Dan's retirement payout and life insurance settlement against the chance that the book would have to be handled by a subsidy publisher. Aging himself, Swallow failed to return the manuscript, write back, or even acknowledge Kroll's letters. Like so many authors, Harry never did hear back from Swallow and finally gave up on the loss of that carbon.[41] There were other editorial nibbles as well as Swallow's, but no one willing to bite. "It's been to 18 publishers," he wrote to Robert toward the middle of the year, "but surely there is a place for a book as well written and intelligent as [this]. I'm doing the unethical thing and doubling up on submissions [i.e., sending the manuscript to two or more at the same time]. I'm going to stay with it till I exhaust the possibilities. . . ." By May 1964 Harry reported to his son that "The Golden Years" had been to twenty-four publishers.[42] It was probably at that point the possibilities had been exhausted and the sheaf was permanently shelved, though as late as March 1965 Harry still held onto a slender thread of hope that the manuscript might see publication.[43]

His personal losses—half his immediate family in less than two years—brought the past into sharper focus, although the outlines were blurred by memory and emotion into something that was more imagined than actual. He tried to compile a book of family remembrances but eventually gave up on the project. It troubled him that he could remember few points about the family's life together that qualified as memorable. With evident melancholy he noted that, consumed with his teaching load at the junior college and absorbed by his own production of salable writing, he had missed out on his own home. The possible consequences of his affections being distracted by a string of mistresses and affairs was ignored without mention. "My thoughts are a stampede of vague longings, of memories, of thanks that I am living, of grief for those who are not," he wrote his two surviving children at Easter.[44]

That sense of family loss and incompleteness finally may have been cathartic for his long-distance relationship as well. Probably during or just after his last extended visit to Morehead in the fall of 1962, Harry and Calia Hicks finally realized that continuing their relationship on the level both wanted was flatly impossible.[45] Harry was too old to offer her a measure of long-term stability; she was too dependent on the small securities of her world with Ben to risk being the one to initiate a divorce. Their intimacies were essentially over, but she and Harry Kroll remained close friends. For a couple more years Harry still visited in Morehead for occasional excursions, limiting his visits to a week or two. They were always happy, productive visits for him, but the drive across Kentucky to Morehead was becoming burdensome. To compensate, Kroll retreated into his memory, continuing to work at "The Golden Years" occasionally among his other manuscripts, tweaking and polishing the narrative and description. Despite the effort, he could not bring it to a state with which he was satisfied.[46]

After 1964, as Harry's relationship with Calia Hicks cooled from intimacy to friendship, and with eye trouble dramatically curbing his driving, Harry did not return to her Kentucky's hills. He was living the lesson he had laid out in what may have been the best short story he ever generated. In "Second Wife" he explored the emotions and opportunisms of older people who marry the young.[47] Now it was he who faced circumstances similar to his opportunistically lecherous Dennis Sawyer of the story. Calia Hicks represented an unattainable ideal of youth and hope.

On the other hand, age had its compensations. Life was markedly slower as a retiree than as a working professor, and it now afforded time to devote to personal interests. He continued to dabble with photography, and often took long weekend day-trips driving through the rural countryside of northwest Tennessee and western Kentucky. Kroll maintained a schedule that allowed him to lecture at workshops and attend professional meetings as frequently as possible in and around the state. After his 1964 summer trip to the Hickses for instance, he taught for a week at Austin Peay University in Clarksville, Tennessee. At the Tennessee Philological Association meeting in Memphis later the same year, he presented a paper entitled "Stuart the Student." honoring Jesse Stuart. Travel, however diverting, did not fill his empty house when he was at home, and when he returned from the Hickses' or the camaraderie of a professional meeting, it was still empty.

With Nettie buried far away in Knoxville and between the occasional summer idylls with the Hickses in Morehead, Harry entertained thoughts of remarrying. He curried a stable of eligible local women in and around Martin, but hesitated making or even discussing the big step. Instead, he shuttled indecisively back and forth across the street from his home on Lovelace Street and his office and typewriter in the old Administration Building on the UTMB campus a few steps to the west. "I always go back to my old wood house and cook my grub and sit and eat my lonely beans, and think 'this is bad, but it's nothing like it could be if I got my hooks on the wrong woman,'" he confided to Robert.[48] Loneliness proved to be only temporary, however. At another Tennessee Philological Meeting in Memphis, Harry took a fancy to fellow attendee and former departmental associate Mildred Payne. Mrs. Payne's husband, a Presbyterian minister in Sharon, a smaller town a few miles south of Martin, had passed away at about the same time as Annette Kroll. She held a master's degree and occupied an associate professorship in the English Department that Kroll previously chaired. Harry had hired her. There is no indication that any impropriety occurred during their departmental service together, but both found themselves in different circumstances four years later. Around Thanksgiving Harry hosted a small house party with Mildred Payne invited as his guest and dinner partner. "From then on it's built up fast as hell," he informed Robert. She was fifteen years younger than he, around sixty. Their relationship deepened in a few months to the point that Harry agonized about asking her to marry him. They must have discussed the matter, because ultimately the couple decided that their separate family obligations were too entrenched and dissimilar to disrupt merely to begin a new marriage. However, to stave off loneliness, the pair established between themselves what he described as "a gentleman's agreement to look after each other," sharing meals at least twice a week and making weekend drives through the countryside. Through the rest of his life the two were frequent traveling companions on research trips and to professional meetings. Harry referred to Mrs. Payne as "the secretary" forever after.[49] Mildred Payne and her close friendship represented something more mature and fulfilling than the desperate closeness he had found with Calia Hicks.

Certainly, having a committed lady friend close at hand breathed new interest into life, and Harry began casting around for a new angle or writing topic. Fiction required too much effort and had become uninteresting for him. Short stories in the rural themes he knew best had no markets to speak of. That left non-fiction, which represented a rather large field.

Bobbs-Merrill had responded with positive interest as early as 1958 when Kroll had floated an outline of Kentucky's "Black Patch" tobacco war.[50] Robert Penn Warren had written a novel *Night Rider* (1939) on the same subject. The book Kroll had in mind was also fictional, a treatment of the Kentucky tobacco growers' violent attempts between 1904 and 1908 to break the strangulating monopoly held by James Duke's American Tobacco Company. Once they got a look at a rough outline for the book, Bobbs-Merrill was no longer interested, neither were other presses he approached the same year, and Harry dropped the project. Ace Books got the next look at the outline and sample pages and determined that "the entire mood of the novel is basically dated. . . . It tends to boil out as being a rich-against-poor novel, a class conflict thing, that is out of keeping with the literary moods of this year, though it would have been all right in the Thirties."[51] With no encouragement, Kroll probably relegated the outline and sample chapters to his box of unsold drafts. They eventually landed at the University of Kentucky Press in early January, 1961.[52] Editor Bruce Denbo liked the idea and wrote that he would be willing to accept the proposal from just the samples, but that the press's academic board would probably quash an acceptance based on its incompletion. Kroll replied hastily the day Denbo's letter arrived with an important explanation of his perspective on writing. He mentioned that he had hewed carefully to the factual line but decided not to add the trappings of academic writing—notes. "I wanted to do more than just write a factural [*sic*] history of a very important historical matter. I wanted to add a third dimension of artistry to the writing," he explained. "I did keep asking myself, 'what will the scholars think of this?' I respect those boys without being one of them. I'm a *creative* writer."[53] Though the University of Kentucky Press ultimately decided the book did not quite fit its criteria, seen in retrospect, the press's interest was encouraging enough that it acted like one billiard ball grazing another, a slight impact which sends the first caroming off on another vector. "I believe that the book would just about pay for itself over a period of time," the editor wrote. Harry's long-buried social conscience, coupled with the prestige of the genuine academic nature of the press, nudged Kroll's attention into a slightly different trajectory, away from historical fiction and toward literary non-fiction.

A year after the University of Kentucky Press had passed on the book, Harry dusted off the idea and submitted the story outline and sixty-page section of sample pages for a manuscript to be titled "The Black Patch Tobacco Wars" to Macmillan in April or May, 1962. He returned from a trip in early July to find an acceptance. "Here I've been going around muttering in my beard that as an author I was washed up, and out of the blue comes this offer of a contract and [an offer for] a $1000 advance," he wrote Robert gleefully. "Of course I have to finish the goddam book, this being only 60 pages and an outline. But that's a small thing."[54] Harry cheerfully accepted a first advance installment of $250 and set to work.

Through the summer of 1962, depressed by the pain of Dan's death that spring, he dawdled daily over his few tobacco-wars pages, filling out the sixty pages into a respectable draft manuscript. In July, Harry drove into Kentucky to do site research in Louisville and then to read the extant manuscript to Calia at her home in Morehead. The travel justified making a side trip to see Jesse Stuart at home in Greenup. A quick stop in Hopkinsville to see trial transcripts in the courthouse on the return journey brought more source material. By August he was home again, cranking out between six and nine pages of text daily. The draft was complete by mid-September, but he hung onto it while some permissions queries remained outstanding, and waiting to see if any ideas for additional sections popped into mind. It was still in his hands late into October, essentially complete but "at that stage when I don't know what the hell else to do to it. I'm just keeping it around because I have till the first of the year to send it in, and maybe I'll think of something to improve it."[55] The ream finally went to the publisher before the end of the month and he sat back impatiently to wait.

Waiting for word, without a writing project at hand, he was taken by a general malaise: "Right now I am idlesome, disliking the thought of writing some short stories, wanting to write a paperback that sprang to my mind and not wanting to get involved with another book. I eat too much and sleep too much, and am lonely. The old house is just as empty as it was in the beginning."[56] To make matters worse, his mornings began with blurred vision that would often simply go away during the day. While he was composing on the typewriter he might also drop in sentences full of nonsensical words. This, too, often simply cleared up on its own.

While Macmillan chawed slowly on the tobacco book, Harry made plans to spend Thanksgiving of 1962 in Morehead with the Hickses, not wanting to drive as far as Maryland to see Robert's family and not wanting to trouble Son and his wife, Nelle, as they completed construction on a new house in Knoxville. As ever, he thoroughly enjoyed the visit to Morehead, though the undercurrents of sadness and discontent were becoming evident between Ben and Calia. At Christmas she wrote Harry, telling him that Ben was talking about leaving but was hesitant to put the family through a divorce.[57] Harry, aware of how the substance of his own marriage had evaporated slowly over the years, hurt for her. In the spring of 1963 a box of Dan's personal effects arrived in Martin, which included the books the father had presented to his youngest son. With Harry Jr. and Robert secure and distant in their young families, Harry felt more deeply alone than he had ever experienced before. The depth of his feeling for his "bastard daughter" can be seen as he re-inscribed to Calia personally the copies of his books once presented to Dan, perhaps the deepest measure expressing how important she had become to him.

Some time in late December or in January 1963, the tobacco war manuscript came back from Macmillan with suggestions for revision. While he could normally pound out revisions in a couple weeks of good work, the historical fiction piece required slow, painstaking work to keep factual errors to a minimum. "It's often cutting, reshaping, putting this in one place after taking it from someplace else." Kroll reworked the entire manuscript and sent it out without much hope before February was half gone. By this time the title had been changed to "Riders in the Night." Macmillan reluctantly returned a rejection on the revision in March with encouragement to submit it elsewhere. Fortunately they did not ask him to return the $250.

By this time, revisions to the early drafts of *Riders in the Night* finally broke the impasse he had experienced over writing short stories. For the first time in years he began cranking out short pieces, submitting his work, and actually selling it, to the surviving juvenile magazines and story papers that still published fictional work, most of it the moral encouragement venues that had changed hardly at all since his youth. "I relearn what I have known two-thirds of my life," he wrote to his second son, "when I produce and peddle I build up my income."[58] Harry still trusted firmly in the writing marketplace and could not see or refused to believe how it had shriveled and contracted. Had he looked at his own sales records he would have noticed that despite his recent success selling short fiction, he was selling only a fraction of the pieces he once had. Since writing was no longer his only means of support, as it had been three decades earlier, he could be content with what money he could make.

Beyond this moderate success with short fiction there were larger creative works, flavored with a trace of bitterness, still in him. In letters to both sons Harry reported in the first week of April 1964 that he had finished "my COW COLLEGE book." The novel, "Cow College Call Girl," was destined for the paperback market. It was a send-up of Kroll's time at the University of Tennessee Junior College in the way that "The Golden Years" had initially been a treatment of Lincoln Memorial University, although he admitted that "the events are purely fiction." He drew heavily on the characters of faculty and administrators he had known at the college. "I put old man Allan in it, and Buck Meek [college Dean Paul Meek], and Maw [Naoma] Green and Myrtle [Phillips]—properly disguised, of course; and I put in myself and sundry other characters, including Dan [Kroll's youngest son] and Evangeline [Dan's wife]." This last-named individual, whom Kroll despised heartily for her divorce of his favorite son, probably provided the title character. "I had myself a good many hearty laughs writing it," he told Robert. "If the sex doesn't scare off editors the thing may sell." [59] His off-handed "if" was an accurate assessment of the manuscript's chances, even in the morals-loosening Beatnik years preceding the Summer of Love. The manuscript never sold, but the work was probably as much a catharsis for the emotional ghosts of his junior college professorial career as it was a serious effort at writing. It was turned down everywhere. A rejection came so quickly from Ace (nine days) that Harry confessed that "I really have lost confidence in it. But so I have in other books, and I keep sending them out."[60]

Meanwhile, Dr. John Hodges, a retiring professor of English at the UT campus in Knoxville, arrived for a visit in Martin. Hodges worked for the university's development council as the coordinator of library development. In the early spring of 1963 Hodges made the branch campus in Martin one of his stops as he toured the state, drumming for any sort of material that would help build the college library at Knoxville into a humanities research institution. One of his stops was a courtesy visit to Kroll's home across the street from campus. Flattered by the attention, Harry rummaged through his box of manuscripts. Hodges returned to Knoxville with the printer's copyedited manuscripts for *Darker Grows the Valley, Share-Cropper,* and *Their Ancient Grudge,* making them among the earliest genuinely literary manuscripts acquired by the institution. Two years later the library would also receive the copyedited pages for *Rider on the Bronze Horse* and *Rogue's Company,* and finally—after publication in 1965—the *Riders in the Night* manuscript as well.[61]

Shortly after Hodges's visit, the small Philadelphia trade publisher Thomas Yoseloff Inc. got an opportunity to consider the tobacco story draft. Yoseloff liked it, but not as a novel, and fortunately he wore two hats. In his separate but coincident responsibility as director of the University of Pennsylvania Press, early in November 1963 Yoseloff offered to publish the book provided Kroll would cut and rewrite the manuscript to treat the subject entirely as non-fiction. Since Harry had stuck to the history, not inserting fictional characters or events this time, the revision was not difficult. "It's a prestige book and the Univ. Penn. Press is a prestige house," he admitted, "and I've said too many times I'd settle for prestige if I couldn't get too much cash." In discussing illustrations, Kroll noted that he had several photographs and additionally sent along as samples a small group of family Christmas cards he had illustrated. He offered to illustrate the book himself with pen-and-ink drawings if the press was interested. They were. After some discussion, they agreed that Kroll would supply not only five illustrations, but also the title page, jacket, and marginal sketches as well.[62] At about the time Harry Kroll hosted the party which connected himself and Mildred Payne, the book had gone to press.

Mildred Payne's companionship coincides, perhaps not coincidentally, with a renewed personal interest in poetry on Harry's part, a form of creative writing he had ignored since his younger days. Whatever the relationship between he and "the secretary" involved, she certainly seems to have stirred a sense of nostalgia in him which was reflected poetically. It was only after their renewed acquaintance that he began writing poems frequently for the first time in nearly forty years. Having neither outlet nor market for poetry, he sent some of it to friend Paul Flowers of the Memphis *Commercial Appeal,* who published a piece occasionally in his daily column on the paper's editorial page. The occasional poem buried in an editorial column was hardly sufficient reward for someone who expected to see his work sell more frequently than it had. But at least the *Riders* book was complete, because Harry and Mildred Payne were already deep into another project, the book which would proved to be not only his last work but also completely out of character, unlike anything else he did in his career.

In the spring of 1960 Kroll generated a query to Joanne Pavincich of *Argosy,* asking if this, the last surviving American pulp story magazine, would be interested in a "jovial satire" of whiskey culture around the distilling center of Bardstown, Kentucky. In his letter to *Argosy* he used an alliterative phrase about "belles, bluegrass, and bourbon" that would be worked into the title of his last book. That story proposal went nowhere, but it awakened his interest in the colorful bit of regional Americana which he would pick up again to better profit a few years later.[63] Based somewhat on his 1960 query to *Argosy,* in 1963, quite on a whim, Harry began writing to various distillery firms around Bardstown and made a number of contacts within the industry there. The queries were intended only to gauge their interest and possible cooperation if he were to write about the industry. To each he asked for their cooperation or suggestions. The responses were encouraging, even flattering, and as always when encouraged, Kroll was hooked by the topic. Harry and "the secretary" Mildred made a research trip to the Kentucky Bluegrass region and to Bardstown specifically, the center of the distilling industry, in June 1964. Though she did not drive, Mrs. Payne lived up to her nickname, handling the appointment calendar, and typing and keeping organized the notes of the interviews Kroll made with the distillery management. By mid-July he had been home long enough to draft the first six chapters of a book.[64]

Upon returning from another trip north and eastward in September he found in his mailbox a contract for the book from Thomas Yoseloff. "I fell all over myself signing and returning [it]," he wrote Robert with pleasure. A few weeks later he soberly noted to his son that this book would be his last. "If I ever get hold of another bear like this by the tail I am to going to turn loose and run like hell. I never dreamed when I got into it that it would involve so goddam much work—and all dealing with people." Though Harry had handled classes, lectures, and conferences for years, the constant interviewing, notes, and parties held for him were a burden. "It reminds me of the old days as a picture man when I used to go into a new community to hit 'em up for pictures" he grumbled to Robert.[65] Still, there was little about which to complain. The distillers were genuinely flattered by professorial attention and Harry was treated like royalty wherever he visited. When Mildred Payne could not accompany him on the second trip through the distilleries in September, one of the firms paid his entire round trip on the railroad, put him up in Louisville's best hotel, and fed him ceaselessly on fine fare. Other than this excursion, most of the rest of his research was handled by correspondence.

Though both trips were just plain fun, the rigors of the road also underscored how old he was getting. "For the first time," he wrote Robert, "I am beginning to feel my age. I may fool people who speak of how young I look, but you can't fool the calendar, not for long." Harry feared that long-distance travel on his own could become dangerous, and his summer trip to see Calia Hicks and her family in Morehead in 1964 proved to be his last. His sight blurred with inconvenient frequency on the Bardstown trip. Most of this he passed off as age, undoubtedly forgetting (or perhaps misunderstanding) his melanoma. In fact, the cancer had been invidiously sending corruptive tendrils through his back, neck, and into his head. "I feel fine but my eyes—my left eye—gives me trouble. My eyes blur at the typewriter and I make lots of mistakes. I find too that I am growing forgetful. . . ." Reluctantly he decided that declining vision meant that his days of making long drives were over. Driving had been one of his personal pleasures for half a century, and he refused to quit without planning one more Kentucky trip with Mrs. Payne for the bourbon book in the closing months of 1964. Because his eyes presented serious trouble frequently, even that trip was eventually cancelled.[66]

There were other telling brushes with mortality. The previous December, Harry's youngest sister Natalie wrote to report on a visit to Charles in Birmingham. Soddy had holed up in his house, unable to make ends meet or care for an ulcerated sore on his leg, but still obsessively buying books. He managed to hang on in his frigid, cluttered house for another year. A week before Christmas 1964, almost exactly a year later, Nattie wrote to tell Harry that Soddy had died in Birmingham of a heart attack at eighty-one. "Soddy and I were once very close," he in turn wrote to Robert soon after. "Then for 30 years I have not seen him and have had few letters from him. I sat a few moments after reading Nattie's letter and tried to grieve. There were no tears for the ancient memories. Just a numb kind of sadness."[67]

Even as he worked on the whiskey book, alternately writing and hunting photographs, and by now seventy-seven himself, Harry was coping with his own increasingly frequent health complications. After the 1965 New Year turned he wrote to Robert about his condition. "I'm with the best specialist in this section and he assures me my eyes are healthy. I find my mind also is slipping. I just can't remember. Oddly enough when I go to the typewriter I find the flow of words comes almost like always; and there would be a lot of comfort in that if I could see to type."[68] New glasses eventually helped his vision tremendously, though they could do nothing to help with manuscript sales. By the middle of the year, tired of writing unsaleable novels, disgusted with fluffy moral stories for the Sunday School papers, and lacking the energy and resources to travel, Harry needed some sort of recreation beyond dinners with Mrs. Payne and watching Nettie's untended flower beds go to weed. After some thought, in the spring of 1965 he began digging through his crate of rejected manuscripts. Like a faded athlete reliving glory days by going through game photos or polishing trophies, Harry turned to his writing for solace and began dispatching his old novel manuscripts one by one to publishers around the country, without any editing or further work. It was not a desperate gamble; he was simply bored and did not have the energy to stir up a new book. Whether or not he acknowledged it, he was turning to the market one final time, hoping that the sale of a manuscript or two this late in life would validate his skill as a writer and reassure him it had not dimmed, that he was still relevant. "They come back," he wrote Robert in Maryland, "usually with a rejection slip; rarely a letter, except from the big houses, where they respect my title of Emeritus Professor of English. . . ."[69] Within a year he had cycled through the stack, all of them once and some several times. Nothing sold. Many were committed to the trash without another glance when they returned.

By now Kroll's interest in photography ebbed and flowed around particular subjects. He was far too disconnected from college students to resume figure photography of the type he preferred. He could no longer drive safely to scout landscape photos. The yard was rough and beautiful in the spring, but close-up photography had never been of interest. He had drawn occasionally but not seriously for years, yet as his eyesight deteriorated, Kroll decided to begin painting. "I have taken up Art oil painting. . . . My plan is to paint pictures for Christmas gifts. . . . My eyes stand up with the brush when they wouldn't with pen-and-ink." "I don't want to write—I'm fed up with writing. I can't sell any of these fiction duds I have, and getting up another non-fiction makes my eyes water worse." He produced a few canvasses and admitted candidly to his son that "they're not exactly awful, but one is close to it."[70] From memory he painted a cabin for Jesse Stuart and mailed it to him. Photographing several of his favorite paintings, these he made into Christmas cards, enclosing a print of each in a preprinted folder.[71]

He continued to work on the stack of material for the whiskey book. "At last I've got off the whisky book materials—manuscript and pictures. I have one more little batch to mail and I hope to do that tomorrow. I had a letter from the publisher this morning. He says he is most anxious to have all the materials in hand. I still have misgivings somehow. When you've had as many disappointments in writing as I have—as well as successes—you somehow run scared all the time. But I have a hunch this book will have sales," he wrote Robert with pride in November 1965. It went to Yoseloff in a massive eleven-pound box of manuscript and photos. Once it was gone, Harry settled back into a malaise and wrote his second son despondently: "With all this work off my hands I now am idle and I'm lost. I hate the thought of writing Sunday school trash. But I have sold a couple [non-fiction] articles with pictures."[72] Slowly he was discovering what the market had been trying to tell writers for a decade, that "nonfiction is so much easier to sell than fiction tha[t] my one regret is that I have not been messing with it for years."

A few idle months later, needing some diversion beyond the records he had played dozens of times, and having purged his file of unsalable manuscripts, he and Mildred Payne decided to work on a book together on a topic that interested both of them, the Pinson Indian Mounds south of Jackson, Tennessee. "You remember our visit some summers ago to the Pinson Indian mounds," Kroll wrote his son Robert in May 1965.

> It dawned on me that there is a book in those piles of dirt. I'd often thought in terms of a mystery fiction, but fiction is so hard to sell and nonfiction apparently relatively easy that I now think of a non-fiction, still with emphasis on the mystery. A deep one is there. I've got some dope and plan to gather some more, and Mrs. Payne and I are going down and get a fresh eye at the place, and methinks I'll address my genius to this project. She's going to do the dull research and I'm going to do the dramatic authoring.[73]

Kroll and Mrs. Payne dabbled for about a year, working on the project just enough to keep it alive while they tripped around the state to professional meetings and weekend dinners.

Life was not quite as bleak as his letters painted. At the suggestion of former student Jesse Stuart, Kroll wrote to John Gilpin of Economy Press in Ashland, Kentucky, in late 1965, inquiring about printing arrangements for a small, privately published book of poetry, illustrated by his drawings. "It would be at my expense, of course. But I have located a one-man print job spot who does nice books at a reasonable price—100 copies cloth for about $250; and I really would like to bring out a collection of the better things I have written over the years."[74] The "better things" were primarily poetry pieces, including some of the illustrated poems done in the 1920s, together with poetry that he had produced over the years for his own pleasure. It is doubtful that the book was actually produced, though the title "Foxfire" appears in a list of Kroll's books in the front of *Mounds in the Mist,* published after his death by coauthor Mildred Payne.

Otherwise, writing, which had defined his life and driven him for nearly fifty years, provided his emotional and professional center, and perhaps wrecked what happiness he might have extracted from family life, was genuinely falling away and he finally let it go without regret. Family correspondence and a smattering of poetry, when a thought came, was about all that dripped through the typewriter.[75] Declining eyesight was the chief reason for its drying up. "These damn eyes of mine!" he wrote Robert in frustration. "The left is pretty much gone for good. Right is normal. I do my seeing with it."[76] "If I cover my right eye it takes a moment for even a dim image to form in the left. It is mottled, very unclear. Sometimes it is clearer than at other times and then be dam if my whole vision isn't worse, for the eyes don't focus together and the dim one blurs the good one."[77]

In December 1965 Harry determined to get some answers about his declining vision. He desperately feared that the loss may have resulted from a small stroke, and that a larger stroke might be in his future. Three days of tests put that fear to rest, but the medical staff concluded that in the socket behind the eye a cyst or tumor was putting pressure on the optic nerve. After a Tennessee Philological Association meeting at Carson-Newman College north of Knoxville, the staff at Baptist Hospital in Memphis put Harry Kroll through skull surgery to remove a cancerous mass behind his left eye in mid-March 1966.[78] Preparing for this, Harry rewrote his will to include Mildred Payne and had the publisher assign royalties accruing from *Bluegrass, Belles, and Bourbon* to her. He also provided a sum for Calia Hicks should she attend graduate school. The collaborative project on the mounds was shelved during his eye surgery in March 1966, but from the hospital Harry penned a note to Robert that "when I get home I'm going to help the lady love cook up a book on the Tenn. Mound Builders."[79] Fortunately, the surgery was successful, but Harry faced the stark inevitability of mortality as the pathologist also identified the mass as melanoma and confirmed its malignancy. He had time left, but not a lot of it. While he was recovering Harry wrote to Son saying that sight was coming back and that he was feeling well, but "all at once I realize I'm an old man."[80]

Based upon Harry's own experiences and the small amount of research Mildred had already compiled, through recovery and the summer he worked on the "Mounds in the Mist" manuscript. "The whole mess fascinates the hell out of me." "The readings on prehistoric redskins I've been doing keeps me entertained many hours of evenings, when I used to brood and bellyache."[81] Work on the mound builders book ground to a halt during the summer of 1966. The temperature in Martin soared and Harry puttered and fretted around the house while Mildred Payne spent six weeks of the season in Memphis, completing some coursework at what was then Memphis State University. By the time she returned to Martin to begin school in September, Harry was pleased to tell his second son that merely two chapters of the book remained to be written. Another letter in early October reported that the book was done and needed only to be shopped around to publishers, although Harry was still borrowing books (perhaps for Mrs. Payne's research) as late as February 1967.[82]

Late in the autumn of 1966 a seventy-eight-year-old Harry Kroll was chipper enough, and seeing well enough, to finally buy himself a new car and to insist that Mildred Payne buy one as well—then learn to drive it.[83] He also commissioned some badly needed repair work on his aging house and took half a dozen of his paintings to exhibit and discuss before the Tennessee Folklore Society meeting at Cookeville.[84] It was his last conference participation. In late November 1966 Harry sent the mound builder book to A. S. Barnes & Co., expecting a rejection. When that came, he reasoned, the manuscript would perhaps go to the University of Pennsylvania Press, as had *Riders in the Night,* and if not accepted there he would begin his rounds of submissions to any press that might show promise. Instead, just before Christmas he reported delightedly to Robert that Barnes had accepted the book immediately but that they wanted a large number of illustrations to scatter through the text. That process entailed an entirely new round of research work. Many of these illustrations Kroll culled from his own photos, taken during a number of trips to the mounds made over the years with his sons and with Mrs. Payne.[85]

Unfortunately his eye began troubling him again that fall; the orbit enlarged rapidly and began sending irregular twinges of pain into his head as he read page proofs for the whiskey book.[86] By November it was evident that the cancer was spreading rapidly and could not be slowed. Harry's doctor was talking about removing the left eye entirely, merely buying Kroll mortal time against the malignancy, but a December visit to his doctor in Memphis cleared up the symptoms of pain and swelling. Kroll took off for a talk before the Press Club in Louisville, Kentucky, to generate interest in the forthcoming publication of *Bourbon, Bells, and Bluegrass* the following March. He was pleased to see his long-time champion, *Commercial Appeal* columnist Paul Flowers in Memphis, who still thought him figure a significant enough to discuss in terms of Kroll's twenty-year-gone contribution to the Southern Literary Festival and to the education of Jesse Stuart, another personal favorite.[87]

The Louisville trip was his last trip over the road. Harry declined quickly during the late spring of 1967. By May 15, x-rays taken by his physician identified the cause of breathing problems and chest pain: the spreading, invasive malignancy had almost completely appropriated his lungs and was quickly spreading deeper into his chest. The next day Kroll went to the Union City hospital, where nearly a quart of fluid was drained from one lung. That procedure, coupled with three heavy prescriptions to stop the fluid's recurrence and additional medication to curb nausea, left him physically wrung out. The doctor suggested surgery, but at seventy-nine Kroll knew that at best he had only a thin chance of surviving. Family and friends began making plans for the inevitable. "All we have is time and your dad's great will," Mildred Payne confided to Robert.[88]

In fact, even as Mrs. Payne wrote to his second son, Harry had barely a month to live. Mrs. Payne drove him to and from the hospital in Union City as necessary, and despite carrying her full course load at the college, became Kroll's nearly full-time caretaker. Between classes and office hours she would cross the street to fix meals and ensure that medication was properly dosed. Friends and neighbors also brought in meals, often remaining to sit and talk as he was able. Kroll weakened steadily as the combination of cancer and medication wrung energy from him. He spent his days on the living room couch, able to move weakly between there, the bathroom, and the dining room table. He could not have written more if he had wanted. "I may be dead when at last royalties show up," he had once grumbled about *Bluegrass, Belles, and Bourbon* to Robert. He was prophetically correct. Kroll received his advance copies of the book, his last completed work, on May 26, two weeks before his death.[89]

It was not a lingering finality. On June 11, 1967, on a clear day in what the sharecropper's boy and Alabama tramp photographer once would have called "laying-by time," Harry Harrison Kroll finally succumbed to the cancer.[90] Harry Jr. came home to Martin from Knoxville for the last time, to accompany his father's body. Two days after Kroll's death a hearse carried his body to Knoxville—Harry finally got out of Martin, Tennessee. He was buried immediately upon arrival after a brief, small memorial service, and was interred beside his wife and Dan in Knoxville's Edgewood Cemetery. Former LMU student Roland Carter drove up from Chattanooga for the interment, almost the only attendee besides Son's family.[91]

What was left of Kroll's legacy as a writer was slim. Harry had purged himself of the lingering ghosts of inefficiency by discarding in the preceding two or three years any of his remaining novel manuscript that would not sell—which turned out to be all of them. Harry had desperately wanted the campus in Martin, which would become the University of Tennessee at Martin a few months after his passing, to hold onto his papers and establish a memorial "Kroll Room" like Murray State University had done for Jesse Stuart and Morehead State University had for James Still. But the Martin campus was unequipped to handle such a gift. There were no rooms to dedicate. The school's first free-standing library building was dedicated only after Kroll's passing. The growing student body crowded into every available corner. The remaining jumbled collection of tear sheets and short-story manuscripts Son and Mildred Payne could gather were dispatched to Memphis State University by Harry Jr. in 1967.

In his last letter to Robert Torrey Kroll, written May 15, 1967 on the morning of a cancer consultation, Harry had noted that the mound builders book was essentially complete. He had decided that if his cancer prognosis looked bleak, the manuscript was sufficiently developed that he would simply pack up the materials and forward them to the publisher, with Mildred Payne's name listed as coauthor, "though I really wish she had done more authoring and less co-ing," he grumbled. Due to complications discovered at that consultation and following several days of varied treatments and side effects, Kroll's physical condition worsened rapidly and the book materials were never shipped. At Kroll's death the book manuscript, photos, and captions were still at his house in Martin. In the disposition of the estate Mrs. Payne committed to carrying the project forward and eventually produced a work of curious coauthorship published two years later. *Mounds in the Mist* stands as his last published monographic work, and her only one.

CHAPTER 5

Harry Harrison Kroll as Litterateur: Lessons

To be considered great fiction, it is said, a story must illustrate or reveal something truthful and universally timeless about the human condition. Harry Kroll understood human circumstances, but rarely and perhaps only accidentally did he lift his eyes from the metaphorical furrow behind his rural plough to squint dimly at larger truths. Kroll saw writing and literature chiefly in the terms almost any poor boy does of opportunity—in terms of money. He preferred to write voluminously rather than exquisitely. Writing was a craft like blacksmithing or business like cotton ginning, not an artistic endeavor. As such, profit required volume, and he generated volumes primarily for the income they promised. Throughout his career he followed what he knew best, and fed the market what he thought it wanted.

Harry Harrison Kroll was a writer who angled for the popular markets. There is little of the self-absorbed, philosophical artiste or literary refinement about him and his stories. Therefore, there is also little point in comparing Kroll with better-known contemporaries in Southern fiction. Kroll would perhaps have liked T. S. Stribling, Frederick Faust (Max Brand), and Cristel Hastings who wrote for the popular press of the day, but he heartily despised high-literary contemporaries like Erskine Caldwell, William Faulkner, and the Agrarians (especially Allen Tate, though he rather liked Donald Davidson). He felt they placed craft above plot and emphasized artistry over experience. Kroll was quite willing to twist and adapt facts and setting to create a fictional story. He felt that his better-known contemporaries were, like Tate, either "nostalgic . . . pretty, one-book aristocrats"; or as with Caldwell and Faulkner, that there was "nothing real in what those people write."[1] Today, as graduate schools tend to teach about literature by studying the work of important individual writers, that expansive economic sea in which most readers and most writers swam, is nearly forgotten and usually ignored. The national popular-fiction markets that have survived have shrunken chiefly to science and fantasy and erotic magazines.

If Harry Harrison Kroll lacks Literary significance, then why present a biography? What do writers of the Kroll variety offer to the study of literature? The key reason is that his career in pulps and story papers reflected one of the circular relationships identified decades ago by Frank Luther Mott: "popular literature—the newspaper, the magazine, the best-seller—has a special and paramount importance because it is popular."[2] In this short concluding chapter, allow me to summarize two broad themes involving minor Tennessee novelist and short-fiction writer Harry Harrison Kroll and his work, which I feel are worth defending.

The first point is that so long as writing and literature are published, literary scholars will do well to explore not merely the linguistic aspects of a writer's art but also their broad economic and social contexts as well. Literary scholarship seems to remember only occasionally that literature is a marketable product in an extensive industry and not merely or even substantively a style or form of expression. Writers driven solely by the need for expression tend to be unpublished. With that in mind, Harry Kroll is emblematic of popular writing during the first half of the twentieth century. Kroll's medium was not in the Literary realm but rather in the vast mainstream of popular literature. Never a significant figure in the American marketplace of books and ideas, he was one of the vast body of other writers whose drops of individuality filled a market-sector ocean of ink. During his lifetime the literary world existed in a constant flux as periods, tastes, and market opportunities reflected dramatic social and economic changes in the real world. Of high culture, critic Fred Lewis Pattee reminded "serious" readers of Kroll's time that "fiction is a fashion that changes often and without apparent reason." Kroll himself was not a high culture or *belle lettres* writer, but rather a writer for the "common condition," via the low-brow venues he knew as a youth. In this Kroll was in good company. Jack London and Willa Cather wrote serials and stories for the popular press well before their careers took off. Of Booth Tarkington, one of the most important turn-of-the-century writers, Pattee himself could only observe, with barely disguised condescension, that Tarkington's legacy was as a "purveyor of entertainment to the commonalty [*sic*]—not a bad achievement, but nevertheless an achievement destined to bring nothing save temporary emoluments."[3]

By the time Kroll began writing seriously, the Roaring Twenties, the Decade of Literature, had begun. No one can over-emphasize the value of experimentation with literary forms that characterized the 1920s. Progressivism crumbled. Its optimistic, expertise-based assumptions did not appear on the Great War's casualty lists, but optimism died even as the speakeasies roared and cheap credit and new factories piled goods higher and higher to bury fear and doubt and dissociation. Paul Hoffman noted that "writers of the 1920s, finding a world that seemed cut free of the past, had to invent new combinations of spirit and matter and new forms of expressing the human drama. They were not aided by any secure ordering of social or religious systems."[4]

Harry Kroll in his natural environment—at his office desk and typewriter, 1949. From the jacket of *Lost Homecoming,* Corbitt Special Collections/University Archives, University of Tennessee at Martin.

It was in the wide-open 1920s that Harry Kroll became a novelist, and if the idea of time and circumstance as literary influence holds true, it should have affected him most greatly. But Harry Kroll had already developed his approach by then, and it had nothing to do with this new sophistication. Writers' sentiments turned toward skeptical, consumeristic modernity far more rapidly than most people recognized. Lynn Dumenil noted that "nineteenth-century success stories posited hard work, sobriety, thrift, and restraint as the keys to personal and business good fortune. And invariably the success in mind was that of the old middle class—material rewards, civic virtue, and personal autonomy[—the kind of stories Harry wrote]. By the 1920s there was a subtle shift. Reflecting in part the popularization of Freudian thought, an important theme became the subconscious, which one writer described as 'an infinite storehouse of intelligence and power' that man could draw upon to 'supply his needs and wants.'"[6] Popular literature and advertising would have readers believe that by exerting enough directed energy, one could will one's way to success in the 1920s.

The reality was that Harry Kroll was nowhere near the cutting edge of 1920s literature. He associated with no literary circle, studied with no practicing writers, and disliked the work of most of those who did not write at his social level. Harry Kroll identified himself as a realist. He viewed himself as less a Southern or Appalachian writer than a writer of rural experience. As a writer, Kroll tended to compose his work in the popular styles and venues that he knew personally—the Horatio Alger fortune story, the romantic novel, and the Sunday School character (morality) tale. Into this he injected the personal experience of himself or others, sometimes idealized but almost always rural, as a framework on which to drape his plots. It worked for awhile. By 1919 Alger's hard-work, up-from-the-grass-roots, formulaic optimism had died in the Belgian mud and on the bayonets of Verdun. The shallow pools of go-get-'em optimism of the 1920s evaporated in the blazing heat of the Depression. Magazines, with a few exceptions, provided escapist reading and no longer pretended to be serious literature. In the world of books and novels it was far worse. "A generation debauched by war was expressing itself in fiction. And there had come novels overloaded with sex, with coarseness, with the logic of futility," mourned one contemporary critic. America was striding self-confidently toward the banal, middle-class consumerism of Sinclair Lewis's *Babbitt.*[5]

A restive, eager, and aspiring middle class was growing out of industrialism, and it looked to reading material to tell it how to act and what to believe. Historian Joan Shelly Rubin observes that during the Gilded Age and after the First World War, adopting a refined literary sensibility was a key development in the creation of an American middle class and in the concepts of gender and race that solidified into structures on which society could prop itself. For a nation and generation which had just industrialized and urbanized, literature and writers were beginning to ask serious questions about what "opportunity" meant in social terms. Harry Kroll was one of these. Rubin misses one important implication of the shift, for in terms of reading, the development of middle-brow literature represented an attempt to move from the working-man's fiction of the story papers toward reading content that would demonstrate competence and literacy worthy of a stake in society. Middle-brow literature became a literature of social and economic aspiration.[7]

Harry Kroll's writing, steeped as he was in the formula fiction of the late nineteenth century, tended to reflect the older literary, class, and gender models with which he was familiar, even as he picked up themes of education, progress, and sophistication. However, even he began to draw upon the new themes of character for character's sake: stories in which the focus shifts toward fulfilling an individual's rise within corporate structure, to "marshal one's innate ability through exercise of will." Joan Rubin argues that the enormously popular Book of the Month Club stands emblematic of the change. Comprehending one's culture and increasing one's market value and social standing could be fostered by reading good books. Rather than reading widely and choosing books oneself, the club offered a shortcut to sophistication by selecting what sophisticated people would be reading. In this way club participation "promised to cure the floundering self's social distress by enabling subscribers to convey the instant and favorable impression required for success in a bureaucratic, anonymous [modern] society." Having worked his way up by dint of labor, just as his characters typically did, Kroll could never quite make the transition to the new frame of reference.[8] He never aspired to status as a high-brow *litterateur;* at best his early work qualified as "middle-brow," and frankly some of his late work was positively salacious.

Though he was a product of his time and place, Harry Kroll never experienced the cultural or emotional disconnection of the First World War which characterized the Lost Generation, nor was he culturally attuned to the unrealistic, socially conservative aspirations of either the decidedly non-agricultural Agrarians or the Confederate Lost Cause myth being created in Nashville during the 1910s and 1920s. Harry's stories were studies in immediacy. There was no moral chaos tearing at his world, requiring re-creation and renewal. His stories were about personal issues: selling walnut logs from the ancestral land; the romantic opportunity in photographing a pretty neighbor for a magazine; marketing the virtues of stone-ground meal; neighbors working out a longstanding disagreement over a property line; pursuing a small-scale business opportunity; integrity; opportunity; and family. Though he wrote in the Southern and Appalachian regional milieus, Harry Harrison Kroll's choices for themes and settings, reinforced by the markets in which he published most of his work, make his *oeuvre* much more closely tied to the idea of rural existence than to distinctly Southern literature. Earlier in his career he wrote fortune stories about young men and women energetically "on the make"; as an older writer Kroll's short stories hinged on the motif of the returned lad, one who has left the farm and returns to it following an education or business success. Someone might argue that in this Kroll exhibits the Agrarian influence of anti-modern wistfulness. It would be more correct to argue that his work is closely associated with the fortune story of popular literature, melded with the very real sense of dispossession that afflicted rural Southern counties, as children after the 1920s moved off their parents' semi-subsistence farms and into towns to pursue jobs as clerks, lawyers, mechanics, construction laborers, and factory hands. In Kroll's stories—virtually all the ones written after World War II—the returnee typically arrives at the home-place without having made his fortune, but often finds that the family smallholding contains a hidden asset of value (coal, placement on a rail or highway through-way, old-growth timber, stone-ground meal, or its picturesque qualities), or discovers that the gangly neighbor girl has grown up fetchingly lovely.

Conversely, because his early novels are strongly autobiographical it could be claimed that Kroll's fiction had always been historical, yet he himself acknowledged that most of his actual writing was only inspired by and thus only loosely based in fact or on a particular place or theme. His work completing Clifford M. Sublette's manuscript for *Perilous Journey* in the early 1940s seems to have shifted his attention or changed his focus as a writer. After this point, Kroll's published manuscripts are tied more closely to factual historical events, though he still took decided liberties with narrative and action, and occasionally introduced additional characters. Focused on place, setting, and circumstance, his literature concerned conditions and opportunity. He criticized opportunism but lauded opportunity. Kroll wanted to be a best-selling author on his own literary terms as a self-contained writer. He seemed to pursue his craft uninfluenced by contemporaries; at least he does not mention them in correspondence or what little of his class material survives. Kroll's effort went into finding a voice, crafting a tale, and selling the manuscript of the moment.

Since the value of writing lay with income rather than in artistic expression, Kroll used and reused characters and settings unsentimentally if a story idea could profitably employ them. For instance, Kroll created a stock character, Uncle Jesse Leverage, who, with his wife Rachael Leverage, appeared as a main character throughout Kroll's pulp stories of the 1920s and '30s. Dennis Sawyer, one of the major characters in Kroll's best-known short story "Second Wife" (1936), also appears in "Solid Through and Through" in a juvenile paper from 1954. Lumber boss Ramsey Turner, a character in Kroll's steamy 1961 *Brazen Dream,* had been featured in 1954 in the juvenile story "For Men Must Work," and had first appeared twenty-one years earlier in "The Good Will Tree."

Settings and other borrowings were also lifted straight from his own experience. "Negative Yes Men," published across two issues of *Try* early in 1941, is a virtually transparent explication of Kroll's own experience as a junior college English instructor, though with an idealized ending, much different than his own situation. Occasionally he might get additional mileage out of reusing the story itself, as he did in "With a Feather in His Hat" and "Old Men Remember." Both stories involve brothers who fought on opposing sides of the Civil War: while visiting a battle site years later they learn that the near miss each vividly remembers actually involved the other—one had fired a shot in a close-fought battle that had creased his own brother fighting in the opposite camp.

The luminescent and somewhat naïve quality to Kroll's short fiction feels entirely absent from his novels. The published novels were written later in his career and for different venues. Many of his novels revolved around themes of the social consequences of poverty in the rural South, a topic he knew from first-hand experience. His settings were typically among the desperately poor sharecroppers in the Mississippi flatland, and the stereotypical blood-feuding mountaineers in Appalachia. His adult characters, even in his Sunday School fiction, tended to be coarse and desperate. There is no

Southern gentry in his writing, and not a hint of tragic nobility in the Southern myth would he have its descendents believe. Those who belong to the monied classes are as libertine and grasping as the desperately poor individuals who constitute most of his characters. Kroll's books are edgy studies of rural figures confronted with or caught in the maelstrom of social class and change. His plotting usually involves one or more rootless characters afflicted with a sense of conflict between opposing obligations to which they aspire or owe allegiance, neither of which may be entirely abandoned nor yet fully integrated—competing families, tensions between social classes, or personal aspirations conflicting with duty or opportunity. Margaret Mitchell's luminous evocation of survivors and martyrs among an utterly imaginary Southern gentry proved far more compelling and socially useful in twentieth century America than Kroll's gritty drawl and in-fighting among neighbors.

Prior to 1927 Kroll was able with some regularity to place work in the second tier of American literature and the core of pre-television popular media: the monthly and biweekly thematic pulp magazines of publishing companies like Street and Smith. Perhaps because of his rural cultural realism, Kroll's writing rarely placed in the national magazines, especially the nation's four most significant venues: *Harper's, Collier's, Saturday Evening Post,* and the *Atlantic.* When the popular demand for casual fiction began drying up under pressure from attention (and recreational discretionary cash) paid to the new media of radio and movies, Kroll's work was close enough to the margin of the publication market that his essentially rural stories were unable to compete for the reduced amount of available story space. Effectively, his work was pushed out in favor of stories that appealed more directly to the reading interests of the increasingly urban consumer. The rural farmer of the mid twentieth century could no longer subsist on a mule-powered smallholding. As a boy Harry had lived the last few years of America's chop-cotton, pine-woods, mountain-fast rural life. As a man, he saw the Agrarians idealize a mythological past of decency and character, but also saw each writer of that group set philosophy aside for Modernity's urban sophistication and conveniences, which produced and marketed their literary conceits. Even in its violent and ugly characters, Harry Kroll had portrayed rural life nostalgically, and the fundamental condition nourishing nostalgia is irretrievable loss. What was left of rurality was by 1960 dominated by commercial agriculture, which was itself a cog or spring in a national economic machine. The literature that informed agriculture had to change as well. It left him dry and frustrated.

Sadly, certain of his *ability,* Harry Kroll never understood the importance of the thematic point, the timeless quality of good literature. Harry Harrison Kroll did not fail at writing; he simply did not succeed at it. His conventionality as a writer and his rusticity as an imagist tied him, despite his technical skill, to the markets of a time that was passing even as he was beginning his career. Focused on breaking in to a market he threw dozens of manuscripts at editors until his work was accepted or he grew weary of being ignored—evidently without studying the market at all. He was myopic in some ways, writing what he wanted and expecting it to sell because of his very real technical ability, rather than looking at a market and seeing if his style or topics needed to shift to fit it more effectively. His nearly thirty books and nine hundred published pieces of short fiction and essays were the moderate triumph of an earlier time and rural past in a modernizing American popular literature.

The second important concluding point concerns the notion of influences on writers. Using Kroll as a focal figure, this point involves the emergence of a modern Appalachian literature. To some extent, scholarly study of the region's recent literature has assumed the Agrarian influence on mid-twentieth-century Appalachian writers in perhaps an unintended teleology: James Still, Jesse Stuart, and Don West attended Vanderbilt, *ergo* their teachers' approaches to literature and language shaped their respective approaches. Scholars regard the Agrarians as literarily important, the reasoning goes, therefore they must also have been influential in their time. Scholars have perceived what they expected to find. With the assumption made, the question then became how that assumed influence was reflected in the language, style, or subject matter of the first group of "modern Appalachian writers."[9] This approach to studying literature privileges the influence of language over other, often larger and more immediate influences on a writer. The overemphasis of language in studying literature is one of the traps inherent in postmodernism, which has become almost a default interpretive setting in higher education in the early twenty-first century. We have gone looking for traces of influence and have shaped our analysis around that search. Admittedly, Stuart himself was profoundly grateful for Davidson's stylistic criticism of "Elegy for Mitch Stuart" and for taking him seriously as a creative writer. But was that an Agrarian influence, or was the encounter (and others like it) merely a beneficial criticism of craft by a more experienced critic and writer? I would argue strenuously for the latter. Theme and approach are often solidified far in advance of stylistic polishing.

This book does not presume to replace the Agrarians with Harry Kroll as prime literary influence on the trio of writers that have been called the "headwaters of modern Appalachian writing." Rather, this study has tried to provide an example of broad, non-literary issues of "significance." I take a position that analysis of influence, motivations, and thinking of writers and writing should be more broadly inclusive, not limited to ideas. This biography provides examples of non-literary but demonstrable historical influences on Kroll's LMU student trio (chapter 2). The ideas and language of literature is only one influence on a writer; economic circumstances of a given moment are another; the vague but real abstractions of personal preference cannot be left out. Using Stuart as an example of this sort of inquiry, Davidson's effect was to polish Stuart rather than to shape him. Stuart shaped himself into a writer well before meeting Davidson at Vanderbilt, by self-directed reading of Robert Burns and Thomas Hardy, his longing and drive for a literary existence, and his deep emotional attachment to the Kentucky hills and the images around him. Later encounters with Kroll, Davidson, and national editors only refined the expressions of what he had developed on his own. Davidson's key contribution to Jesse Stuart was to encourage him to think in terms of markets for high-culture literature rather than the popular literature of Harry Kroll, or the "little magazine" movement of tiny, literary niche publications. Thus, we would do well to ask what *besides* literature influenced writers like James Still, Jesse Stuart, and Don West—who only later in their careers came to be considered Appalachian writers—rather than accept Agrarian influence as an article of faith and examine *how* that influence was manifest. It makes for messier biography, but a much more human and rewarding understanding of writers and writing.

Harry Harrison Kroll was among the last writers of the generation that produced the half-century high period of American popular literature between 1880 and 1930. His career spans two of the three major shifts in the country's literary industry during the twentieth century: the heyday and precipitous decline of the fiction magazine market during the late 1920s, and the rise to prominence of nonfiction in the book market and solidification of the paperback market by the 1950s. It would have been exceedingly unusual for any author of his generation to pursue a career long enough to cross the century's third watershed, the shift to digital media in the 1990s, which fueled an even larger explosion of niche publishers and small-scale publication. John Cheever, who began a writing career in the late 1950s and died in 2009, came the closest. The dramatic changes in markets and reading and literacy that undulated through Kroll's lifetime have not ceased. Literature is organic, growing out of the soil of human experience. Harry Kroll sowed his work in the rural settings he knew best as a young adult and kicked at the comparatively poor crop he reaped, but he did not mind toiling in the hardscrabble field of literature, where there is always work for new field hands.

NOTES

Most major archival collections documenting Harry Kroll and his work are divided between institutions. Harry's surviving book manuscripts are among the Special Collections holdings at the University of Tennessee, Knoxville, and at the Mississippi Department of Archives and History in Jackson, Mississippi. The Kroll papers themselves are divided between personal and family correspondence at the University of Tennessee at Martin, and his short-fiction literary manuscripts at the University of Memphis, each of which has duplicates of the other's holdings. The Jesse Stuart papers represent a special case. A collection of Stuart's letters is at the University of Louisville and others exist among the papers of individuals to whom he wrote, others are in the holdings of the Jesse Stuart Foundation in Ashland, Kentucky, but the bulk of Stuart's papers were given by the author to Murray State University in Murray, Kentucky. However, in 2008 that institution signed a long-term loan agreement for the Stuart papers with Morehead State University. At the writing of this book the collection is at Morehead, but because title to the collection legally remains with Murray State University, it is cited there in the notes.

Chapter 1 • A Poor-Man's Boy, 1888–1920

1. Unless otherwise cited, biographical data from chapter 1 is taken from *I Was a Share-Cropper* (Indianapolis: Bobbs-Merrill, 1937), 251–63, 276–302; "Looking Back," *Author and Journalist* 32, no. 11 (Nov. 5, 1947): 5–7; Harry Harrison Kroll (hereafter, HHK) to Dear Boys, May 13, 1962, Robert T. Kroll papers, Martin, Tenn. (hereafter cited as RTK Papers).

2. "My Father," *Esquire* 5, no. 1 (Jan. 1936): 72; Pedigree Resource File, disk 9, PIN 118299; Twelfth U.S. Census (1900), Dyersburg city, district 16, sheet 4; Natalie Kroll Piske interview by Harry Kroll Jr., ca.1975, transcript in the untitled Robert T. Kroll autobiography, RTK papers. He questions the accuracy of his aunt's memories.

3. The description quoted is from *I Was a Share-Cropper,* 64. Being of German extraction, the family thinks that Caroline's family name, Cripe, may have been spelled *Kreipe* by earlier generations. Twelfth U.S. Census (1900).

4. Roger E. Sappington, "Church of the Brethren," *Encyclopedia of Religion in the South,* ed. Samuel S. Hill (Mercer Univ. Press, 1984), 163–64. Cf. *Yearbook of American Churches* (Nashville: Abingdon Press, 1933).

5. Natalie Piske interview, 3. Her memory seems to be the only record of Jimmy's birth. In the 1900 census the number of children born to Caroline and the number living are both listed as four. Family tradition lists HHK's birthplace as near Vincennes, in the toe of Indiana's boot; a contemporary biography

for which Kroll supplied the data specifies the Blackford County location. "Harry Harrison Kroll," *Wilson Library Bulletin* 19, no. 5 (Jan. 1945): 308.

6. Soddy to Hatch, n.d., Kroll papers, Martin.

7. J. Wayne Flynt, *Poor but Proud: Alabama's Poor Whites* (Tuscaloosa: Univ. of Alabama Press, 1989) charts the changes in some detail; Jacqueline Jones, *The Dispossessed: America's Underclasses from the Civil War to the Present* (New York: Basic Books, 1992), 81–89.

8. James M. Neff, *Southern Almanac and Hand Book: Containing Valuable Information Concerning the Climate, Soil, and Resources of One of the Best Portions of the Great South* (Fruitdale, Ala.: Brethren's School Company, [1896]); N. R. Baker, *The Southern Almanac and Hand Book for the Year 1897* (Fruitdale, Ala.: Brethren's School Company, 1897); *Announcement of the Brethren's School Company and Catalog of Schools, Third Year, 1897–1898* (Fruitdale, Ala.: Brethren's School Company [printed: Citronelle, Ala.: Citronelle Call], [1897]), 2–3. The only recorded copies of these brochures exist in the collection of Elizabethtown College, Elizabethtown, Pa., and I am grateful to Peter DePuydt for research help. N. R. Baker served as the State Supervisor of Rural Schools after 1911. Alabama Dept. of Education, *Annual Report, 1911,* 16–17.

9. *Share-Cropper,* 3–50; Baker, *Southern Almanac,* 36; Roger E. Sappington, *The Brethren in Tennessee and Alabama* (privately published, ca. 1988), 85–88.

10 "I Was a Share-Cropper," manuscript, Univ. of Tennessee Special Collections, Knoxville; Twelfth U.S. Census (1900).

11. Dyer County tax book, 1898 (dist. 4), p. 79; 1899, p. 92; 1900 (noted "over age" in "total taxes" column), microfilm, Tennessee State Library and Archives, Nashville.

12. Flynt, *Poor But Proud,* 192.

13. *Share-Cropper,* 84; "Good, Solid Work," *Tennessean Magazine* (May 1, 1949): 32.

14. I will only mention a few pieces of germane scholarship on the topic of books and reading, including *Print in Motion: The Expansion of Publishing and Reading in the United States, 1880–1940,* ed. Carl F. Kaestle and Janice A. Radway (Chapel Hill: Univ. of North Carolina Press, 2009); Michael Denning, *Mechanic Accents: Dime-Novels and Working-Class Culture in America* (New York: Verso, 1987); Christopher P. Wilson, "'Magazining' for the Masses," *The Labor of Words: Literary Professionalism in the Progressive Era* (Athens: Univ. of Georgia Press, 1985), 40–62; and James L. W. West, *American Authors and the Literary Market Place since 1900* (Philadelphia: Univ. of Pennsylvania Press, 1988); and their excellent bibliographies.

15 The market on east Court Street was identified by Dyersburg local historian Darrell Butler from an advertisement in the *Dyersburg Times,* May 14 and Oct. 15, 1891.

16. I know of no actual documentation for a specific body meeting at the time, but the Brethren pamphlets cited earlier were printed in Fruitdale and Citronelle and distributed by the Brethren School Company. Both Fruitdale and Citronelle still have small but active Brethren congregations. Regrettably, a fire in the 1960s consumed most records of the Fruitdale congregation; another in 1980 robbed us of Citronelle's collection. Personal communication of Steven Petcher and Dorothy Quimby, Citronelle, Ala., Mar. 30, 2005.

17. J. Wayne Flynt, *Dixie's Forgotten People: The South's Poor Whites* (Bloomington, Ind.: Indiana Univ. Press, 1979); Flynt, *Poor But Proud.*

18. Flynt, *Poor But Proud,* 4–11.

19. Flynt, *Poor But Proud,* passim.

20. Natalie Piske interview, 5. The town was formed around 1900 for workers of the Yellow Pine Lumber Company. Around 1904 the company evidently sold out or reorganized as the E. W. Gates Lumber Company. U.S. General Land Office, *State of Alabama: Compiled from Official Records of the General Land*

Office, Geological Survey and Other Sources [map] (Washington, D.C.: Dept. of the Interior, 1915); Thomas Lawson Jr., *Logging Railroads of Alabama* (Cabbage Stack Press, 1996), 200.

21. Unless otherwise noted, details and quotes about this period are taken from an extended letter to Kroll's sons describing his photographic tramping, courtship, and marriage. HHK to Dear Boys, May 13, 1962, Kroll papers, Martin, and RTK papers. Their route south and then north along the rail line as photographers is extracted from that letter and from Charles B. Kroll to HHK, [Dec. 24], 1960, Calia Hicks papers, University of Tennessee at Martin.

22. John Simpson Graham, *History of Clarke County* (Birmingham: Birmingham Printing Co., 1923), 202, 219.

23. *Catalogue of the Alabama Normal College* (Livingston, Ala., 1906); HHK to Son, Dec. 28, 1961, Kroll papers, Martin; "Rise of Writer Reads Like Fiction," unidentified clipping (perhaps from *Baldwin Times [Bay Minette, Ala.]*), byline dated Nov. 16, probably 1932, in scrapbook A, leaf 45, Kroll papers, Martin.

24. *Share-Cropper,* 250.

25. HHK to Dear Boys, May 13, 1962, RTK papers.

26. Thirteenth U.S. Census (1910), Marengo County, Ala., precinct 11.

27. *Share-Cropper,* 251; Wilson, *Labor of Words,* 93–94.

28. HHK to Dear Boys, May 13, 1962, Kroll papers, Martin, and RTK papers.

29. *Share-Cropper,* 253.

30. Wilson, *Labor of Words,* xi, 198–200, 203 n. Other studies of value include Ronald Weber, *Hired Pens: Professional Writers in America's Golden Age of Print* (Athens: Univ. of Ohio Press, 1997); Sarah Wadsworth, *In the Company of Books: Literature and Its "Classes" in Nineteenth-Century America* (Amherst: Univ. of Massachusetts Press, 2006).

31. Black schools in the county averaged merely eighty-four school days annually. B. F. Gilder, "Marengo County," 95–96; "Number of Schools Taught," 138; and "Enumeration, Enrollment," 134; in *Annual Report of the Department of Education of the State of Alabama for the Scholastic Year Ending September 30, 1910* (Montgomery, 1910).

32. *Share-Cropper,* 261–63.

33. Fellowship application, 1935, J. S. Guggenheim Foundation archives, New York; "Over the Mountain," *Editor* 86, no. 6 (Aug. 10, 1929): 104–5; *Share-Cropper,* 279–280.

34. Alabama Dept. Education, *Annual Report, 1909,* 24; *1910,* 19; *1911,* 6; *1914,* 7.

35. Marriage record book W, p. 202, Clarke County courthouse, Grove Hill, Ala.; *Clarke County Democrat* 55, no. 3 (May 25, 1911): 4; Kroll, "Honeymoon Summer," *Progressive Farmer* 55, no. 6 (June 1940): 7, 22–23, 42.

36. *Share-Cropper,* 275, 325–27; Harry Kroll, *Lost Homecoming* (New York: Coward-McCann, 1950), 3–5; Flynt, *Poor but Proud,* 174–81. Darius died June 28, 1911 (Jefferson County, Ala. death certificates, vol. 9, no. 452). Special thanks are due Beverly Key for her generous act of random kindness in locating this document.

37. "Average Yearly Salary of Teachers," Alabama Dept. Education, *Annual Report, 1913,* 176–79. Knowing where he taught, it is possible to trace the scope of his school career in the statistical tables found in the *Annual Reports,* something I will not do in detail.

38. Alabama Dept. Education, *Annual Report, 1913,* 34.

39. Alabama first-grade teacher's certificate #1405, dated July 23, 1913, Kroll papers, Martin.

40. Deed dated Sept. 16, 1913, deed book OO, p. 360, Marengo County courthouse, Linden, Ala.; "Letters from Our Readers: Winter of 1917, Really a Dilly," *Commercial Appeal (Memphis, Tenn.),* Jan. 28, 1962, section 4, p. 3.

41. "Winter of 1917, Really a Dilly," *Commercial Appeal (Memphis, Tenn.),* Jan. 28, 1962.

42. Alabama Dept. Education, *Annual Report, 1915,* 13; "Consolidation," *Annual Report, 1917,* 20–22.

43. Peabody College transcript, Kroll papers, Martin; Deed dated May 31, 1919, deed book VV, p. 530, Marengo County courthouse, Linden, Ala. Kroll's transcript represents almost the only chronological window into this period of his career, but errantly lists the examination site as "Dixonville, Alabama," a town on the Florida border, when it should have been Dixons Mills.

44. "Creating the George Peabody Campus, 1911–1930" and "The Academic Side, 1914–1930," both in Paul K. Conkin, *Peabody College: From a Frontier Academy to the Frontiers of Teaching and Learning* (Nashville: Vanderbilt Univ. Press, 2002), 210. The college itself was still relatively new, with the new campus (adjacent to Vanderbilt) dating from 1911. Quite a good account of the beginnings of the school reform movement in Tennessee where Kroll would soon land can be found in Jeanette Keith, "The Battle for the Schools," in *Country People in the New South: Tennessee's Upper Cumberland* (Chapel Hill: Univ. of North Carolina Press, 1995), particularly 131–36.

45. *Nashville City Directory, 1926,* vol. 58 (Nashville: Marshall-Bruce-Polk Co., 1926), 9. Cf. Harold E. Holland, "Religious Periodicals in the Development of Nashville, Tennessee as a Regional Publishing Center, 1830–1880," DLS thesis, Columbia Univ., 1976, 872–75, citing Constantine G. Belissary, "The Rise of Industry and the Industrial Spirit in Tennessee, 1865–1885," *Journal of Southern History* 19, no. 2 (May 1953): 193–215.

46. *Southern Agriculturist* 49, no. 17, 18 (Sept. 1, 15, 1919).

47. "Looking Back," *Author and Journalist* 32, no. 11 (Nov. 5, 1947): 5; Guggenheim Fellowship application, 1935; "Over the Mountain," *The Editor* 86, no. 6 (1929 Aug 10): 104–5.

48. *The Railsplitter* (Harrogate, Tenn.: Lincoln Memorial University, 1928), unpaged; Fourteenth U.S. Census (1920), Houston County, Ala., "Beat 13" or enumeration district 158 for Columbia, sheet 7; "Autobiography of Harry Harrison Kroll, Jr.," ca. 1989, RTK papers, 2. Harry Jr. cites his dad's position in the opposite direction at Cuevas, Mississippi, a mile or two inland from the Gulf and just off St. Louis Bay. Harry Jr.'s attribution seems to have been made only on the strength of his memory as a toddler and is disproven by the census entry.

49. "Autobiography of Harry Harrison Kroll, Jr.," 1.

50. "Looking Back," *Author and Journalist* 32, no.11 (Nov. 5, 1947): 5–7. Kroll held onto the typed pages until at least the writing of this nonfiction article, when he mentioned both manuscripts with obvious fondness. It might have been discarded with the other unsold manuscripts between 1965 and 1967; by the time his few surviving manuscripts were deposited by Harry Jr. at the University of Memphis a year later, its fate was unknown.

Chapter 2 • More than One Kind of Education, 1921–1935

1. The city population enumerated in the 1920 census was 118,342. *Fourteenth Census of the United States,* vol. 3, "Population" (Washington, D.C.: GPO, 1922), table 10, p. 970; Louis M. Kyriakoudes, *The Social Origins of the Urban South: Race, Gender, and Migration in Nashville and Middle Tennessee, 1890–1930* (Chapel Hill: Univ. of North Carolina Press, 2003).

2. Donald Davidson, *Southern Writers in the Modern World* (Athens: Univ. of Georgia Press, 1958), 21.

3. Jesse Stuart, "Foreword," *Beyond Dark Hills,* 2nd ed. (New York: McGraw-Hill, 1972), xii. He was correct, but mostly because the Fugitives were no longer meeting at the time Stuart attended Vanderbilt, not because they were unwelcoming.

4. HHK to Jesse Stuart, [Apr. 21, 1941], Stuart papers, Univ. of Louisville.

5. Wadsworth, *In the Company of Books,* 98. See also Kaestle and Radway, *Literacy in the United States.*

6. Richard S. Lowery, *"Littery Man": Mark Twain and Modern Authorship* (New York: Oxford Univ. Press, 1996), 21.

7. *Bulletin: George Peabody College for Teachers,* new series, 7, no. 4 (Mar. 1919): 12.

8. Peabody College, *Bulletin 1920–1921,* 8, no. 4 (Mar. 1920): 53; *Bulletin, Summer 1922* 11, no. 1 (May 1922): 78; *Bulletin, 1922–1923* 10, no. 5 (Mar. 1922).

9. "Twelve hours, however, of electives, to be counted toward the B.S. degree, may be allowed from the courses belonging to the Knapp School or the School of Practical Arts when these courses are of advanced scientific or cultural character." *Bulletin of Vanderbilt University* 21, no. 2 (March 1921): 73.

10. Ibid., 84–85. Vanderbilt archivist Kathleen Smith notes that Moss taught only 1920–21.

11. Stuart, *Beyond Dark Hills,* 2nd ed., xiii.

12. J. R. LeMaster, "Jesse Stuart's Poetry as Fugitive-Agrarian Synthesis," in *Jesse Stuart: Essays on His Work,* ed. J. R. LeMaster and Mary Washington Clark (Lexington: University Press of Kentucky, 1977), 28; The same view is taken in James M. Gifford and Erin R. Kazee, *Jesse Stuart: An Extraordinary Life* (Ashland, Ky.: Jesse Stuart Foundation, 2010).

13. Barry D. Riccio, "Popular Culture and High Culture: Dwight Macdonald, His Critics and the Ideal of Cultural Hierarchy in Modern America," *Journal of American Culture* 16, no. 4 (winter 1993); James Seaton, "Critical Theory and Popular Culture: The Example of Marcuse," *Markham Review* 9 (Fall 1979) examine the divide, though. William Darby, *Necessary American Fictions: Popular Literature of the 1950s* (Bowling Green, Ohio: Popular, 1987); Joan Shelly Rubin, *The Making of Middle-Brow Culture* (Chapel Hill: Univ. of North Carolina Press, 1992).

14. Alastair Fowler, *Kinds of Literature: An Introduction to the Theory of Genres and Modes* (1982; New York: Oxford Univ. Press, 1987), 20. I disagree with Leavell that Davidson suggested Stuart adopt a manuscript submission and publication process; Stuart cites Kroll's example but never mentions Davidson in that regard. Frank Leavell Jr., "Jesse Stuart at Vanderbilt," *Jack London Newsletter* 10, no. 2 (May–Aug 1977): 84-93.

15. "Autobiography of Harry Harrison Kroll, Jr.," 1.

16. "Harry Harrison Kroll Addresses Woman's Press and Author's Club," unidentified clipping, scrapbook A, leaf 62, Kroll papers, Martin.

17. Charles M. Harvey, "The Dime Novel in American Life," *Atlantic Monthly* 100 (July 1907): 37–45.

18. James L. W. West III, "The Magazine Market," *The Book History Reader,* ed. David Finkelstein and Alistair McCleery (London: Routeledge, 2002), 269–76. An excellent contemporary comment on the comparative market in Britain is supplied by Q. D. Leavis, *Fiction and the Reading Public* (1932; New York: Russell & Russell, 1965). Summaries and studies of select elements of the U.S. market are available, but thus far no one has tackled its massive history.

19. *Peabody Reflector,* 1st series, 4, no. 5 (Nov. 1, 1922).

20. Jane Kirkland Graham, *Viola, the Duchess of New Dorp: A Biography of Viola Roseboro* (Danville, Ill.: Author, 1955), 23–31, 198–201; HHK, "The Law and Evidence," *McClure's* 1, no. 1 (May 1925): 62–74. Robert H. "Frank" Leavell is not close contemporary Frank Hartwell Leavell of the Baptist Sunday School Board, one of Kroll's early publishers. To confuse things further, Frank Hartwell Leavell Jr. was a later Vanderbilt student and Jesse Stuart biographer.

21. Viola Roseboro to Professor Leavell, Oct. 4, 1922, Kroll papers, Martin.

22. Ibid.

23. Ibid.; "What the White Man Wants," *Peabody Reflector,* 1st series, 3, no. 2 (Aug. 1, 1922): 10.

24. *Share-Cropper,* 288–90.

25. "He Didn't Know the Alphabet Until He Was 21; Now He's a Professor," *Des Moines Register,* Dec. 2, 1928.

26. *Share-Cropper,* 290.

27. *Peabody Reflector,* 1st series, 5, no. 11 (Oct. 1923): 13; and 6, no. 3 (Mar. 1924): 18.

28. Agnes Chrietzberg, "A Chance to Play," *Kentucky Humanities* 1 (1999): 18–22. Since Kroll's time the town has steadily lost population.

29. Robert L. Brandfon, *Cotton Kingdom of the New South: A History of the Yazoo-Mississippi Delta from Reconstruction to the Twentieth Century* (Cambridge, Mass.: Harvard Univ. Press, 1967); James C. Cobb, *The Most Southern Place on Earth: The Mississippi Delta and the Roots of Regional Identity* (New York: Oxford Univ. Press, 1992).

30. *Share-Cropper,* 295.

31. *Share-Cropper,* 294–96.

32. "Getting into Print" (1903), quoted in Wilson, *Labor of Words,* xiv.

33. Kroll acknowledged that his "autobiography" was heavily fictionalized, but enough factual details can be corroborated from other sources to verify that the account of his career in Lula, as recorded in *Share-Cropper,* 293–96, is generally accurate.

34. Excellent factual assessments of the economic circumstances that Kroll was decrying may be found in E. A. Boeger and E. A. Goldenweiser, "A Study of the Tenant Systems of Farming in the Yazoo-Mississippi Delta," *U.S. Dept. of Agriculture Bulletin* 1269 (1924); E. L. Langford and B. H. Thibodeaux, "Plantation Organization and Operation in the Yazoo-Mississippi Delta Area," *U.S. Dept. of Agriculture Technical Bulletin* 882 (May 1939). Kroll's own summary account of Lula appears in *Share-Cropper,* 292–96. A closer account of this latter work may be found in the critical bibliography of the next section.

35. *Share-Cropper,* 295–96.

36. Viola Roseboro to HHK, Feb. 11, 1925, Kroll papers, Martin; *Share-Cropper,* 297.

37. The only complete file of the *Editor* I have been able to locate is at the Library of Congress.

38. J. A. Bryant Jr., *Twentieth Century Southern Literature* (Lexington: Univ. Press of Kentucky, 1997), 44.

39. Donald Davidson to Mr. [James I.] Finney, Nov. 6, 1930, Donald Davidson papers, Vanderbilt Univ., Nashville.

40. William Boozer, "Late Talks with Allen Tate," *New York Times Book Review,* Apr. 8, 1979, cited in *I'll Still Take My Stand,* ed. Frank E. Smith (Vicksburg, Miss.: Yazoo Press, 1980), 7. As the South's major literary movement of the time, the Agrarians are critiqued briefly in Irene and Allen Cleaton's *Books and Battles: American Literature, 1920–1930* (Boston: Houghton Mifflin, 1937), 229–32. Later scholars are more kind in taking the group seriously, including Louise Cowan, *The Fugitive Group: A Literary History* (Baton Rouge: Louisiana State Univ. Press, 1959); *Literature of Tennessee,* ed. Ray Willbanks (Mercer Univ. Press, 1984); Paul Conklin, *The Southern Agrarians* (Knoxville: Univ. of Tennessee Press, 1988); Mark G. Malvasi, *The Unregenerate South: The Agrarian Thought of John Crowe Ransom, Allen Tate, and Donald Davison* (Baton Rouge: Univ. of Louisiana Press, 1997); and Paul V. Murphy, *The Rebuke of History: The Southern Agrarians and American Conservative Thought* (Chapel Hill: Univ. of North Carolina Press, 2001). Individual biographies and bibliographies are available as well. No one has yet fitted the group into the Southern conservative movement of the time.

41. Allen Tate, Donald Davidson, and John Crowe Ransom to Stringfellow Barr, Sept. 20, 1930, Davidson papers.

42. John A. Simpson, *Edith D. Pope and Her Nashville Friends: Guardians of the Lost Cause in the* Confederate Veteran (Knoxville: Univ. of Tennessee Press, 2003); Caroline E. Janney, *Burying the Dead but Not the Past: Ladies' Memorial Associations and the Lost Cause* (Chapel Hill: Univ. of North Carolina Press, 2008); Karen Cox, *Dixie's Daughters: The United Daughters of the Confederacy and the Preservation of Confederate Culture* (Gainesville: Univ. Press of Florida, 2003); Francesca Morgan, *Women and Patriotism in Jim Crow America* (Chapel Hill: Univ. of North Carolina Press, 2005); W. Fitzhugh Brundage, "White Women and the Politics of Historical Memory in the New South," in *Jumpin' Jim Crow: Southern Politics from Civil War to Civil Rights,* ed. Glenda Gilmore, Bryant Simon, and Jane Dailey (Princeton: Princeton

Univ. Press, 2000), 115–39; Joan Marie Johnson, *Southern Ladies, New Women: Race, Region and Clubwomen in South Carolina, 1890–1930* (Gainesville: University Press of Florida, 2004); Paul V. Murphy, *The Rebuke of History: The Southern Agrarians and American Conservative Thought* (Chapel Hill: Univ. of North Carolina Press, 2001). During the 1960s Davidson was a key figure in the Tennessee Federation for Constitutional Government, a white-supremacist group.

43. Quentin Reynolds, *The Fiction Factory; or, From Pulp Row to Quality Street: The Story of 100 Years of Publishing at Street & Smith* (New York: Random House, 1955), 46.

44. "Mr. Stuart's Review," in an untitled publisher's promotional folder for Kroll's *The Usurper* (Bobbs-Merrill, 1942), copy in Kroll papers, Martin.

45. Letter in "Experience Exchange," *Editor* 68, no. 9 (Feb. 28, 1925): 72.

46. Weber, *Hired Pens,* 88–91. Faust's rigor put Kroll's daily output to shame.

47. The *Clarksdale Register,* the county's only newspaper, does not survive between 1922 and 1925, so Kroll's scrapbook clippings remain the only documentation of his effect on Clarksdale.

48. "Lula Educator Honored," *Commercial Appeal (Memphis, Tenn.),* [ca. Nov. 1924]. Kroll scrapbook A, leaf 97, Kroll papers, Martin.

49. One grammatical and stylistic critique survives, in H. M. Hamilton to My dear Kroll, Jan. 4, 1926, Kroll papers, Martin.

50. HHK, "A Comparison of Upper and Lower Southern Folk Speech," master's thesis, Peabody College, 1925.

51. *Share-Cropper,* 295.

52. A typographic correction on Kroll's surviving transcript shows an erasure of a "4" and a retyped "5," and his diploma is dated in the verbose style of such things "the twenty-sixth day of August in the year of our Lord nineteen hundred twenty five." Kroll papers, Martin.

53. HHK to Miss Pfeiffer, June 21, [1956], Kroll Papers, Martin; and HHK to Beatrice Creighton, Apr. 11, 1959, Kroll papers, Martin; "Community High School," in *Bedford County Tennessee: Family History Book,* ed. Dick Poplin (Paducah, Ky.: Turner Publishing, 2002), 81.

54. Poplin, ed., *Bedford County,* "Community High School," 81.

55. Ibid.; play handbill dated Apr. 15, [1926], in scrapbook C, Harry Harrison Kroll papers, Univ. of Memphis Special Collections. No Shelbyville newspapers survive for the period. Interestingly, "Peckerwoods" is given as the earliest story title in 1929, four years after this performance, which is clearly "The Cabbin [*sic*] in the Cotton."

56. "Autobiography of Harry Kroll, Jr.," 4–5, RTK papers; Charles Wolfe, *Rutherford County: 200 Years of Our County* (n.p., n.d.); Tony Russell, *Country Music Records: A Discography, 1921–1942* (Oxford: Oxford Univ. Press, 2004), 574. Harry's brief tenure with the pair has no documentation beyond Harry Jr.'s memory.

57. *Mountain Herald* 29, no. 2 (Feb. 1926): 9. Unquestionably the best treatment of this broad process is Earl J. Hess, *Lincoln Memorial University and the Shaping of Appalachia* (Knoxville: Univ. of Tennessee Press, 2011).

58. *Exponent of Lincoln Memorial University* 6, no. 2 (June 1925): 13; Oscar Graeve to HHK, Aug. 28, 1926, Kroll papers, Martin.

59. "The Golden Years," p.7, paper read before the Tennessee Philological Association, Lincoln Memorial Univ., Feb. 24, 1956, in scrapbook 273, Jesse Stuart papers, Murray State Univ., Murray, Ky. Only after his marriage, as Torrey tired of explaining how to pronounce his name, did he give up and go by Robert; Harry always wrote to his second son as "Torrey," by which he had been known through his growing-up years.

60. Robert T. Kroll autobiography, 4–5.

61. "Golden Years," p. 5, Stuart scrapbook 273, Murray State Univ.

62. Decades later Still admitted offhandedly that he had been in a Kroll class but specifically denied being influenced by his teaching as well as all others. Since he moved in the Danforth circle this is undoubtedly correct. James Still, "An Interview with James Still," *Appalachian Journal* 6, no. 2 (winter 1979): 136–37; Chris Green, "Headwaters: The Early Poetics of James Still, Don West, and Jesse Stuart," in *James Still: Critical Essays on the Dean of Appalachian Literature,* ed. Ted Olson and Kathy H. Olson (Jefferson, N.C.: McFarland & Co., 2007), 29, 38.

63. Stuart, *Beyond Dark Hills* (1972), 165.

64. Jesse Stuart, "Jesse Becomes an Editor," *Lincoln Memorial University Alumnus* 21, no. 2 (winter 1972): [unpaged]; later quoted in H. Edward Richardson, *Jesse: The Biography of an American Writer, Jesse Hilton Stuart* (New York: McGraw-Hill, 1984), 68–69; Elizabeth Lamont, "1920s LMU and the Flowering of Appalachian Literature," *Emancipator* (online only), http://www.lmunet.edu/campuslife/emancipator/lamont.php (cited Nov. 15, 2010).

65. "Mr. Stuart's Review," in an untitled publisher's promotional folder for HHK's *The Usurper* (Bobbs-Merrill, 1942), copy in Kroll papers, Martin.

66. Jesse Stuart, *To Teach, To Love* (New York: World Publishing, 1970), 117.

67. Jesse Stuart, *Harvest of Youth* (Howe, Okla.: Scroll Press, 1930; Berea, Ky.: Council of the Southern Mountains, [1964]); Don West, *Crab Grass* (Nashville: Trevecca Art Print Shop, 1930).

68. Her letters may be found among the James Still Collection, 61STL, Camden-Carroll Library, Morehead State University, Morehead, Ky.

69. James J. Lorance, "Expanded Horizons: Lincoln Memorial University as Seedbed of Creativity, 1926–29," in *A Hard Journey: The Life of Don West* (Urbana: Univ. of Illinois Press, 2007), 12–18. Cf. Jesse Stuart, *The Year of My Rebirth* (New York: McGraw-Hill, 1956), 262. While biographies of the major figures who intersected at LMU are available (Still, Stuart, West, and now Kroll), only Liz Lamont has really explored the history and influences of the competing LMU salons, and only part of that work has been published. Elizabeth Lamont, "Don West's Undergraduate Days at Lincoln Memorial University: The Record vs. the Myth," *Appalachian Heritage* 36, no. 4 (Fall, 2008): 40-47; "An Unsung Appalachian Literary Heritage: The Significance of James Still's Undergraduate Experience," *Appalachian Heritage* 38, no. 4 (Fall, 2010): 32-37; Lamont, "1920s LMU." A full-scale book would be a rich treasure.

70. Frank H. Leavell Jr., "The Literary Career of Jesse Stuart," PhD dissertation, Vanderbilt University, 1965, 44–46; HHK, "Stuart the Student as I Remember," in Hensley C. Woodbridge, *Jesse Stuart: A Bibliography* (Harrogate, Tenn.: Lincoln Memorial Univ., 1960), xviii.

71. Dora Byron, "For Sale: One Ivory Tower," *English Journal* 37, no. 6 (June 1948): 310–14; HHK, "Stuart the Student as I Remember"; HHK, "Jesse Stuart: The Student I Remember," manuscript, p.5, Calia Hicks papers. The manuscript is an early draft for the published version and includes a number of details and stories not included in the final text. Jesse Stuart, "Lessons in a Liberal College Education," *Saturday Review* 29 (Feb. 16, 1946): 26; Leavell, "Jesse Stuart," 47.

72. Jesse Stuart, "The Crazy Professor," *Esquire* 11, no. 4 (Apr. 1939): 72–73, 179–80. West almost certainly did not dismiss Kroll or his approach as "capitalist"; that is likely Stuart projecting his personal disagreement with his former friend's leftist radicalism.

73. Don West, "Harry Harrison Kroll: An Essay," *Appalachian Mountain Books* 2, no. 2 (1986), reprinted in *No Lonesome Road: Selected Poems and Prose,* ed. Jeff Biggers and George Brosi (Urbana: Univ. of Illinois Press, 2004), 18–20; Chris Green, "Truth, Poetry, and Don West," *Appalachian Heritage* 36, no. 4 (fall 2008): 51–59; Elizabeth Lamont, "Don West's Undergraduate Days at Lincoln Memorial University: The Record and the Myth," *Appalachian Heritage* 36, no. 4 (fall 2008): 40–47. Chris Green is correct that West's more significant influence was found in the School of Religion at Vanderbilt, where he did *not* study writing, but the theme was already well established earlier at LMU.

74. "Mr. Stuart's Review," in an untitled publisher's promotional folder for Kroll's *The Usurper* (Bobbs-Merrill, 1942), copy in Kroll papers, Martin; Leavell, "Jesse Stuart," 43–44.

75. Cf. "Powdersmoke and Manhood," *Complete Story Magazine* 9, no. 2 (Sept. 10, 1926): 85–91; "Once a Hillsman," *Complete Stories* 9, no. 5 (Dec. 1926): 98–105; "The Return to the Brute: A Feud Story of the Southern Mountains," *Everybody's* 57, no. 3 (Sept. 1927): 165–72; "Over to Poorvalley," *Peabody Reflector and Alumni News* 4, no. 1 (Jan. 1931): 10, 12–13; "Two-Way Vengeance," *Complete Stories* 31, no. 2 (Mar. 15, 1933): 114–23.

76. *Exponent of Lincoln Memorial University* 8, no. 2 (June 1927): 40. Class numbering changed during the time Kroll taught at LMU. When he came in 1926, freshman composition was taught in English 1, 2, 3; when he left in1928 the same series was numbered English 11, 12, 13.

77. Campbell's goal was "to produce slick or pulp magazine writers who sell immediately and often," wrote Alfred A. Knopf's book scout Herbert Weinstock twenty years later. "Report on trip to Tulsa and Oklahoma City," Apr. 1950, box 537, fd. 7, Alfred A. Knopf records, Harry Ransom Humanities Research Center, Univ. of Texas, Austin.

78. *Mountain Herald* 30, no 6 (Sept. 1927): 2. Mrs. Grannis was married to the head of the Biology Department, chaired the faculty publicity committee on which Kroll served, and since April 1926 had edited the *Mountain Herald,* the campus's equivalent of a development/alumni magazine. Kroll was appointed as assistant in time for the publication of issue 10 (Dec. 1926). His name last appears on vol. 30, no. 6 (Sept. 1927), after which it was issued only under direction of Grannis and French instructor Dr. Lucia Danforth.

79. HHK to Jesse Stuart, Jan. 1, 1953, in Leavell, "LCJS," quoted in Richardson, *Jesse,* 78.

80. HHK to Jesse Stuart, Jan. 13, [1942], Stuart papers, Univ. of Louisville. The discussion with Smith happened while he was teaching at the Huckleberry Writers' Colony outside Asheville, N.C. HHK to Jesse Stuart, [Sept. 13, 1943], Stuart papers, Univ. of Louisville.

81. Quoted in Richardson, *Jesse,* 78; [Harry Kroll Jr.] to Pat [Hundley], Aug. 1, 1976, Harry H. Kroll Jr. papers, Univ. of Tennessee at Martin; *Mountain Herald* 30, no. 7 (Oct. 1927): 10.

82. "Autobiography of Harry Harrison Kroll, Jr.," 7, RTK papers.

83. "Golden Years," 4, Scrapbook 273, Stuart papers, Murray State Univ.

84. Ibid.

85. H. M. Hamilton to HHK, Sept. 12, 1927, Kroll papers, Martin.

86. Frances L. Phillips to HHK, Nov. 1, Nov. 9, 1927, Kroll papers, Martin.

87. Frances Phillips to HHK, Jan. 9, Feb. 7, Feb. 20, 1928; William Morrow to HHK, Feb. 20, 1928, Kroll papers, Martin.

88. The only contemporary inscription located thus far is James Still's copy at Morehead State University. Stuart related the book's reception at LMU in a promotional piece for one of Kroll's later books. See note 65.

89. "'Insider' Produces Genuine Novel of Mountain People," *Nashville Tennessean,* Sept. 16, 1928; Frances Phillips to HHK, Oct. 10, Nov. 2, 1928, Kroll papers, Martin.

90. Frances Phillips to HHK, Nov. 2, 1928, Kroll papers, Martin.

91. Frances Phillips to HHK, Jan. 28, 1929, Kroll papers, Martin.

92. Stuart, review of *The Usurper,* in an untitled Bobbs-Merrill promotional folder for the book, Kroll papers, Martin.

93. A consideration of the sort of religious culture Kroll had offended, along with the implications and applications of religion, is addressed in Jeanette Keith, "Following the Old Paths: The Family, Religion and Politics in the 1920s," in *Country People in the New South: Tennessee's Upper Cumberland* (Chapel Hill: Univ. of North Carolina Press, 1995), 183–210. Tennessee's culturally conservative Upper Cumberland re-

gion is just south of where Kroll had taught in Woodburn, Ky., and a few counties west of Lincoln Memorial University. An excellent general summary of the tradition-bound socioeconomics of the region at the time Kroll was at LMU can be found in the concluding pages, 208–10. Earl Hess takes issue with this view. Hess, *Lincoln Memorial University,* passim.

94. J. H. Moore reminiscences, LMU Archives, Carnegie-Vincent Library, Harrogate, Tenn.; Lorance, *Hard Journey,* 15 ; "Golden Years," p. 8, scrapbook 273, Stuart papers, Murray State Univ.

95. "Mountain Writer Is Visitor in City," *Nashville Tennessean,* Sept. 4, 1928.

96. "Teacher Can Spoil Talents of Mountain Folk By Too Much 'Learnin,' Says Author Here," *Nashville Tennessean,* evening edition, Sept. 3, 1928, 7. Surprisingly the book makes these points so subtly as to be effectively imperceptible. Cf. *Mountainy Singer,* 217–35.

97. *Foxfire* as an educational approach, its illustrated oral history book series, magazine, and overall celebration of "plain living," is well known. The desperate teacher who engaged his students noted that in teaching a traditional English curriculum, "I had bored them terribly." *Foxfire,* ed. Eliot Wigginton (Garden City, N.Y.: Anchor Books, 1972), 9–14; cf. *Foxfire: 25 Years,* ed. Eliot Wigginton and students (Garden City, N.Y.: Anchor Books, 1991). For a comparison see Benedict Anderson, *Imagined Communities: Reflections on the Origin and Spread of Nationalism,* 2nd ed. (London: Verso, 1991), chap. 8.

98. Nearly thirty years after leaving Lincoln Memorial, Kroll began writing of his experiences in a manuscript titled "The Golden Years." It was widely praised by the former students to whom he showed it, but never managed to find a publisher. A partial photocopy of the manuscript, perhaps a third of the pages, may be found in the Martha A. Whitt papers, Univ. of Tennessee at Martin. She was given a duplicate of the original typescript as biographical background by Mildred Payne after Kroll's death. She eventually discarded pages lacking biographical data, leaving behind an imperfect but tantalizing picture of Kroll's perspective on that time, particularly regrettable since Payne's original typescript has never been found.

99. "Autobiography of Harry Kroll, Jr.," 7; *Iowa Wesleyan News,* Jan. 14, 1929. My thanks to college archivist Lynn Ellsworth for identifying and locating IWC local material.

100. *Share-Cropper,* 297.

101. "Harry H. Kroll, Mountaineer Author of Tennessee, Heads Wesleyan Journalism Dept.," *Ottumwa Courier,* Oct. 26, 1928, clipping in Scrapbook 1, [p. 86], Kroll papers, Martin; Board of Trustees minutes, Feb. 10, 1929, Iowa Wesleyan College Archives, Mt. Pleasant, Iowa; "Looking Back," 5–7; "Daddy lost his job at Iowa Wesley in May to the son of the president," recalled Harry Jr. "The boy had graduated from school and needed the job" ("Autobiography of Harry Harrison Kroll, Jr.," 7). However, the IWC president, James Ephraim Coons (who served 1928–35), was new himself; the board chairman between 1921 and 1930 was Carl S. Williams. Harrell did not have connections with either, so Harry Jr.'s memory must have been faulty. Lucia Danforth to James Still, Oct. 16, [1930]; Nov. 1, 1931; May 11, 1941, James Still collection.

102. Program dated May 10, 1929, scrapbook C, Kroll papers, Memphis.

103. T. S. Stribling, quoted in Kenneth W. Vickers, *T. S. Stribling: A Life of the Tennessee Novelist* (Knoxville: Univ. of Tennessee Press, 2004), 119.

104. "Short Stories Bring the Most," unidentified clipping (probably from a Fairfield, Iowa, paper), Scrapbook A, [p. 90], Kroll papers, Martin. Since publishers regularly bought more than they published, many might have appeared later or not at all. My tally of published short matter currently known stands at ninety-six.

105. Quoted in "The Author as Producer," trans. Anna Bostock, *Understanding Brecht* (London: NLB, 1973), 94.

106. Lee Smith, address at Third Annual Appalachian Heritage Literary Festival, Harrogate, Tenn., June 14, 2008. Lee tells me she got this statement straight from a speaker at the Hindman School the preceding year but neglected to record the source.

107. Paul M. Hirsch, "Cultural Industries Revisited," *Organizational Science* 11, no.3 (May–June 2000): 356–61.

108. Fred Lewis Pattee, *The New American Literature, 1890–1930* (New York: Century, 1930), 311.

109. Warren Susman, *Culture and Commitment, 1929–1945* (New York: Braziller, 1973), 8. David E. Kyvig, *Daily Life in the United States, 1920–1940* (Chicago: Ivan R. Dee, 2004) provides a useful survey of this period.

110. Alice Marquis, "Written on the Wind: The Impact of Radio," in *Hope and Ashes: The Birth of Modern Times* (New York: Free Press, 1986), 15–49. The sociology of radio's influence prior to broadcast networking is addressed in Catherine L. Covert, "'We May Hear Too Much': American Sensibility and the Response to Radio, 1919–1924," in *Mass Media between the Wars: Perceptions of Cultural Tension, 1918–1941,* ed. Catherine L. Covert and John D. Stevens (Syracuse: Syracuse Univ. Press, 1984), 199–220. Cf. William C. Ackerman, "Dimensions of American Broadcasting," *Public Opinion Quarterly* 9 (spring 1945); Gerald Nachman, *Raised on Radio* (New York: Pantheon, 1998). Scholars have not noticed one important caveat to this woe-betide hand-wringing in the Cheney Survey of the book industry: that the personal involvement (activity) of individual book readers had not changed much. The real issue was that these new competing activities were preventing new readers from developing at the same rate as before. Cheney, *Economic Survey,* 52–56, 59.

111. Marquis, "Sound and Fury: Hollywood and Writers," *Hope and Ashes,* 54–55, citing figures from Robert McLaughlin, *Broadway and Hollywood: A History of Economic Interaction* (New York: Arno Press, 1974), 91–97.

112. Edward Bok, *The Americanization of Edward Bok* (New York: Scribner's, 1920), 292–93.

113. Pattee, *New American Literature,* 312. Stories under each of these names are among the tear-sheets he retained, which are today in the Kroll papers, Memphis. Robert V. Kramer, "Stolen Stamps"; Graham Black, "The Rut"; Stanley Bright, "A Business of His Own," *Fame and Fortune Magazine* 24, no. 2 (Oct. 1928, 2nd number). Multiple placements were exceptional. "Wesley Hen*shaw*" was another popular writer and not a Kroll pseudonym.

114. Marshall Smith, "Writer Fired from Job After Job, Makes Living on Success Stories," *Memphis Press-Scimitar,* Mar. 14, 1932.

115. Fellowship application, 1935 Guggenheim Archives; John Simon Guggenheim Memorial Foundation archives, New York. Copies at the Univ. of Tennessee at Martin..

116. *Bulletin of Peabody College,* new series, 19, no. 4 (April 1930): 16.

117. Matriculation records, Vanderbilt Univ. Registrar's Office, Nashville. Thanks to Peggy Downing for help with these. Stuart rarely mentioned his education at Peabody in later years and patriotically claimed he was forever a "Vanderbilt man" to Donald Davidson. Elizabeth Lamont observes that he was writing to LMU claiming identical sentiments at the same time. Jesse Stuart to Donald Davidson, Nov. 17, 1934, Davidson papers.

118. Frances Phillips to HHK, Nov. 7, 1929, Kroll papers, Martin.

119. John Tebbel, *A History of Book Publishing in the United States: The Golden Age between the Wars, 1920–1940,* vol. 3 (New York: R. R. Bowker, 1978), 559–60.

120. Frances L. Phillips to HHK, May 26, 1927, Kroll papers, Martin.

121. Frances Phillips to HHK, July 1, 1930, Kroll papers, Martin.

122. Fellowship application, 1935 Guggenheim Archives; *Share-Cropper,* 301.

123. Frances L. Phillips to Mr. Kroll, May 26, 1927; Jacob Baker to Mr. Kroll, June 17, 1927; Grinelle Vernon to Professor Kroll, Aug. 25, 1927, Kroll papers, Martin.

124. S. S. Mims to HHK, Jan. 7, Feb. 1, 1928, Kroll papers, Martin; "Harry Harrison Kroll's Own Story of How He Wrote 'Cabin in the Cotton,'" undated, unidentified clipping in disbound scrapbook C, Kroll papers, Memphis.

125. "The Opening Wedge," *Young People's Weekly* 43, no. 12 (Mar. 23, 1929): 5, 7.

126. Richard R. Smith to HHK, Sept. 25, 1930; James Van Toor to HHK, Oct. 3, 10, 1930, Kroll papers, Martin.

127. James Van Toor to HHK, Nov. 12, 1930, Kroll papers, Martin.

128. R. R. Smith to HHK, Aug. 3, 1931, Kroll papers, Martin.

129. R. R. Smith to HHK, Aug. 27, 1932, Kroll papers, Martin.

130. Tebbel, *Book Publishing,* 3:570–771.

131. R. R. Smith to HHK, Sept. 22, 1931; R. R. Smith Inc. to HHK, Oct. 2, 1931, Kroll papers, Martin; "The Weekly Record," *Publishers Weekly,* Oct. 31, 1931.

132. Dick [R. R. Smith] to HHK, Dec. 24, 1931, Kroll papers, Martin.

133. Fellowship application transcription, 1931, John Simon Guggenheim Memorial Foundation Archives, New York. Kroll listed Richard R. Smith, William Morrow & Co.; personal references were Bruce R. Payne, Edgar A. Wright, O. C. Ault of Peabody, and Charles D. Lewis of the Teachers College in Murfreesboro (now Middle Tennessee State Univ.). Morrow's and Lewis's responses were the two that undercut him.

134. Dick [R. R. Smith] to HHK, Feb. 4, 1932, Kroll papers, Martin; "Peckerwoods: An Impressive Story of the Cotton-fields," *Morning Post (London),* Feb. 16, 1932; "Realism before Heroics," *Western Mail (Cardiff, Wales),* Mar. 3, 1932, in Kroll Scrapbook A, leaf 58, Kroll papers, Martin.

135. Dick [R. R. Smith] to Harry, July 15, 1932, Kroll papers, Martin.

136. Dick [R. R. Smith] to HHK, Mar. 7, 1932, Kroll papers, Martin.

137. *San Francisco Chronicle,* Jan. 3–26, 1932, in Kroll Scrapbook A, leaf 47, Kroll papers, Martin.

138. HHK to Jesse Stuart, Dec. 18, [1940], Jesse Stuart papers, Univ. of Louisville. Tate's review, "A Mississippi Dreiser," appeared in the holiday book section of the *Nation* 133, no. 3465 (Dec. 2, 1931): 614–15.

139. Ray Long & Richard R. Smith Inc. royalty statement, July 31, 1932, Kroll papers, Martin.

140. O.H. Cheney, *Economic Survey of the Book Industry, 1930–1931,* 1949 reprint (New York: R. R. Bowker, 1949), 50–51; Ann Watkins, "Literature for Sale,"(1941) in *Bowker Lectures on Book Publishing* (New York: R. R. Bowker Co., 1957), 100; "Author Buys Greater Hudson Eight," *Tennessean,* Nov. 13, 1931; Julian Lee Rayford, "Jesse Stuart: Kentucky's Immortal Chronicler," *American Book Collector,* Jesse Stuart number (Sept. 1958): 5–7.

141. HHK to Son, Dec. 28, 1961, Harry Kroll Jr. papers.

142. Ray Long to HHK, Oct. 21, 1931, Kroll papers, Martin.

143. "Harrison Kroll, Noted Writer Will Make His Home in Murfreesboro," "Noted Writer Arrives in Murfreesboro With Family to Make New Home Here," unidentified clippings, Scrapbook A, [pp. 46, 49], Kroll papers, Martin. The concluding chapter "Little Man, What Now?" of James D. Hart, *The Popular Book: A History of America's Literary Taste* (New York: Oxford Univ. Press, 1950), 246–82, provides a remarkable assessment as well as figures documenting the fall and shifts in American reading habits during this period.

144. Data from the Margaret Herrick Library, Academy of Motion Picture Arts and Sciences, Beverly Hills, Calif.; film notice, *New York Times,* Sept. 26, 1932; film review by Mordaunt Hall, *New York Times,* Sept. 30, 1932.

145. John C. Rodger telegram to HHK, Sept. 8, 1932, Kroll papers, Martin; "Preview Down South," *New York Evening Post,* Sept. 24, 1932.

146. *Weekly State Gazette (Dyersburg, Tenn.)* articles "Moves Cabin in Cotton Forward to September 26," Sept. 15, 1932; "To Be Proud Of," Sept. 22, 1932; "Furniture Store Has Best Cabin" and "Gala Event for Author Reaches End Here Today," Sept. 29, 1932. HHK, *Lost Homecoming,* 7.

147. William Morrow to HHK, Feb. 20, 1928, Kroll papers, Martin.

148. Dick [Smith] to HHK, Dec. 14, 1932, Kroll papers, Martin.

149. Dick [Smith] to HHK, Nov. 28, 1932, Kroll papers, Martin.

150. Dick [Smith] to HHK, Dec. 14, 1932, Kroll papers, Martin.

151. Ibid.

152. Gertrude Algase to HHK, Jan. 20, 1934, Kroll papers, Martin.

153. Copy of Samuel Sloan to Verne Porter, Dec. 27, 1935, Kroll papers, Martin.

154. "Kroll, Harry Harrison," Guggenheim Archives, New York. Copies at the Univ. of Tennessee at Martin.

Chapter 3• College Professor, American Novelist, 1936–1957

1. Both quoted in David Welky, *Everything Was Better: Print Culture in the Great Depression* (Urbana: Univ. of Illinois Press, 2008), 2–3.

2. Michael Barone, *Our Country* (New York: Free Press, 1990), 95–96.

3. W. Everett Derryberry was a graduate of the University of Tennessee who played football for Major Neyland and later served as president of Tennessee Technical College in Cookeville between 1949 and 1974.

4. Paul Meek to Charles Bell Burke, Dec. 10, 1935, and Burke to Meek, Dec. 19, 1935, Chancellor's Records, Univ. of Tennessee at Martin Archives, Martin, Tenn. University policy stipulated that faculty credentials had to be cleared with the chair of the appropriate academic department in Knoxville before a hire could be made in the Junior College at Martin.

5. "Two Instructors Added to UTJC Teaching Staff," *Volette (Martin, Tenn.)* Jan. 20, 1936. An article about the new course catalogue in an April issue notes that Kroll had "assumed his duties at the beginning of the Winter quarter, 1935." The primary documents cited above clearly prove the later statement an error. See "New Catalog Contains Changes," *Volette (Martin, Tenn.),* Apr. 27, 1936.

6. In 1972 the campus became the University of Tennessee at Martin.

7. Despite Kroll's opinion of his student, Carter's sole publication I have been able to locate is "English Grammar with a Halo," *College English* 7, no. 3 (Dec. 1945): 165–66.

8. Richardson, *Jesse*, ch. 9, 10.

9. *Volette (Martin, Tenn.),* May 2, 15, 1938. The title varies in order in virtually every contemporary source in which it is mentioned.

10. This trip, its purpose, and the relationship can be no more than inferred from the letter of Jessica Mannon to Mrs. Kroll, Nov. 12, 1936, Kroll papers, Martin.

11. Ibid.

12. HHK to Torrey, [Nov. 9, 1963], RTK Papers. See also chapter 2, note 59.

13. D. L. Chambers to HHK, July 31, Aug. 26, 1937, Kroll papers, Martin.

14. D. L. Chambers to Mrs. Kroll, Oct. 23, 1937, Kroll papers, Martin.

15. Ibid.

16. Viola Roseboro to HHK, May 30, 1925, Kroll papers, Martin.

17. Receiving Record of "Four-Square Mark" and "My Folks," dated Nov. 6, 1936, Bobbs-Merrill records, Lilly Library, Indiana Univ., Bloomington.

18. Contract, Kroll papers, Martin; *Volette (Martin, Tenn.),* Jan. 18, 1937.

19. Richard L. Saunders, *Harry Harrison Kroll: The Works* (Caramon Press, 2009), 202–5.

20. Kroll's books are treated in chronological detail in Saunders, *HHK Works.*

21. Paul Hoffman to HHK, Mar. 22, 1937, Kroll papers, Martin. A reader's report by Jessica Mannon in the Bobbs-Merrill materials at least provides a solid plot summary and character outline (Bobbs-Merrill records, 104: 17). Like so many other pieces of Kroll's unpublished works, none of the manuscript survived to the present.

22. Charles A. Madison, *Book Publishing in America* (New York: McGraw-Hill, 1966), 258–61; Jack O'Bar, "A History of the Bobbs-Merrill Company, 1850-1940: With a Postlude through the Early 1960s," Ph.D. dissertation, Indiana University, 1975.

23. Receiving Record for "Four-Square Mark" and "My Folks," Nov 6, 1936, Bobbs-Merrill records.

24. Paul Hoffman to HHK, Mar. 22, 1937, Kroll papers, Martin; HHK to Jesse Stuart, [Apr. 21, 1942], Stuart papers, Univ. of Louisville.

25. HHK to Son, Dec. 28, 1961, Kroll papers, Martin. Robert Torrey Kroll's copy of the book, which he annotated while trying to resolve family chronology—finally giving up in frustration—is at Special collections/University Archives Univ. of Tennessee at Martin.

26. Cf. Margaret Vandiver, *Lethal Punishment: Lynchings and Legal Executions in the South* (New Brunswick, N.J.: Rutgers Univ. Press, 2006), 199. The postcard is laid in an anonymous family photo album, a modern photograph of which is in the hands of Dr. Vandiver. The victim's name, date, location, photographer, and precisely the comment which re-appears in Kroll's book, "This is the way we protect our women," are lettered onto the postcard negative. Kroll, by this time, was already teaching school in Alabama and would not have been anywhere nearby when the lynching happened.

27. "My Mother," *Atlantic Monthly* 160, no. 2 (Aug. 1937): 249–53; "My Father," *Esquire* 5, no. 1 (Jan. 1936): 72, 144.

28. Paul Hoffman to Mr. Kroll, Mar. 22, 1937, Kroll papers, Martin.

29. John Mullan, *How Novels Work* (New York: Oxford Univ. Press, 2006), 81, 84.

30. D. L. Chambers to HHK, July 1, 17, 1937, Kroll papers; Soddy to Harry, June 22, [1937], Kroll papers, Martin.

31. Penciled notes on the "Share-Cropper" manuscript, Univ. of Tennessee, Knoxville.

32. HHK to Maw, n.d. (2:16), Kroll papers, Martin.

33. Quoted in Edward Cary Royce, "Social Change and the Constriction of Possibilities: The Rise of Southern Sharecropping," Ph.D. thesis, SUNY Stony Brook, 1983, 330–33.

34. HHK to Bruce F. Denbo, Jan 8, 1961; William H. Jesse to HHK, Apr. 2, 1947, Kroll papers, Martin. The manuscript is now MS 4 at the Hodges Library, Univ. of Tennessee at Knoxville.

35. "I wrote it in 15 days, the first draft. Now I plan a summer over in the North Carolina mountains to whip it into shape." HHK to Jesse Stuart, [July 7, 1943], Stuart papers, Univ. of Louisville.

36. Query to Stella dated June 20, [1947], "Kroll, Harry Harrison—Correspondence, 1940–1948," Bobbs-Merrill records.

37. Cited in Hart, *Popular Book,* 201.

38. Mitchell relied heavily on the reminiscences of Theodore Roosevelt's Confederate-leaning mother and their family's Bulloch Hall summer-home community of Roswell, Georgia, for her novel. David G. McCullough, *Mornings on Horseback* (New York: Simon & Schuster, 1981), chap. 2.

39. Simpson, *Edith D. Pope,* passim.

40. Donald Davidson to Mr. Finney, Nov. 6, 1930; Allen Tate, Donald Davidson, John Crowe Ransom to Stringfellow Barr, Sept. 20, 1930, Davidson papers. James I. Finney was publisher of the *Tennessean* and Davidson's boss. This letter cost Davidson his column and newspaper job.

41. Alice Payne Hackett, *Seventy Years of Best Sellers, 1895–1965* (New York: R. R. Bowker, 1967), 153–55.

42. Michael Korda, *Making the List: A Cultural History of the American Bestseller, 1900–1999* (New York: Barnes & Noble, 2001), 81.

43. Hart, *Popular Book,* 265.

44. Ray Long to HHK, Oct. 21, 1931, Kroll papers, Martin.

45. HHK, "The Historical Novel," in *Four Talks on Writing Delivered at the Southern Literary Festival* (Blue Mountain, Miss.: Southern Literary Festival, 1947), 10.

46. HHK to Jesse Stuart, [Apr. 21, 1942], Stuart papers, Univ. of Louisville.

47. Everett Derryberry to Paul Meek, June 14, 1938; Paul Meek to Everett Derryberry, June 16, 1938, Everett Derryberry papers, RG 27 (118:6), Tennessee Tech Univ. Archives, Cookville, Tenn.; *Volette (Martin, Tenn.),* Sept. 30, 1946.

48. HHK to Jesse Stuart, [May 18, 1943], Stuart papers, Univ. of Louisville.

49. HHK to Jesse Stuart, [July 1943], Stuart papers, Univ. of Louisville.

50. "Kroll Winds Up Busy Season of Talks," *Volette,* May 2, 1941. Notices about many of these appear in the *Volette.*

51. "Coahoma" subject file, Mississippi Dept. of Archives and History, Jackson, Miss.

52. HHK to Jesse Stuart, [Apr. 21, 1942], Stuart papers, Univ. of Louisville. The final version of the manuscript is among the holdings of the Mississippi Dept. of Archives and History.

53. "Index of Spring Titles," *Publishers' Weekly,* Jan. 27, 1940; "Kroll Will Speak Before A.A.U.W," *Volette (Martin, Tenn.),* Mar. 4, 1940; "The Weekly Record," *Publishers' Weekly,* Mar. 30, 1940.

54. Lucia Danforth to James Still, Aug. 10, 1940, James Still collection.

55. Maximilian Becker to HHK, Feb. 26, 1940, Kroll papers, Martin.

56. HHK to Jesse Stuart, Aug. 20, [1941], Stuart papers, Univ. of Louisville.

57. Cf. "Negative Yes Men," *Try* 4, no. 3, pt. 2 (Mar. 9, 1941): 2–3, 11, 14–15.

58. HHK to Jesse Stuart, [May 18, 1943], Stuart papers, Univ. of Louisville.

59. The tale unfolds in a series of letters from Lucia Danforth to James Still between 1930 and 1941 in the James Still collection.

60. "Martin Boy Writes from Montreal," *Weakley County Press (Martin, Tenn.),* Nov. 14, 1941. As a British Army signals officer Harry Jr. installed the radio communication network on the Normandy beachhead at Omaha Beach on D+1. He was wounded by shelling and released (not discharged) from service. At home in the U.S. he was quickly picked up by Philco Radio, put in an American uniform without rank as a contract specialist, and sent to the Pacific to install radio communications at the heavy bomber base on Tinian. Thus he served in both theatres of war. Despite his wound and honorable service, the British government overlooked the service of non-Commonwealth volunteers in their forces, and because he was technically a civilian specialist and not a ranked soldier, Harry was denied access to both the G. I. Bill and a British military pension. Harry Kroll Jr. scrapbook in possession of Nelle Kroll, Knoxville.

61. George M. Horton, "Strolling Through the Years at UTJC, UTMB, and UTM," unpublished typescript, vol. 2, p.103, George Horton papers, Special Collections/University Archives, Univ. of Tennessee at Martin.

62. HHK to Jesse Stuart, [1943], Stuart papers, Univ. of Louisville.

63. Madison, *Book Publishing in America,* 261.

64. "Kroll, Harry Harrison—Reader's report, Untitled teacher story", Bobbs-Merrill records.

65. Hart, *Popular Book,* 273. The whole of chap. 14, "Little Man, What Now?," provides an excellent summary of the shift in reading tastes and book buying from the Depression to postwar world, with a sprinkling of hard facts cf. Tebel, *Book Publishing,* 3:427.

66. HHK to Jesse Stuart, [Apr. 21, 1942], Stuart papers, Univ. of Louisville.

67. Untitled *Usurper* promotional material, Kroll papers, Martin.

68. Bess Jones, "Kroll," *Saturday Review of Literature* 24, no. 5 (May 24, 1941): 10.

69. An internal sales summary generated by Bobbs-Merrill calculated that 5,376 copies had sold between its release with the spring books of 1942 and June 1947. Query to Stella dated June 20, [1947], "Kroll, Harry Harrison—Correspondence, 1940–1948," Bobbs-Merrill records.

70. D. L. Chambers [DLC] to HHK, Mar. 3, 1942, Kroll papers, Martin.

71. *Volette (Martin, Tenn.),* July 13, 1942; *Charlotte Observer (North Carolina),* Aug. 11, 1940. A summary history drawn from Haynes's self-published autobiography *True Early Adventures in Florida Days and Mountain Country* (Hendersonville, N.C.: Author, n.d.) can be found in Jennie Giles, "Camp Memories," *Times-News (Hendersonville, N.C.),* Dec. 6, 1992.

72. HHK to Jesse Stuart, [June 25, 1942], Stuart papers, Univ. of Louisville.

73. HHK to Dear Sir, Mar. 10, 1943, Kroll papers, Martin. The book is dated 1943 on the title page, which was probably a copyright registration issue.

74. DLC to HHK, Apr. 15, 1943, Kroll papers, Martin. Four years later, after returns from bookstores and other venues were factored into the sales figures, the book was calculated to have sold 5,404 copies of the press run. Query to Stella dated June 20, [1947], "Kroll, Harry Harrison—Correspondence, 1940–1948," Bobbs-Merrill records.

75. *Volette (Martin, Tenn.),* Oct. 12, 1942; HHK to Jesse Stuart, [May 3, 1943], Stuart papers, Univ. of Louisville; Cheney, *Economic Survey,* 85.

76. Query to Stella dated June 20, [1947], "Kroll, Harry Harrison—Correspondence, 1940–1948," Bobbs-Merrill records.

77. *Volette (Martin, Tenn.),* Feb. 7, 1944.

78. Dan to HHK, Aug. 20, 1945, Dan Kroll letters, Univ. of Tennessee at Martin.

79. HHK to Jesse Stuart, [July 7, 1943], Stuart papers, Univ. of Louisville.

80. Letter to the editor titled "Novels About The South," in column "Tell It To Old Grandma," *Montgomery Advertiser (Ala.),* [Mar. 1944], in scrapbooks C, Kroll papers, Memphis.

81. Personal communication with the author, June 10, 2008.

82. *New Yorker,* Mar. 17, 1945, p.95.

83. The unpublished material is housed in the Kroll papers, Memphis, donated by Harry Jr. in 1967.

84. HHK to Jesse Stuart, Dec. 18, [1940]; Jan. 18, [1941]; Aug. 20, 1941; [Apr. 11, 1942]; [May 3, 1943]; Stuart papers, Univ. of Louisville.

85. "Faculty Changes," *Volette (Martin, Tenn.),* Nov. 13, 1944; HHK to Jesse Stuart, June 30, [1944], Stuart papers, Univ. of Louisville.

86. Kroll papers, Memphis; Jessica Mannon to HHK, Jan. 6, 1942, Kroll papers, Martin; reader's report "Kroll, Harry Harrison—Untitled teacher story", Bobbs-Merrill records. Kroll did not feel strongly enough about the story to even finish it, but was too attached to let it go. The ribbon copy of the untitled partial manuscript is probably the one which remained in the hands of Harry Jr. until 2002; it is now among his father's manuscripts at the Univ. of Memphis.

87. An undated internal transmittal memorandum notes that the manuscript had been "brot in by author" and that it lacked a title. Rosemary to HHK, Mar. 1, 1946, Kroll papers, Martin; undated transmittal memo, "Kroll, Harry Harrison—Witch's House readers' reports," Bobbs-Merrill records. The Bell Witch story has been both recounted and debunked dozens of times. Contemporary but fantastic accounts include M. V. Ingram's *An Authenticated History of the Famous Bell Witch: The Wonder of the 19th Century, and Unexplained Phenomenon of the Christian Era* (Nashville: Rare Book Reprints, 1961) and Richard Powell's own account in *The Bell Witch: An American Haunting,* ed. Brent Monahan (New York: St. Martin's Press, 1997).

88. Rosemary to Mr. Chambers, Oct. 16, 1946, "Kroll, Harry Harrison—Correspondence," Bobbs-Merrill records.

89. Ibid.

90. HHK to Jesse Stuart, [June 1, 1943], Stuart papers, Univ. of Louisville.

91. Walter Sanders, photographer, "*Life* Visits the Hatfields and McCoys," *Life* 16, no. 21 (May 22, 1944): 108–16.

92. HHK to Rosemary, [Mar. 14, 1947], Kroll papers, Martin. *Their Ancient Grudge* was reprinted with a new introduction by the Univ. of Tennessee Press in 2008.

93. Blee and Billings, "Where 'Bloodshed Is a Pastime,' " 122. See also chap. 2, n. 70.

94. "Index to Spring Books," *Publishers' Weekly,* Jan. 26, 1946; "Writers of Tennessee," in *Tennessee: A Guide to the State* (New York: Viking, 1939), 150; DLC to HHK, Jan. 15, 1946; and HHK to DLC, Jan. 17, 1946, Kroll papers, Martin.

95. DLC to HHK, Oct. 19, 1946, Kroll papers, Martin; Query to Stella dated June 20, [1947], "Kroll, Harry Harrison—Correspondence, 1940–1948," Bobbs-Merrill records. Though it was the most recent book on the sales list it still ranked fourth at that date, behind *Fury in the Earth* by only 236 copies.

96. Jesse Stuart to Dear Teacher and Friend, Apr. 14, 1967, Kroll papers, Martin. The novel was republished with a new introduction in 2007.

97. HHK to Oliver Evans, Apr. 29, [1948]; HHK to Evelyn, [Apr. 1948], Kroll papers, Martin.

98. Undated letter draft, [ca.1945], Dan Kroll letters.

99. Jesse Stuart to HHK, Aug 31, 1934, and Stuart to Merton S. Yewdale, Sep. 28, 1934, Jesse Stuart Foundation, Ashland, Ky.; Yore Errant Son to Daddy, Sept. 5, 1945, Dan Kroll letters. Dorothy Dix was a popular advice columnist of the time.

100. HHK to Dan, May 6, [1950s], Kroll papers, Martin.

101. Rebel Forrester at the Harry Harrison Kroll memorial, Feb. 18, 1988, tape transcript, UTM Archives.

102. *Lost Homecoming,* 304–5.

103. Ruby Nell Stroud Riley (UTJC class of 1942), personal communication with the author, July 19, 2004.

104. Cf. HHK to Torrey, [June 30, 1958], [July 31, 1965], RTK papers. This assertion is supported by hints in a number of Harry's letters from the mid-1940s into the 1960s, and several photographs in a privately held scrapbook of a former Kroll student from a local family in Martin. The photos' subject and scrapbook's keeper has passed away, and I have not yet located a woman who has described this activity.

105. J. Stevens to HHK, Jan. 11, 1952, Kroll papers, Martin.

106. Dan to HHK, Aug. 20, 1945, Dan Kroll letters.

107. A. A. van Duym, "Where Is the Book Business Heading?," in "Strictly Personal," *Saturday Review of Literature,* Nov. 24, 1945; Henry C. Link and Harry Arthur Hopf, *People and Books: A Study of Reading Habits and Book-buying Habits* (New York: Book Industry Committee, Book Manufactures Institute, 1946), 9, 22, 122, 138–66.

108. Link and Hopf, *People and Books,* 56, 113, 122; Dorothy V. Knibb, "Reading Trends Stir Book Trade," *Domestic Commerce* 33, no. 11 (Nov. 1945).

109. Jessica Mannon to HHK, Jan. 6, 1942, Kroll Papers, Martin cf. O'bar, "Bobbs-Merrill," 27n.3.

110. Kroll wrote less as a regional Southern writer than what I would identify as a "ruralist," but Leigh Ann Duck, *The Nation's Region: Southern Modernism, Segregation, and U.S. Nationalism* (Athens: Univ. of Georgia Press, 2006) usefully illustrates some of the broad literary changes across time in regionally defined themes Kroll employed. C. W. Sullivan III, "Robert Heinlein: Reinventing Series Science Fiction in the 1950s," *Extrapolation* 47, no. 1 (spring 2006). Cheney, *Economic Survey,* 21ff provides an excellent summary of the geographic distribution of book buying in the country during the 1930s, which had only become more concentrated.

111. HHK to Jesse Stuart, [May 18, 1943], Stuart Papers, Univ. of Louisville.

112. Jack Heflin, "Southerner Dares to Write Wholesomely," quoting an uncited source in a review of Verner Bull, *Swamp Water* (Little, Brown, 1941) in *Commercial Appeal (Memphis, Tenn.),* May 11, 1941; HHK to Henry Holt & Co., Jan. 18, 1946, Kroll Papers, Martin. Cf. O'bar, "Bobbs-Merrill," 27n.3.

113. HHK to DLC, Jan. 28, [1948]; J. Stevens to HHK, Jan. 11, 1952, Kroll Papers, Martin.

114. Watkins, "Literature for Sale," *Bowker Lectures,* 109.

115. Welky, *Everything Was Better,* 150–59. Cf. William Darby, *Necessary American Fictions: Popular Literature of the 1950s* (Bowling Green, Ohio: Bowling Green Univ. Press, 1987); "Distribution of 'Literate' Population," and "Distribution of Urban Population," Cheney, *Economic Survey,* 21, 23; Kenneth C. Davis, *Two-bit Culture: The Paperbacking of America* (Boston: Houghton Mifflin, 1984).

116. Figures cited in Welky, *Everything Was Better,* 161.

117. Rosemary to HHK, Apr. 15, 1948, Kroll papers, Martin.

118. Weinstock, "Report on trip to Louisville, St Louis, Dallas, Austin, San Antonio, Houston," Feb. 1951, Alfred A. Knopf records, Harry Ransom Humanities Research Center, Univ. of Texas, Austin, 537:7.

119. Korda, *Making the List,* 100, 104.

120. Jesse Stuart to Robert L. Kincaid, May 8, 1947, Jesse Stuart Collection, LMU Archives, Harrogate, Tenn. Kroll seems to have been unaware that Peabody College professor Alfred Leland Crabb was writing on the same topic. *Journey to Nashville: A Story of the Founding* (Indianapolis: Bobbs-Merrill, 1957).

121. Mrs. John Lawrence Merritt to HHK, Aug. 14, 1947, copy, Kroll papers, Martin.

122. DLC to HHK, Sept. 15, 1947, Kroll papers, Martin.

123. HHK to Mrs. John Lawrence Merritt, Sept. 22, 1947, Kroll papers, Martin.

124. HHK, undated letter fragment to Mrs. John Lawrence Merritt, [ca. Sept. 17–24], 1947, Kroll papers, Martin.

125. HHK to DLC, [1948] Jan. 28, Kroll Papers, Martin.

126. Rosemary [York] to HHK, Apr. 15, 1948, Kroll papers, Martin.

127. HHK to Rosemary [York], [Apr. 17], Apr. 18, 1948], Kroll papers, Martin.

128. Rosemary [York] to HHK, Apr. 21, 1948, Kroll papers, Martin.

129. Undated reader report signed "Rosemary," in "Kroll, Harry Harrison—Men of Empire, readers' reports," Bobbs-Merrill records.

130. Undated reader report signed "GVRjr.," in "Kroll, Harry Harrison—Men of Empire, readers' reports," Bobbs-Merrill records.

131. Rosemary [York] to HHK, Oct. 21, 1948, Kroll papers, Martin.

132. Harcourt, Brace and Company to HHK, Nov. 3, 1948; Louis Collins to HHK, Nov. 24, 1948, Kroll papers, Martin.

133. J. B. Lippincott Co. to HHK, Jan. 28, 1949; Bertram Lippincott to Mr. Kroll, Feb. 28, 1949; Doubleday & Co to HHK, Mar. 23, 1949; HHK to A. A. Wyn, June 27, [1949]; A. A. Wyn to HHK, July 22, 1949, Kroll papers, Martin.

134. Franz Horch to HHK, Sept. 14, 20, 1949; HHK to Mr. Horch, Sept. 17, [1949], Kroll papers, Martin.

135. *Dear Writer* (Martin, Tenn.: Author, [1949]).

136. Photo in Harry Kroll Jr. papers.

137. *Commercial Appeal (Memphis, Tenn.),* [after June 30], 1949.

138. HHK to Pat Trafager, Sept. 16, [1949], Kroll papers, Martin.

139. HHK to Goldbeck, Apr. 24, [1950], Kroll papers, Martin.

140. Polly S. Pierson to HHK, Aug. 16, 1950; HHK to Polly Pierson, Aug. 9, [1950]; Coward-McCann royalty account statement, Feb. 20, 1951, Kroll papers, Martin.

141. Lloyd E. Smith to HHK, July 5, 1951; HHK to Lloyd E. Smith, July 7, [1951]; HHK to Bureau of Copyrights, July 7, 1951; Dan Kroll telegram, July 9, [1951], Kroll papers, Martin.

142. These letters are interspersed with others of July 1951 in the Kroll papers, Martin.

143. G. Mallett Prevost to Dan Kroll, Feb. 8, 1952; Dan Kroll to HHK, Feb. 10, 1952; Dan Kroll telegram, Feb. 13, [1952], Kroll papers, Martin.

144. James Van Toor to HHK, Oct. 16, 1930, Kroll papers, Martin.

145. HHK to Lloyd E. Smith, July 12, [1951]. These manuscripts, dating to January, 1952, are in the Kroll papers, Memphis.

146. HHK to Lloyd E. Smith, July 26, [1951], Kroll papers, Martin. The emendations make the paperback a new but unstated second edition rather than a simple reprint.

147. His changes to the text are found among the Kroll papers, Memphis. The specifics are catalogued in *HHK Works,* 118. Lloyd E. Smith to HHK, May 5, 1952; Western Printing & Lithographing Co. remittance advices dated May 9, 1952, and Oct. 7, 1952, Kroll papers, Martin.

148. HHK to Jesse Stuart, [June 1, 1943], Stuart papers, Univ. of Louisville. Cf. Patrick Hundley, "Harry Harrison Kroll's Unknown Vendetta Against Allen Tate," *Southern Literary Journal* 10, no. 2 (spring 1978): 134–43.

149. Kroll's Philological Association address can be found in scrapbook 273, Jesse Stuart papers, Murray State Univ.

150. Jesse Stuart to HHK, 1956 May 18, 1956, Calia Hicks papers, Martin.

151. Arnold Hano to Mr. Kroll, Feb. 17, 1953; Knox Burger to Mr. Kroll, Mar. 10, 1953; Margaret Pawl to Writers' Service, May 12, 1953, Kroll papers, Martin.

152. HHK to Donald Wollheim, Feb. 7, [1955], Kroll papers, Martin.

153. Jesse Stuart to Robert Kincaid, Oct. 12, 1956, LMU Archives.

154. The first volume was *Summer Gold* (Westminster, 1954), and the sequel volume was *My Heart's in the Hills* (Westminster, 1956).

155. HHK to Miss Pfeiffer, July 30, [1955], Kroll papers, Martin.

156. Donald I. Fine to HHK, Oct. 21, 1957, Kroll papers, Martin.

157. *This Is Your Life* official Website, http://www.thisisyourlife.com/tiyl.html?id_tiyl=1215TL384031, cited Apr. 16, 2008.

158. *This Is Your Life,* episode YLN285, aired Feb. 12, 1958, http://www.classictvinfo.com/ThisIsYourLife/TIYLEpisodeList.htm, cited Apr. 16, 2008.

159. Harry Platt to HHK, Mar. 26, 1958, Kroll papers, Martin.

160. "Honeymoon Summer," *Progressive Farmer* 55, no. 6 (June 1940): 7, 22–23, 42; HHK to Son, Dec. 28, 1961, Kroll papers, Martin.

161. *Volette (Martin, Tenn.),* May 20, 1958. Aloha Oe was an annual memorial event at both university campuses, at which the "torch of service" was symbolically passed to upcoming students by the graduating class. It was discontinued in Martin after 1969.

Chapter 4 • Professor Emeritus, 1958–1967

1. HHK to Torrey, [June 30, 1958]; and Mamma to Dear Children, June 26, [1958], RTK papers.
2. Barbara Johnson to HHK, July 29, 1958, Kroll papers, Martin.
3. Walter Campbell to HHK, Aug. 16, 1957; Louise Robertson to HHK, May 9, 1958; Anne Tiffany to HHK, June 6, 1958; Judith Schmidt to HHK, Aug. 9, 1958, Kroll papers, Martin.
4. HHK to Torrey, [June 30, 1958], RTK papers.
5. Paul J. Vanderwood, *Night Riders of Reelfoot Lake* (Memphis: Univ. of Memphis Press, 1969).
6. HHK to Torrey, [Nov. 9, 1963], RTK papers.
7. "3 Authors Discuss Books For Peabody Graduates," *Nashville Banner,* May 29, 1959.
8. *Contemporary Authors Autobiography Series,* vol. 17 (Detroit: Gale Research, 1993), 231–48.
9. Claudia Hicks interview transcript, Aug. 28, 2006, Special Collections/Univ. Archives, University of Tennessee at Martin. Kroll later worked the epigram about Kentucky men and women into "Licking River Revisited," *Southern Folklore Quarterly* 26, no. 3 (Sept. 1962): 246–51.
10. Jesse Stuart to James Still, Aug. 7, 1959, James Still collection.
11. Beatrice Creighton to HHK, Apr. 8, 1959, Kroll papers, Martin.
12. HHK to [Temple Baker], [Dec. 1965], James Still collection. The Morehead staff are not quite sure how this letter got to Still.
13. HHK to Dan, May 6, [1960 or 1961], Kroll papers, Martin. Cf. Dan to Pop, Oct. 3, [1945], Dan Kroll letters.
14. "The Iron Weed," Calia Hicks papers.
15. "Honeymoon Cabin," typed manuscript, Calia Hicks papers. A manuscript for another suggestive poem, "Ask Me Not to Go," is also in the Hicks papers; it was published in the *Commercial Appeal (Memphis, Tenn.),* Apr. 24, 1967.
16. HHK to Nattie [Natalie], Jan. 30, [1961], Kroll papers, Martin.
17. "Licking River Revisited," *Southern Folklore Quarterly* 26, no. 3 (Sep 1962): 246–51.

18. Baby to Papa, n.d., in "Correspondence from Calia Hicks," Kroll papers, Martin; his letters and postcards are in the Calia Hicks papers; Jesse Stuart to HHK, May 2, 1962, Kroll papers, Martin.

19. "Glaspy letters" file, Kroll papers, Martin.

20. HHK to Douglas S. Kennedy, July 4, 1960; H. M. Mason to HHK, Aug. 4, 1960; John M. Ross to HHK, Sept. 1, 1960, Kroll papers, Martin.

21. HHK to George Wiswell, Aug. 18, 1960; Michael St. John to HHK, Aug. 23, 1960; Bill Helmer to HHK, Oct. 24, 1960, Kroll papers, Martin.

22. HHK to A. M. Birnbaum, July 12, 1960; A. M. Birnbaum to HHK, Aug. 4, 1960; HHK to Birnbaum, Aug. 13, [1960]; Birnbaum to HHK, Sept. 15, 1960; HHK to Noah Sarlat, Nov. 16, 1960 (which provides more detail on his plans for the piece); undated purchase offer for "Action at Johnsonville," Kroll papers, Martin.

23. J. Edward Lantz to HHK, Mar. 21, 1950, Kroll papers, Martin.

24. Margaret Norton to HHK, May 5, 1960; Mary Pool to HHK, Sept. 13, 1960, Kroll papers, Martin.

25. HHK to Mr. Austin, Jan. 4, 1961; Gerald Austin to HHK, Feb. 15, 1961, Kroll papers, Martin.

26. James Henle to HHK, Sept. 16, 1960, Kroll papers, Martin.

27. Thomas J. Anderson (*Farm and Ranch*) to HHK, Jan. 12, 1961, Kroll papers, Martin.

28. Donald A. Wollheim to HHK, Dec. 16, 1960, Kroll papers, Martin.

29. Royalty statement for *Brazen Dream,* Jan–Jun, 1962, Kroll papers, Martin.

30. HHK to Torrey, [Jan. 29, 1962]; HHK to Torrey, [Mar. 26, 1926], RTK papers.

31. Mom to Son and Nelle, Feb. 1, [1961]; HHK to Tom Anderson, May 12, [1961], Kroll papers, Martin.

32. HHK to Dan, Apr. 30, [1961], Kroll papers, Martin; *Lost Homecoming,* 43.

33. HHK to Son, Dec. 28, 1961, Kroll papers, Martin.

34. HHK to Dan, May 6, [1961], Kroll papers, Martin; HHK to Dear Boys, May 13, 1962, RTK papers.

35. HHK to Calia and Frank [Hicks], [Aug. 12, 1961], Calia Hicks papers.

36. HHK to Torrey, [Oct. 7, 1961], RTK papers.

37. Robert T. Kroll to HHK, Feb. 23, 1962; HHK to J. Willard Nalls, Jr., Nov. 18, [1962], Kroll papers, Martin.

38. HHK to Son, Feb. 19, [1962], Kroll papers, Martin.

39. HHK to Torrey, [Jan. 29, 1962], RTK papers.

40. HHK to Torrey and Edie, [Mar. 26, May 26, 1962], RTK papers.

41. Swallow was dedicated to putting out good literature and was not a vanity publisher, but was often required to rely on his authors for financial help in producing and disseminating their work. HHK to Torrey, [Apr. 13, May 26, 1962], RTK papers.

42. HHK to Torrey, [May 3, 1964], RTK papers.

43. HHK to Torrey, [Mar. 21, 1965], RTK papers.

44. HHK to Torrey and Edie, [Apr. 23, 1962], RTK papers.

45. Only two letters from Calia to Harry survive, both undated but written around Christmas and probably in 1962.

46. Mildred Y. Payne to Martha A. Whitt, Oct. 22, 1973, Martha A. Whitt dissertation notes, Special Collections/Univ. Archives, Univ. of Tennessee at Martin; Martha Ann Whitt, "The Poor White in the Major Novels of Harry Harrison Kroll" (dissertation, Univ. of Alabama, 1974), 269. The "Golden Years" was the only unpublished manuscript to survive the general purge of his unsold work during the author's last two years. A copy of the final manuscript survived as late as 1974 when former colleague and confidante Mildred Y. Payne generated a photocopy (probably from a carbon in her own keeping) as background material for Martha Ann Whitt, a Univ. of Alabama graduate student and later UT Martin faculty member. The location of Payne's original manuscript, if it survives, is unknown today. Regrettably, Dr. Whitt's duplicate was weeded heavily to reduce file space; she discarded pages that did not contain

straightforward biographical data or clues. The sheets that did survive, probably about a third of the manuscript's leaves, remain in her manuscript collection at UT Martin.

47. "Second Wife," *Atlantic Monthly* 158, no. 4 (Oct. 1936): 432–41.

48. HHK to Torrey, [Mar. 9, 1963], RTK papers.

49. HHK to Torrey, [Feb. 6, 1964], RTK papers.

50. Harry Platt to HHK, Mar. 26, Apr. 1, 1958, Kroll papers, Martin.

51. Donald A. Wollheim to HHK, Feb. 3, 1959, Kroll papers, Martin.

52. Betsy Boyd to HHK, Sept. 16, 1960; Bruce F. Denbo to HHK, Jan. 4, 1961, Kroll papers, Martin. *A Restatement of Policy* (Univ. of Kentucky Press, 1953), with Denbo's letter in the Kroll papers, suggests why Kroll's book did not quite fit their publication criteria.

53. HHK to Bruce F. Denbo, Jan. 8, 1961, Kroll papers, Martin.

54. HHK to Torrey and Edie, postcard postmarked July 9, 1962, RTK papers.

55. HHK to Torrey, [Aug. 20, Sept. 22, Oct. 8, 1962], RTK papers.

56. HHK to Son and Torrey, [Oct. 6, 1962], RTK papers.

57. Baby to Papa, [1962], Kroll papers, Martin.

58. A. L. Hart Jr. to HHK, Mar. 26, 1963, Kroll papers, Martin; HHK to Torrey, [July 13, 1963], RTK papers.

59. HHK to Torrey and Edie, [Apr. 6, 1964], RTK Papers; HHK to Son, [Apr. 4, 1964], Kroll papers, Martin.

60. HHK to Torrey, [May 3, 1964], RTK papers.

61. *Volette (Martin, Tenn.),* Feb. 12, 1963. Cf. "Library to Get Endowment Funds," *Volette,* Feb. 18, 1964.

62. Thomas Yoseloff to HHK, Nov. 14, 1963, Kroll papers, Martin. The balance of the correspondence may be found among several letters in the same folder and the one following in the Kroll papers, Martin.

63. HHK to Joanne Pavincich, July 5, 1960; Ruth Scheidt to HHK, July 20, 1960, Kroll papers, Martin. The motivation was Paul Green's "symphonic drama" *The Stephen Foster Story,* based on the life of the Kentucky resident and American composer, which had opened in Bardstown the previous summer. Bardstown was not only the home of Stephen Foster but the center of Kentucky's distilling industry. The play was published as *The Stephen Foster Story: A Symphonic Drama Based on the Life and Music of the Composer* (New York: Samuel French, 1960). The show has been edited over the years and is now *Stephen Foster: The Musical,* still performed during the summers at My Old Kentucky Home State Park in the J. Dan Talbott Amphitheatre. Kroll also tried to interest *Escapade* magazine in the story, which was willing to see it; HHK to Douglas Allen, Aug. 30, [1960]; Joan Werner, Sept. 1, 1960, Kroll papers, Martin.

64. HHK to Torrey and Edie, [July 13, 1964], RTK papers.

65. Postcards postmarked Sept. 10, 1964, and Oct. 8, [1964], RTK papers.

66. HHK to Torrey, [July 13], Oct. 8, [Dec. 18], [1964], RTK papers.

67. Natalie Arnold to HHK, [Dec. 1963], Kroll papers, Martin; HHK to Torrey, [Dec. 25, 1964], RTK papers.

68. HHK to Torrey, [Jan. 30, 1965], RTK papers.

69. HHK to Torrey, [Apr. 28, 1965], RTK papers. "I don't think I want to get into another book. But I wasn't built to loaf and invite my soul. I can't invite my soul that way. I'm peddling all my rejected book manuscripts just for the hell of it. I'd like to see if it's possible any longer to sell one of my novels."

70. HHK to Torrey, [Aug. 25, 1965], RTK papers.

71. An example to 1959 Morehead attendee Temple Baker may be found in the James Still collection.

72. HHK to Torrey, [Feb. 17, Feb. 26, Apr. 19, 1965], RTK papers.

73. HHK to Torrey, [May 19 or 31, 1965], RTK papers.

74. HHK to Son and Torrey, Jan. 16, 1966, RTK papers.

75. HHK to Torrey, [Nov. 10, 1965], RTK papers.

76. HHK to Torrey, [Nov. 26, 1965], RTK papers.

77. HHK to Torrey, [Dec. 13, 1965], RTK papers.

78. HHK to Torrey, [Jan. 16, Feb. 5, 1965], RTK papers.

79. HHK to Torrey, [Mar. 28, 1966], RTK papers.

80. HHK to Son, [May 5, 1966], Kroll papers, Martin; HHK to Torrey, [Apr. 1, 1966], RTK papers.

81. Daddy to Son, May 5, 1966, Kroll papers, Memphis; HHK to Torrey, [June 4, 1966], RTK papers.

82. William Fitzgerald to HHK, Feb. 23, 1967; Daddy to Son, [Sept. 6, 1966]; Daddy to Son, [Oct. 6, 1966], Kroll papers, Martin.

83. HHK to Son, [Oct. 6, 1966], Kroll papers, Martin.

84. HHK to Son, [Oct. 30, 1966], Kroll papers, Martin.

85. HHK to Torrey, [Nov. 19, Dec. 17, 1966], RTK Papers. A few of these are now in the Kroll papers, Martin.

86. Daddy to Son, [Oct. 30, 1966]; HHK to Son, [Nov. 9, after 1966], Kroll papers.

87. "Greenhouse," *Commercial Appeal (Memphis, Tenn.),* Apr. 22, 1967.

88. HHK to Torrey, [May 15, 1967]; Mildred Payne to Torrey, June 2, 1967, RTK papers.

89. Mildred Payne to Torrey, June 2, 1967, RTK papers.

90. Certificate of Death, Tennessee Dept. of Public Health, Nashville.

91. "Kroll Piece Brings Praise," *Tennessee Alumnus* 67, no. 1 (winter 1987): 32.

Chapter 5 • Harry Kroll as Litterateur: Lessons

1. HHK to Jesse Stuart, Dec. 18, [1940], Stuart Papers, Univ. of Louisville.

2. Frank Luther Mott, *Golden Multitudes: The Story of Best Sellers in the United States* (New York: R. R. Bowker, 1947), 2, quoted in Welky, *Everything Was Better,* 216.

3. Pattee, *New American Literature,* 79.

4. Frederick J. Hoffman, *The Twenties: American Writing in the Postwar Decade,* rev. ed. (New York: Free Press, 1962), 434.

5. Pattee, *New American Literature,* 461; Sinclair Lewis, *Babbitt* (New York: Harcourt, Brace and Co., 1922).

6. Lynn Dumenil, *The Modern Temper: American Culture and Society in the 1920s* (New York: Hill and Wang, 1995), 87.

7. Lawrence W. Levine, "The Folklore of Industrial Society: Popular Culture and Its Audiences," *American Historical Review* 97, no. 5 (Dec. 1992): 1369–99; Joan Shelly Rubin, *Middle-Brow Culture.*

8. Rubin, *Middle-Brow Literature,* 98–110; Dumenil, *Modern Temper,* 87.

9. Jim Clark, "'Unto All Generations of the Faithful Heart': Donald Davidson, the Vanderbilt Agrarians, and Appalachian Poetry," *Mississippi Quarterly* 58 (winter 2004): 299. Clark errs in assuming West's writing was influenced by the Vanderbilt English Department—he was a Divinity School student—although he is correct that "if West felt obliged to define himself against the Agrarians, that too is a kind of influence." I agree, though feel that this reflected primarily an issue of class distinction and not a literary one.

INDEX

Never Been Rich was designed and typeset on a Macintosh OS 10.6.7 using InDesign CS5 software. The body text is set in 10.25/13.5 Minion Pro and the display type is various weights of Minion Pro. This book was designed and typeset by Barbara Karwhite and manufactured by Thomson-Shore, Inc.